EAST ANGLIA AGAINST THE TRICOLOR, 1789-1815

An English Region and the Conflict with Revolutionary and Napoleonic France

Further details of Poppyland Publishing titles can be found at
www.poppyland.co.uk
where clicking on the 'Support and Resources' button will lead to pages
specially compiled to support this title.

POPPYLAND
PUBLISHING

Orme's representation of the Battle of Copenhagen. The British fleet sailed from Yarmouth Roads under the command of Hyde Parker and Nelson.

The circular battery at Harwich, the Redoubt, is the most massive of the fortifications surviving much as it was in Napoleon's time. It was built next to the sizeable Harwich army camp at Beacon Hill. The fort and the Martello towers were an insurance against the new fleet Napoleon built at Antwerp and in Dutch ports after the battle of Trafalgar.

On the other side of the estuary from Harwich harbour was Landguard fort, seen on the Martello tower map opposite. Today's Landguard fort was substantially rebuilt in Victorian times.

Arwarton
Creek

Shotley

Shotley
Point

N.º 33   N.º 34

N

Shotley Gate

M

5

5   **6**

Harwich
4

5

Harbour

Bobus Hole

3

Harwich

Seroge Rd.

Walton
Ferry

1   6   **L**   N.º 35

3

Blonfields

4

3

Barracks

N.º 32
N.º 31

Signal
House

1½

Walton L.t Street

Foot Rock

4

1½

Languard
Common

Altar

Languard   4

Fort

N.º 36

O   N.º 37   N.º 38   N.º 39

P

Q

Felixstow

N.º 40

round

5

2

3

Picture credits:

Author: 37, 61, 109 (bottom and bottom margin), 156
Author's Collection: 3, 6, 7, 31, 56, 63, 65, 67, 68, 69, 75, 103, 106, 108, 109 (top margin), 114, 119 (top), 123 (bottom), 138, 146, 148, 150, 154, 181
Cyril Crawford Holden Collection: 77
Derek Hayes Collection: 97 (top margin)
Frank Meeres: 64
Gary Rossin: 60 (both top)
Hampshire County Council ©. Provided by the Hampshire Cultural Trust: 168 (both)
Mike Page: iv, vi (top left), 157
National Archives: v, 15, 16, 17, 160, 161, 164 (top), 165
National Portrait Gallery: 4 (both), 5 (both), 8 (both), 11, 31, 32, 33, 93
Nelson Museum: 97 (top)
Norfolk Museums Service 179
Paul Damen: 60 (bottom)
Poppyland Publishing: Cover, v (top right), 62 (margin), 87, 97 (bottom margin), 111, 123, 184, 190, 191
Poppyland Publishing Collection: 57, 62 (top and bottom), 70, 107, 109 (top margin), 119 (middle margin), 123 (top and middle margin), 136, 143, 164 (bottom)
Randall/Salter Magic Lantern Slide Collection: viii (bottom right)
Robert Malster Collection: 78, 79, 80, 81, 163
Ron Fiske Collection: 46, 47, 54, 100

The maps on pages 190 and 191 contain OS Data © Crown copyright and database rights 2016.

Contents

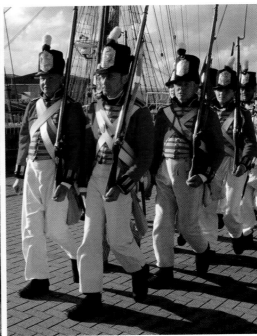

Above: Re-enactors recall the West Norfolk Militia, marching on the Yarmouth quayside.
Left: The Martello tower, Tower Q, at Felixstowe, now converted into a residence.
Below: Militia volunteers on parade on the west cliff top at Cromer.

Introduction

A history of Eastern England's part in the worldwide tumult of 1789-1815 has to be about more than Admiral Nelson, Tom Paine and the Martello towers. These are just three pieces in a jigsaw, most of which got so hidden away as to be almost lost.

Nelson and Paine left the region early on – to follow diametrically opposite paths till they died far from home – one the supreme national hero, the other England's most controversial political exile. They will of course play their roles in this book, but not central ones. For one thing many very authoritative and detailed biographies of them have been published in recent years. As for the Martello towers, though apparently a necessity at the time, they appeared late on, were never put to use, and so feature here only in a subsidiary way.

The missing mass of the jigsaw includes the local army and militia garrisons, which for almost 20 years stood guard against a French and Dutch invasion, which on three occasions was actually almost (though not quite) scheduled. It also includes the sea war, because the Royal Navy was based off Yarmouth for most of the same period for the same reason, but also to escort merchant shipping to and from London and the Baltic, enforce a blockade of enemy seaborne trade, and hunt hostile privateers.

Thomas Paine of Thetford, with the hindsight of history the most influential of the East Anglian writers of the 18th century. His words of *Common Sense* would contribute greatly to the constitution of the United States of America and he narrowly escaped the guillotine when in France at the end of the century. Two centuries later the greater part of his words are accepted as the core of democracy.

Within one year (1797) the Yarmouth squadron was caught up in the largest mutiny in British naval history yet also crushed the Dutch fleet in the Battle of Camperdown. Later it was eastern England's first line of defence against Napoleon Bonaparte's vast invasion schemes. East Anglia was also a naval and army launchpad for British landings as far apart as Egypt, Denmark and Portugal – one of the least remembered pieces of the jigsaw, and as if barely anyone could now recall that the Allied air forces flew from East Anglia in the Second World War.

But I shall not limit the story is to the army and navy. Before the fighting with France and her allies began a bitter civil war of ideas and words broke out in East Anglia, to a degree which might surprise those who imagine it to have been the tranquil land of Gainsborough, Constable and Crome. Ranged on one side were the conservative loyalists who, after initial sympathy in many cases, reacted with panic to the French Revolution: people such as the Suffolk agricultural writer Arthur Young, the Norfolk M.P. William Windham, and indeed Horatio Nelson himself. On the other were Paine (who most wholeheartedly identified himself with the new France, as he once had with the new America), the great Norfolk landowner, agricultural improver and M.P. Thomas Coke, and the radical intellectuals and artisans of Norwich, who so alarmed the government that William Pitt denounced it as "the Jacobin City". The voteless, or those whose right to participate in public life did not match their education and ambition, were convinced that those in power were using the revolution and war as pretexts to block enlightened reform and consolidate their own position.

Class hatreds were bound up with this war of words, and economic distress was soon mixed in as well. Landowners very visibly prospered while their labourers sank deeper into a poverty verging on starvation. Local manufacturing industry, already in decline, was hit by the loss of markets, so poorer and even lower-middle classes of townsmen were radicalised. Inflation, new taxes, and loss of public faith in the banks and the currency caused panic and discredited a government whose main achievement so far had been to revive and stabilise the economy.

Had radical protest, Franco-Dutch invasion plans, bad harvest and financial crisis coincided in time – instead of coming in admittedly close succession – authority and law and order in the region might well have broken down and ever since the tricolor instead of the Union flag might have flown over the town halls of Norwich, Bury and Ipswich, the stately homes been abandoned ruins, and the eastern counties been "départements" of an English republic.

Why events played out in this way will be a main focus of this book.

Other jigsaw pieces will be fitted in too – the Continental refugees (some of them royal) fleeing from revolution, the diplomats who came and went through local ports to negotiate the alliances and treaties which were meant to keep France in check, the enemy prisoners of war who were gathered in a great camp near the Fens, the violence between the various resident soldiers and sailors, and sometimes local civilians, which added to the wartime crime waves.

I became interested in this period of local history after researching eastern England's experience of the 20th century world wars and wondering what parallels could be drawn with this earlier age. My efforts to make sense of it still feel incomplete, and the conclusions I have drawn about people and events tentative. My research has been mainly archival – with the old newspapers stored in various libraries and online, long out-of-print memoirs and biographies, and the documents at the National Archives in Kew at the core. But I must add my thanks for informative conversations with Messrs. David Addy, John Collins, Robert Malster, Vick Miller, Andrew Phillips, Terry Reeve, Margaret Stone (for the loan of research notes by the late Claude Dove), Peter Stibbons of Poppyland Publishing, and many of the staff at Kew.

News from the Revolution 1

"The absolute power of the French King verges to a close".

So said the *Ipswich Journal* on 11th July 1789. The *Journal* was a Suffolk weekly newspaper consisting of a single folded sheet of four pages, all printed in the same small type, and read by a few thousand local gentry, merchants and clergymen. Its momentous words were hardly an East Anglian journalistic scoop, because it was merely reprinting the *Sunday Post* from London, made up of official British government information. However what the *Journal* had told the county was that the French Revolution had begun.

The same day the *Norfolk Chronicle*, a more left-wing Norwich-based paper which had already praised the American Revolution, was even more excited about the French, dismissing any doubts some Britons might have as "too ridiculous to be considered".

In its next edition but one the *Ipswich Journal* assumed that its readers had already heard about the storming of the Bastille on the 14th, because it reported the arrest of its governor. (In fact he had been beheaded by the mob). It continued: "by the French mail which arrived today we learn that in Paris everything is in the utmost confusion". And on 8th August it sagely declared:

"The political phaenomenon exhibited by France at this moment is perfectly unparalleled throughout the annals of history".

Meanwhile two East Anglian intellectuals had been eye witnesses.

Dr Edward Rigby, Norwich medical scientist, had gone over to France especially to study the great meeting of the Estates General which King Louis XVI had convened in May, and then watched the summer's unfolding events. He was utterly charmed by it all, and came back enthusing about "an event which will contribute to the happiness and prosperity of millions" and claiming that henceforth Frenchmen and Englishmen would be brothers in freedom.[1]

Arthur Young, agricultural writer of Bradfield Combust, near Bury St Edmunds, was more cautious and less emotional. He had been on two study tours of France already, and noted the lazy arrogance of the less enlightened nobility and the poverty of some of the peasantry. Coincidentally just starting his third visit, he arrived in Paris as the Estates General was gathering at Versailles. Writing up the events in his diary, like Rigby he recognised how radical the changes were, and broadly approved, dismissing King Louis as

Edward Rigby is remembered in this plaque in Norwich.

Arthur Young, agricultural writer from near Bury St Edmunds, had twice previously visited France and made a timely arrival for his third visit.

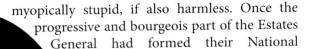

myopically stupid, if also harmless. Once the progressive and bourgeois part of the Estates General had formed their National Assembly, and were in control, he set off eastwards. At Strasbourg he heard about the fall of the Bastille, and, wondered whether France would settle down with its new-found freedoms or lurch into civil war.[2]

Back in East Anglia, as throughout England, the French news was mostly greeted with optimism and satisfaction. A France which was no longer a dictatorship, no longer dominated by an aristocratic military caste and persecuting Catholic church, was welcome to Britons of all classes and political persuasions.

For a century the Whig party had been dominant in Norfolk, first in government, more recently in opposition. They were not democrats, nor sprung from the lower classes. Their leaders inhabited palatial mansions, set in the finest landscaped parks and adorned with Classical columns, orangeries, Chinese porcelain collections and gilt-framed ancestral portraits. But they did believe in limiting the power of the Crown and in the freedom of the individual. In 1788 they had celebrated the centenary of their Glorious Revolution, in which the "Popish tyrant" King James II (son of the beheaded Charles I), had been forced into exile by the Dutchman William of Orange and England had adopted a constitution guaranteeing Parliament, the Protestant religion, and various civil rights. For years their leader in the Commons, Charles James Fox, had been sniping at George III. His constant theme was that the King's hostility towards the American colonists, his bribed MPs and voters, his taxes, his corrupt East India Company, and his standing army, posed a threat to the liberty established in 1688.

Thomas Coke would toast the American revolution at Holkham Hall and was the most influential resident of Norfolk at the time of the French revolution.

Fox had no stauncher supporters than in Norfolk. Chief of these was Thomas Coke, of Holkham Hall near the north coast. Coke (pronounced "Cook") was the wealthiest and most influential resident of the county. Aged 35, he was a descendant of the great anti-royal lawyer of the 17th century, Sir Edward Coke. In 1784, along with a 100 other Whigs, he had lost his Commons seat in the landslide which confirmed in office the King's recently appointed boy-wonder William Pitt the Younger. Coke's junior schoolmate at Eton, and Norfolk landowner neighbour, was William Windham of Felbrigg Hall. Having survived the 1784 holocaust, and held his Norwich seat, he had continued to second Fox's blistering attacks on the King and his ministers in the Commons.

William Windham of Felbrigg Hall (below)was another forthright voice in parliament in intially welcoming the French revolution.

It was natural that Coke, Windham and their Whig friends would feel sympathetic towards the French. The disempowering of an absolute monarch, the religious liberty, the establishment of a "free" parliament, the talk of rights – all this was so akin to 1688 and the American Revolution of 1776. In August 1789, when the French National Assembly abolished feudal ranks, powers and privileges, Windham went over to Versailles to see for himself. Like Arthur Young, he sympathised with the ideals but was unsure about the rowdy and vengeful tone and as to how it would all turn out.

No community in Great Britain was more enthusiastic about the events in France than Dr Rigby's Norwich. The third-largest city in the country, with a large, well-educated and go-ahead middle class, and thousands of proud but impoverished cloth weavers, it was already home to a formidable circle of radical thinkers who despised arrogant and stupid kings, lords and bishops, looked beyond narrow English traditions to enlightened foreigners, and longed for the day when the long-downtrodden subject would become a free citizen. Almost all were Dissenters, that is, radical Protestants who boycotted the official Church of England and met for worship and discussion in their own chapels.

Many were Unitarians. This sect believed that Jesus was a divinely-inspired man, not God masquerading as human, that God loved all mankind, and had no plan to punish them, and that heaven could be created in this world by human action. It preferred the people to their rulers, science to superstition and change to tradition. At its elegant Octagon Chapel, at Colegate, could be found the Taylors, Aikins, Barbaulds, Aldersons and Martineaus – professional people addicted to books, debates and lofty thoughts. Dr Aikin, who practised at Yarmouth and was married to a Barbauld, was a poet and essayist who later founded the *Monthly Review*. John Taylor was a hymn writer. William Taylor, apart from being a textile merchant and a friend of Dr Rigby, was a Continental traveller and the first English student

Edward Rigby, Norwich scientist and physician, had witnessed events unfolding in France and felt that they would lead to the greater freedom of the French and British people. His portrait can be seen at the Norfolk and Norwich University Hospital.

of German literature. Dr Alderson's daughter Amelia was a budding author.[3]

Also enthusiastic were the Norwich Quakers, with their rejection of all compulsion, hierarchy and ceremony in religion, and their belief in inner conviction and free discussion. Their most eminent local members were the Gurney family, famously trustworthy bankers and kindly landowners, who owned a town house in Magdalen Street and a new country mansion at Earlham (later part of the University of East Anglia). John Gurney was the proprietor of the bank. His daughter Elizabeth was, under her married name Fry, later to be a famous prison reformer.

A third pro-French group were the Baptists of St. Paul's Chapel, who believed religious belief must be a free choice, instead of being forced upon the individual. Their ministers were Mark Wilks and Joseph Kinghorn. Most were rather less educated and affluent than the members of the other two denominations.

Bishop George Horne preached vehemently against the radical and revolutionary voices to be heard in the dissenting chapels.

4th November 1688 was the date William had landed in England, and as its 101st anniversary came round the Whigs commemorated it with toasts, speeches and pamphlets. But this time their core message was that the British should renew their libertarianism from the inspiration of contemporary France. William Taylor formed a Revolution Society. In the spirit of the Whig "Glorious Revolution" apologist at his most radical, it pointedly declared that all political authority stemmed from the people, that abuses of power justified revolt, that speech and the press must be free, and that the government-corrupted and controlled "rotten boroughs" should be democratised.

Free and fair elections had not, in reality, been part of the "1688 Constitution". But they were now the leading radical demand. In East Anglia most men at Norwich, Sudbury and Colchester were entitled to vote. (Women were of course excluded). At Ipswich, however, only about a quarter were, in rural Suffolk one in seven, at Harwich and Thetford one in 20, and at Bury St Edmunds just one in 50. The four little villages – officially "boroughs" – of Orford, Aldeburgh, Dunwich and Castle Rising, with a combined population of about 2,000, sent to Westminster the same number of MPs as the four largest towns in the region, with their combined population of 75,000.[4] Most Suffolk and Essex MPs were government hirelings, and in no sense *represented* the people of their constituencies. Although local Dissenters were allowed to vote if they met their constituencies' particular property qualification (that is, in most places if they were well-off) they were still excluded from all public office (as MPs, mayors, magistrates, and jurors) by the 17th century Test and Corporation Acts.

Coke and Windham, though not in favour of one-man-one-vote democracy, had pledged to scrap these statutes and to shift seats from the government-controlled mini-boroughs to the larger towns. In case some of its readers thought that the French were only concerned with abstract political rights of no concern to practical folk, the *Norfolk Chronicle* approvingly told its readers that they had also scrapped the tithes (church local taxes) and game laws which the poorer East Anglian country folk so hated.

The democratic thinking of Norwich was spreading to other towns. On 4th January 1790 Thomas Nash, of Royston, founded a Cambridgeshire Constitutional Society, and organised its first meeting at the *Black Bull* tavern in Cambridge, with the agenda of vetting parliamentary candidates in the elections scheduled for that June and pressurising them to be loyal to 1688. That spring William Taylor's son, William jr, also set out for Paris to sample the National Assembly debates, and came back full of enthusiasm for its recent *Declaration of the Rights of Man and the Citizen*. His account of the visit was serialised by the *Cambridge Chronicle*.

The existing British constitution was however so weighted that the mid-1790 general election returned the Pitt "Tory" government with a very secure majority. Coke retook one of the Norfolk seats, but all the government men were returned. From their pulpit in Norwich Cathedral Bishop George Horne and his chaplain William Jones warned their congregation not to heed the radicalism spouted in the Dissenting Chapels and Whig clubs a few streets away.[5]

William Pitt the Younger, in the watercolour by James Gillray which can be seen at the National Portrait Gallery in London. Pitt was Prime Minister from 1783 to 1801 and then again from 1804 to 1806.

That November of 1790 the Norwich Whigs and radicals joined in scornfully rejecting the right-wing tract which the celebrated Anglo-Irish writer and MP Edmund Burke had published in response to more pro-revolutionary sermonising by the London Unitarian Dr Richard Price. Burke, defender of the American Revolution, critic of English misrule in Ireland and India, and opponent of the slave trade, had until recently been a Whig as radical as Fox, Coke and Windham. But all along he had harboured a dislike of superficial drawing-room liberalism, a love of tradition, and a feeling that natural instinct, not theory and reason, ruled humanity. Now his *Reflections on the French Revolution* utterly dismissed the very "enlightened" ideas which other Whigs found so congenial. He argued that 1789 was the very opposite of 1688, not a Gallic version of it. He depicted French royalty, nobility and clergy as refined and gentle beings, in the clutches of a vulgar middle class on the make and a subhuman mob. He dismissed the human rights proclaimed in Paris as so much empty and pretentious claptrap. He predicted that the French Revolution would become a bloody tragedy for France and a menace to England.

The Norfolk leftists rallied round Fox when he had a blazing row with Burke in the Commons. They got into the rather silly habit of congratulating and thanking Burke for exposing the stupid prejudice of the political right by writing in such far-fetched terms. Windham made a point of making another visit to the French National Assembly, and applauded the grand ceremony in which they, King Louis, and his ministers, swore allegiance to their new

Charles Fox was the principal voice of the radical opposition in parliament.

quasi-democratic constitution. He thought the occasion somewhat mobbish, with the royals humiliated and the audience vulgar, but still felt that "we lose nothing of the solid advantages and privileges that the new system can promise".[6]

Back in Norwich Bastille Day (14th July) 1791 was widely celebrated. The *Norfolk Chronicle* published a song called *The Trumpet of Liberty*, written by John Taylor. The Baptist Mark Wilks preached that the Revolution was orderly, high-minded and above all part of God's plan. He and other Norwich radicals held a celebratory dinner at the *Maid's Head* inn. That night, a 100 miles away in Birmingham, another Unitarian intellectual, the scientist Dr Joseph Priestley, was the target for a right-wing rentamob reacting to his recent statements that royalty were scum and Christ was a revolutionary. They smashed up his house and library and nearby Dissenting chapels. Wilks, Kinghorn, and other Norwich leftists met at Dr Martineau's to organise a sympathy message and a financial contribution, while at Great Yarmouth Independents (Congregationalists), Baptists and Quakers united to send him a solicitous goodwill message.[7]

It is odd that perhaps the two most internationally renowned Britons of the era were both Norfolk men – Admiral Nelson from Burnham Thorpe and Tom Paine from Thetford. Paine, a self-educated one-time corset-maker and Customs officer, had been inspired to emigrate to America by a meeting with the Pennsylvania politician-scientist Benjamin Franklin. He had famously written in defence of the American Revolution and fought in George Washington's army. During the period of reconciliation between Pitt's Britain and the USA he had returned to live in London. Stung into fresh action by Burke's *Reflections*, late in 1791 he went back into print with his *The Rights of Man*, the most readable and popular book written so far on the French Revolution. It sold in its many thousands and naturally came into the hands of the Norwich Revolution Society.

Fanny Burney, born in King's Lynn, recorded many events over the revolutionary period and on meeting Bonaparte, regarded him as an enlightened reformer.

Paine had inspired radicals in the capital to form the London Society for Constitutional Information – or London Corresponding Society – in order to learn from the French and tell them about oppression and injustice in this country. Both London and Norwich groups began to widen their appeal by inviting uneducated workers and craftsmen to their meetings and telling them their rights and potential power – indeed spreading "political information" to the masses became their main activity. In March 1792 the Norwich Society wrote to its London equivalent, asking the latter to enrol 12 of its leaders as members – among them Thomas Goff (the Norwich chairman), William Taylor sr, the Baptist Wilks, and the Norwich secretary Charles Basham. Goff, who signed the letter, cited Paine and the radical writers James Mackintosh and Joel Barber as their inspiration. However he struck a note of moderation by rejecting violence and class war and saying that all hard-working and decent folk, "from the richest merchant to the poorest mechanic", would benefit from a great national Convention which would draft a new and democratic American or French-style constitution.[8]

Although they were much smaller and less active, comparable societies were also starting up at Yarmouth, Ipswich, Woodbridge and Bury St Edmunds, and corresponding with Norwich.

It was this homegrown campaign for egalitarian democracy which first generated a right-wing reaction among our upper classes, months before the French Revolution's violent surge to the left. On 25th April 1792 William Windham argued in the Commons in favour of slave trade abolition, and then five days later against his fellow Whig Lord Grey's proposal for electoral reform, which (he claimed) "tended to raise and excite amongst the people an universal discontent, where none existed previously".[9] Next month Arthur Young called for the English gentry to form a force of armed and mounted volunteers, while many other East Anglian men of property applauded King George III for his recent proclamation against "sedition".

The Norwich radicals were in any case about to overreach themselves. Humanitarians and liberals, they supposed the French revolutionaries to be the same. They interpreted French anarchy as freedom, French vengefulness against the old privileged orders as social justice, and French mob hysteria as Christian community. They had therefore not foreseen the turn events in France were about to take. That spring the republican factions took over the country and invaded Belgium, then ruled by Austria, the birthplace of Queen Marie Antoinette. Austria and Prussia counter-invaded. The Prussian commander, the Duke of Brunswick, threatened dire retribution if the French harmed their by now helpless royal family. Then, in August, a Paris mob stormed the Tuileries Palace, massacred its garrison of Swiss Guards, and arrested the royals. Early that September the Norwich Revolution Society nonetheless signed the most revolutionary statement so far published on this side of the water. This open letter told Parisians:

> "While foreign robbers are ravaging your territories under the specious pretext of justice, cruelty and devastation lead on in the van, while perfidy with treachery bring up the rear … we can inform you, friends and freeman, that information makes a rapid progress among us: and the conjoint reign of ignorance and despotism passes away. Men now ask of each other, what is freedom? What are our rights? … Frenchmen, you are already free, and Britons are preparing to become so".[10]

The letter began to circulate just as the Paris mob were mass-murdering in the prisons, palaces and streets, King Louis was deposed and the republic declared. Tom Paine identified himself with these developments by travelling round Suffolk praising the Revolution and then accepting election to the National Convention, as the new republican legislature was called, as deputy for Calais.

Prime Minister Pitt, part cautious liberal reformer, part glacial numbers man, had so far been unmoved. His right-hand man Henry Dundas had become alarmed, however, getting the Attorney-General to issue an official condemnation of the *Rights of Man* and ordering the Dover Customs to search its author's baggage on his way over to Calais. (Paine responded with a cheeky letter of protest written to Dundas in person).[11]

But the anxiety and alarm were not solely whipped up by higher authority: they spread of their own accord. When the King's-Lynn-born writer Fanny Burney visited the Hawkins family at Halstead, Essex, that September she found the Reverend Hawkins busily writing essays about the French atrocities. Moving on to Bradfield Combust in October to stay with Arthur and Mrs Young, she found that:

> "Mr Young is a severe penitent for his democratic principles, and has lost even all praising for the 'Constituant Révolutionnaires' who had 'taken him in' by their doctrines".[12]

Young's French émigré friend the Duc de Liancourt, then living in nearby Bury St Edmunds, had told him about the brutal murder of his cousin back in France. His earlier back-of-the-mind doubts about the Revolution had been vindicated, and he was planning the Burke-style pamphlet *The Example of France, a Warning to Britain.*

Though quite unconnected, that same month a mob at Yarmouth ransacked the town's food market (several were later tried and a violent woman was transported to New South Wales). The East Anglian propertied and business classes were thereby reminded that violence could happen here too.[13]

However, it was the strategic threat of the Revolution spreading from "the mouth of the French cannon" which finally pushed Pitt off the fence that autumn. In November the French defeated the Austrians at Jemappes, and quickly occupied Brussels, Ghent, Ostend, Namur and Antwerp. Buoyed up by these victories, their National Convention voted that wherever their armies advanced, they would depose and dispossess the existing governments and give their populations liberty. They also reopened the estuary of the River Scheldt, hitherto closed to foreign shipping for the security of Britain and her Dutch allies.

On 8th December the Government, "by the King's proclamation", mobilised the local civilian Militia all along the east and south coast, as far inland as Cambridgeshire. In justifying this, Pitt referred to "persons within the kingdom acting in concert with persons in foreign parts, who intend to subvert the laws and established Constitution of the realm".[14] It was clear that military force would be used against home-grown dissidents should they feel inspired to rise in support of the revolutionary menace spreading north-eastwards just across the North Sea.

In traditional Whig fashion Coke joined Fox in opposing what they called a blatant attempt to introduce military dictatorship and shackle the country to Austro-Prussian despotism. The Norwich radicals were even more vocally opposed. But Windham admitted that he had been short-sighted in his earlier dalliance with the radicals, and voted with the government.

Ten days later a London court tried the self-exiled Thomas Paine in absentia for "seditious libel" against the King (though not for treason). The prosecutor, none other than Edmund Burke, quoted Paine's references to the King as a "tyrant", and the court convicted the author. Significantly Burke had pointed out that Paine had rejected the 1688 Revolution and Constitution as denials, not vindications, of liberty, thereby driving a wedge between

During Thetford's Thomas Paine's significant and lengthy initial stay in America his *Common Sense* and *Crises* writings led the reasoning and reinforcement for the country's independence. movement. Paine returned to England and when charged with sedition, he joined a revolutionary faction in France.

him and such moderate or "constitutional Whig" admirers of the French Revolution as those at Norwich.[15]

It now seemed as if every outraged gentleman, Anglican clergyman, magistrate, burgess and journalist who could put pen to paper was submitting his piece of Burke-derived loyalist and anti-revolutionary rhetoric. The *Ipswich Journal* published a letter signed by "Briton". He attributed "inequality of rank and fortune" to "varying personal talents and exertions", and condemned "those opinions conveyed in the terms *Rights of Man* – liberty and equality – No King – No Parliament – and others of the import". He called for a defence of "liberty and property against the artful attacks of levellers and republicans which are calculated to undermine the happiness and prosperity of the people".[16]

On 24th January 1793 the guillotining of King Louis three days previously was reported in the East Anglian papers, which expressed a new-found sentimental sympathy for this hitherto-denigrated Bourbon. The *Journal* commented:

> "(his) conduct … must reflect eternal honour to his memory, and consecrate his fate to the pity and admiration of every succeeding age, while those who have condemned him shall be regarded as objects of detestation and abhorrence".[17]

Local readers also learned that the French ambassador had been ordered to leave the country by 1st February. Coincidentally that same day France declared war on both Britain and Holland. In its next issue, on 6th February, the *Journal* devoted more space to further eulogies for the French king and condemnations of his killers than to the outbreak of war. "True Briton", writing to it from Chelmsford, said: "philosophers and philanthropists enforce their opinions by the pike and the dagger, those infernal substitutes for reason and argument". He accused the French revolutionaries of "every crime in which the Prince of Darkness can delight", and asked: "What punishment should be inflicted on assassins who have deluged that country in blood?" claiming that in addition to "the cruel butchery of the innocent monarch" 28,000

At the grand Holkham Hall, toasts had been drunk in earlier decades to the success of American independence and Thomas Coke was one of those who expressed initial sympathy for the French revolution.

Frenchmen had been massacred so far. The paper dedicated a poem to the deceased "Most Christian King", with the refrain: "Farewell, thou extremely tortured soul, farewell!" It also printed Mrs Crouch's Covent Garden song of sympathy for Marie Antoinette: "See Austria's daughter, Gallia's queen, with haggard face and altered mien". It added that several women in her audience had fainted and that there was not a dry eye in the house.[18]

That same week more loyal messages flooded into Westminster, and the newspapers, from almost every city, borough and rural hundred in the country. To take one East Anglian example, a meeting at Clare (Suffolk) chaired by the Harwich MP and Pitt-loyalist John Robinson said:

> "We the Merchants, Gentry, Clergy, Yeomanry, Tradesmen and other inhabitants of Risbridge do unanimously declare our sincere and firm attachment to the constitution of the kingdom, formed in remote time, improved in succeeding ages, and established in the Glorious Revolution of 1688".[19]

Most Norwich Whigs and radicals remained unmoved, but even there such Burkean sentiments were gaining ground. The city's new mayor, John Harvey, hosted a big loyalist dinner to condemn the radicals then commemorating the third Bastille anniversary. The existing Norwich Tory clubs had recently published a declaration of their loyalty to the established Constitution and resolve to uphold "peace, order…true liberty and Security of Property". The City Corporation also sent in a typical loyal address.[20]

In just six months there had been a great shift in British educated and propertied-class opinion, and a total collapse in Anglo-French relations. The remaining East Anglian admirers of the Revolution had been overtaken by events, discredited (in the eyes of most), and isolated. And, of course, there was now a war.

The Beginning of the Sea War 2

War between Britain and France was hardly an unknown quantity in 1793. It was the sixth such conflict in less than a century, and the fifth had only ended ten years previously, when France – and later also Spain and Holland – fought on the side of the American rebels. But, in the words of Edmund Burke, this new struggle was "a war against an armed principle" – that is to say, an ideological one. The enemy were posing as the would-be liberators of Britons, and, revolutionary excesses notwithstanding, there were still many Britons who believed them. So, as the Militia Acts and loyal addresses said, at least *potentially* this could be a civil as well as a foreign war.

However it was reassuring for King, Pitt and British establishment that, unlike in the previous conflict, we had many foreign allies. By March 1793 the anti-French Revolution "Coalition" included most of Europe. As its contribution to what was meant to be a combined offensive to eject the French invaders from Belgium and Germany Pitt despatched a large part of the British Army to southern Holland, and put one of the King's younger brothers, Frederick Augustus Duke of York, in command of it. At the King's suggestion three of his Guards battalions went over first, shipping from Greenwich on 26th February. Three more foot regiments followed a few days later.

Because it linked Pitt's government and military depots with his armies and allies on the Continent the road from London to Harwich – and later on to Yarmouth – became the most strategically important in the country. From these two East Anglian ports the Post Office "packet boats" plied to and from Holland and Germany. For the next 20 years along this route travelled sealed copies of treaties, high-level secret military orders, news of great battles, and British government propaganda, as well as generals, troops, admirals, diplomats, government couriers and exiled kings. Apart from Britons, the travellers included Dutchmen, Germans, Scandinavians, Russians, French émigrés and even Turks. Their emblazoned coaches rumbled through the high streets of the Essex towns – leaving Colchester down East Hill and past the bullet-riddled timber-framed Siege House of English Civil War fame.

The journey from London could be done in 12 hours, though some chose to break the journey at Ingatestone or Witham. The turnpike road was well maintained. Passengers enjoyed the scenery, especially after reaching the Stour valley at Manningtree. They were always struck by the setting of Harwich, on its little peninsula almost surrounded by sea and broad estuaries, but also usually dismissed the little town itself as dirty and badly built. Both out- and inbound passengers stayed for at least one night at the *White Hart* or *Three Cups* inns. The outbound ones had to visit the Post Office to buy a travel permit. The innkeepers sold them food and drink for their voyage, shrewdly failing to state their hefty prices till after bringing out their orders. The Customs Officer visited to search their baggage – a nuisance that some were able to avoid by paying a half-crown bribe. The packet captain came to the inns to collect them when he was due to sail, accompanied by boatmen and porters who, for more payments, carried the luggage on board. The packet boats themselves were sleek, low-built, two-masted craft, rigged like yachts. In 1793 they were the *Diana* (captained by Philip Deane), the *Dolphin* (Matthew Flyn), the *Princess of Orange* (Cyprian Bridge), and the *Prince of Wales* (Thomas Hearne). Their captains were part of the town's little elite of voters and borough councillors. Mostly they had inherited their posts from their fathers and held them for life. Hearne, the senior captain, although dogged by suspicions of smuggling, had gone to sea locally at the age of ten. A 1794 passenger described him as "a rough sailor, a man of few words who never for one instant left the deck night or day".[1] Bridge's grandson became a Victorian admiral.

Besides her captain, a packet standardly carried a crew of one mate, two stewards and 13 sailors, and had been armed with half a dozen 6-pounder and 4-pounder guns and the same number of "swivels", little rotatable guns bolted onto the gunwales and firing bags of small iron balls. A packet had about 23 bunks, but took many more passengers who had to sleep on the cabin floors. She was a mail boat as well as a passenger vessel, and carried government despatches which were kept in lead-weighted bags ready for dumping overboard should capture by the enemy threaten.

For the first two years of the war, as in peace, the packets' Continental terminus was the small port of Helvoetsluys, about 25 miles west of Rotterdam at the entrance to the Old Maas river. (The New Maas, on which Rotterdam stands, had been silted up and the great channel of the New Waterway not yet dug). There were two sailings each way per week – on Wednesdays and Saturdays on the second (afternoon or evening) tides. The crossing took from two to four days, according to the wind – if this was blowing from the east the boats had to wait at Harwich, while a westerly wind correspondingly delayed departure from Holland. In the first week of war the Dover-Calais packets were sent round to Harwich. The Harwich ones were employed taking despatches to Lord Auckland (the former William Eden), ambassador at The Hague, who quoted them in an address he gave to the Dutch States General.[2]

On 14th March a third military convoy, of seven ships, left Harwich for Holland with an escort of three frigates from the Nore. It carried army horses and another diplomat, the Earl of Elgin, British ambassador to the Austrian Netherlands and the future purchaser of the Elgin Marbles. Just after it had unloaded in the Maas news was received that the French general Dumouriez had been defeated by Marshal Saxe-Coburg's Austrians at Neerwinden, east of Brussels, forcing him to abandon his invasion of Holland.

The outbreak of war found the 34 year-old Captain Horatio Nelson living on half pay and in semi-retirement with his wife Fanny in his parents' old vicarage at Burnham Thorpe near the north Norfolk coast just one mile from Coke's Holkham Hall. Horatio had met and married Fanny, then a widow with one son, while serving in the West Indies nine years earlier. In February 1793 he had just been given command of the 64-gun "4th rate", *Agamemnon*, then laid up in the Medway. About half her proposed 500 crew were provided by the Admiralty, via the Nore "receiving ship" HMS *Sandwich*. The rest he had to enlist from the London river, north Kent and East Anglia, some volunteers

Burnham Thorpe parsonage, birthplace of national hero Horatio Nelson; the building no longer stands but a plaque on a wall marks the site. The future vice-admiral's father was Norfolk country parson Rev. Edmund Nelson.

Part of Nelson's first crew muster roll on the *Agamemnon* at the outbreak of war in 1793. This page concludes with his signature.

incentivised with "bounties", some "impressed" (rounded up by press gangs). He recruited all his officers from neighbours in Norfolk – together with his young servant, William Hoste, son of the rector of Tittleshall and many years later a celebrated captain in the Adriatic and admiral. About a third of his seamen were also East Anglians. The ship's muster roll for that winter lists nine men impressed at Harwich, several dozen at Yarmouth, and others at Lynn. Individuals had originated from Cambridge, Wymondham, Wells, Sculthorpe, Creake, Houghton, Ringstead and Terrington (Norfolk), Ipswich, Stradbrooke, Houghton and Woodbridge (Suffolk), and Colchester and Great Oakley (Essex) – along with the more far-flung Isle of Skye, Philadelphia, Virginia and Naples. Nelson sent round some, along with his baggage, from Wells on a cutter he had hired. Having fitted out and stored at Sheerness he left for the Mediterranean.[3]

The press gangs which Nelson relied on were part of the Navy's "Impress Service", set up by one of Pitt's acts of parliament in 1790. It had three East Anglian bases: Lynn (i.e. King's Lynn), Yarmouth and Harwich, commanded respectively by Captain Isaac Prescott, Captain James Glasford, and Lt William Collis.[4] They were authorised to conscript any young mariners they found in their ports and neighbouring areas, provided these were British, able-bodied, and not employed on government service. Their recruits would

William Hoste attended the same North Walsham school that Nelson had been at. At his most significant frigate battle later in the conflict he would lead his squadron with the signal "Remember Nelson".

A page from the muster roll of the *Agamemnon*, with many Norfolk place names in the places of birth. Two of the crew listed are from Nelson's own birth village.

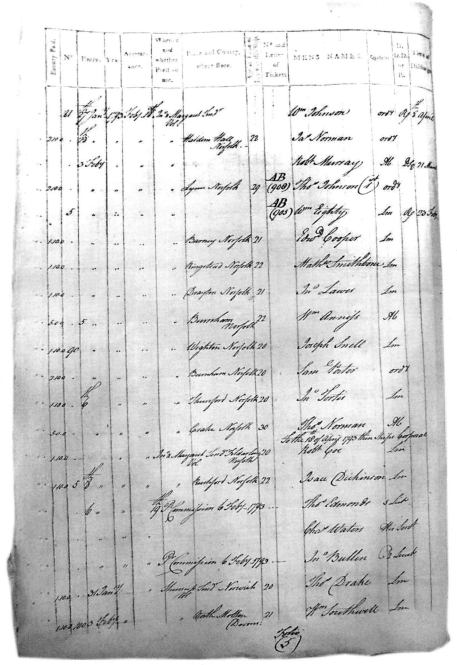

then find themselves on the first available coastwise naval cutters headed for the Thames or Medway, and would be helping to man whichever ship was next to put to sea. In the 20th century world wars naval conscripts were summoned to drafting bases with printed call-up papers and free train passes evenly and fairly distributed throughout the country – including inland and to "landlubbers" – and then given several months shore training. But in 1793 most seafarers were illiterate, postal services and communications did not exist in the modern sense, there were no shore training establishments, and so this sort of treatment was understandable. After all, the inland brothers and cousins of the "victims" were quite likely conscripted into the Militia.

Nonetheless the Impress Service was hardly popular. The 1790 act had been passed in response to a threatened war with Spain over their seizure of British ships in Nootka Sound, on the far-distant Oregon Pacific coast. That war had never broken out, but, in proportion to the numbers of men called for by Pitt, there had been more volunteering and less impressment than for this new French war. Whether this was because the French enemy was seen as more dangerous, or because fighting a supposedly free people had less appeal than fighting a Catholic monarchy, is unknown. When Captain Lecky's 16-gun *Racehorse* sloop fitted out on the Tyne during the first fortnight of war she waited on the Impress Service to draft local men. She was then witness to a disturbance so serious that it was immediate national news, demanding the attention of the Government, the Admiralty, and the newspapers, including those down in East Anglia. The Newcastle and Sunderland coal miners and iron smiths had just gone on strike over wages and food prices, and their defiance had immediately spread to the Tyne and Wear seamen who crewed coal ships down to London. When the press gangs tried to enter Newcastle they were chased out and threatened with death. The town's mayor appealed to Dundas to send regular troops to keep order, doubting the reliability of the militia. In the end the sailor protesters signed a petition of grievances which the mayor thought had quietened them down, but the *Racehorse* got no conscripts and had to content herself with a group of hired volunteers which had gathered on the beach at South Shields.[5] When Collis turned up at the *Royal Oak* pub in Harwich in 1794 landlord Cole scared him into hasty retreat.[6]

Only a very small part of the Royal Navy was actually in the North Sea – as opposed to the dockyards and fitting out ports in the Thames and Medway – in 1793. However London was already the world's largest commercial port, and most of the shipping from Northern Europe approached it along the east coast. As in the 20th century world wars, by far the largest single cargo involved was coal from Newcastle and Sunderland, because by now all of London and every town in southern England relied on it for heating, metal forging and smithing, baking, and brewing, even though coal-fired transport and electricity were still unknown. Thousands of coal brigs, each carrying 100-200 tons, unloaded in the Thames alone in a year – scores per week. And so, as in the world wars, the east coast coal route, past East Anglia, offered an obvious and easy target to enemy raiding ships – and brought the war, as opposed to war preparations, to at least the edge of the region. However, unlike in the 20th century, these raiders were not warships, aiming to sink the merchantmen, but civilian-manned privateers, licensed by the revolutionary authorities to capture them, bring them back home, and sell them and their cargoes.

It is some sort of tribute to the otherwise crude and shambolic early British war organisation that a system of merchant convoys was already emerging – based, of course, on experience from the many earlier conflicts with the French and Dutch. In the 20th century large shore naval and civilian offices, coded telephone and radio messages, legal compulsion, pages of complex standing orders, flotillas of escort destroyers and corvettes, and strings of naval bases, would have been involved. But in February 1793, without any of this, and almost spontaneously, many east coast shipowners, ships' captains and merchants were grouping their vessels by the dozen, even the hundred, in

The officers of the *Agamemnon*.

harbour and waiting on the arrival of a warship or two for escort. This involved them getting the town's naval agent or mayor to send a paper message down to London, and the Admiralty then sending one of its ships to the harbour concerned.

From the outset, the privateers avoided these convoys and swooped on ships sailing independently and unescorted. On the morning of 8th February several of them started to chase merchant ships in the Dover Strait and on the eastern edge of the Thames Estuary. One northbound merchant brig, the *Robert and Mary*, was hailed and shot at 15 miles north-east of the North Foreland. She escaped, but a boy in the crew named Allen Hall was wounded in the leg, and when she reached Orfordness two days later he was landed in a boat and taken to a surgeon in Ipswich. Two days later his ship came into Yarmouth and reported the incident to the local Customs. Just as she was doing so a small southbound brig from Sunderland, carrying coal to London, was chased into Harwich harbour, whereupon her pursuer was seen making off to the south-east.[7] On 21st February the "posts" from London reported that these privateers had been fitting out at Dunkirk and Calais, and, according to the 19th century French historian Gallois, twenty-six left Dunkirk alone by the end of the month.[8]

On the 22nd Captain Alexander Fraser's 14-gun *Savage* sloop, the only one the Royal Navy had had in the North Sea at the outbreak of war, was cruising between Margate and Orfordness, covering the Duke of York's second convoy, when she came across a Portuguese trading brig homeward-bound from Amsterdam. Her captain told Fraser he had spotted a French privateer nine miles to seaward. The *Savage* headed in that direction and caught sight of the raider, but lost her.

On the morning of Sunday the 24th civilians onshore at Lowestoft spotted a suspicious brig and dogger about six miles out to sea. Soon afterwards a large convoy of colliers came down from the north, having left Tyne and Wear after the rioting there. Some of the Lowestoft men rowed a boat out to alert their escort, which was none other than the *Racehorse*. She diverted to seaward, spotted the brig, evidently a privateer, chased for three hours, but eventually lost her and continued south with the convoy. That afternoon another privateer was spotted heading for a King's Lynn commercial brig leaving Southwold's little harbour. She managed to get back into port, but the French came so close their four swivels could be seen and their (English) shouts heard.

Next day the *Savage* spotted what was probably this same privateer about ten miles east of "Leostoffe", as Fraser called Lowestoft. After a short pursuit during which the *Savage* fired two of her guns, she boarded and captured the Dunkirk privateer *Custine* – together with one British commercial brig which the Frenchman had seized. The French captain, Thomas Ballan, had with him a crew of 26. Two days later Fraser landed these prisoners and the crew of the brig at Yarmouth. Apparently his crew had been excessively celebrating, because his log records that en route he ordered one of his marines to be given 12 lashes, and on leaving for Flushing on the 28th inflicted another twelve on a seaman, and six each on another four – all for drunkenness. As for the captured Frenchmen, Ballan and three others were released on parole, the rest detained.[9]

Ironically that same day, off Yarmouth, a Danish brig bringing timber to London was captured for the second time, having been captured three days earlier in the same area, then retaken and released by one of the Duke of York's troop convoy.

On 3rd March a London-bound collier and some Harwich cod smacks passing through Yarmouth Roads told local boatmen that they had seen enemy privateers in action off Cromer. They reported that a French schooner had seized three or four fishing smacks near the Well Bank, and that a lugger privateer had taken two colliers. On the 5th Captain Thomas Williams' *Lizard* sloop, then in the heart of the North Sea about a hundred miles north of Yarmouth, intercepted the French eight-gun brig privateer *Sans Culotte* and bombarded her with chain shot. The French quickly hauled down their flag. Williams put a petty officer and eight men onto his prize, and brought Captain Charles Bacquelin and all 42 of his crew onto his own ship. Next day, ten miles from Yarmouth, *Lizard* found a second privateer, *Le Vaillant Custine* (two guns, ten swivels) and again opened fire. Soon the raider, Captain Louis Jack, and his 38 crew were in her possession. On the 8th the British frigate and her two prizes anchored off Yarmouth. Both privateers were from Dunkirk. Two local yawls came out with a file of Marines to bring the 81 captives into harbour, while the prizes sailed on to the Thames. The Yarmouth prison records tell us that the two French captains were paroled and six of their men were allowed back to Dunkirk, though in some cases not for two years.

Simultaneously Captain Lansdaine's *Iris* frigate was dealing with what was probably the lugger privateer just reported at Yarmouth. On 6th March, north-east of that port, she opened fire on a lugger which was with a brig. Boarding the latter, she found her to be the *Trouw Parochie*, a Dutchman which had been returning to Amsterdam from Lisbon, but was now controlled by a French prize crew. Removing the Frenchmen, she took the brig in tow and headed on to the Nore. Next afternoon, coming up the Swin about seven miles off the Clacton shore, she again sighted the lugger, which must have been following her. Casting off the tow, she used seven guns to force the raider *La Communitée* to "strike her colours". Two days later she anchored herself, her prize and her recapture at the Thames entrance, and handed over her prisoners to HMS *Terrible*.[10]

The two *Custines* were named after the former aristocrat who had led the revolutionary army to victory at Jemappes and taken Belgium. Several Channel privateers had been given the same name. But, after defeat in Germany a few months later the hero of the hour was recalled to Paris, put on show trial, and guillotined. Such was the Revolution.

While the *Childers* frigate was escorting troop transports over to Holland on the 14th she captured and scuttled the Dunkirk privateer *Triton* halfway between the Naze and the Maas. One week later the *Cleopatra* frigate, then about seven miles east-south-east of Lowestoft, unsuccessfully pursued the Dunkirk privateer *Trois Amis* (rendered in English as "Three Brothers"). The following day she recaptured the *Peggy*, a merchantman from Port Glasgow, which had been seized by this privateer and remanned with seven of her crew while bringing rice from Charleston, South Carolina, to Bremen in north-west Germany.

Meanwhile the *Lizard* was cruising about 30 miles south of Harwich. On the 22nd she joined up with the *Cleopatra*, used four guns to stop a dogger which *Trois Amis* had captured and remanned, and put an officer and five of her own men on board. Two days mornings later, nearby, she found a lugger flying the English flag, forced her to heave to, and thereby captured *Trois Amis* and the 15 crew she still had on board. In the afternoon she fired at another vessel which got away, conferred with the *Niger* frigate, mistakenly shot at a Harwich packet, and, at twilight, captured a Hamburg brig being sailed by five more men from *Trois Amis*. Next morning (the 25th) she came across a Dutch brig, manned yet again by a prize crew from that privateer, fired three guns, and recaptured her. Soon afterwards some Ostend fishing boats came in sight. As that Flanders port was still French-occupied *Lizard* seized one along with her six crew. The 26th and 27th were decidedly stormy, forcing the frigate and her two prizes and three recaptures to anchor in Hollesley Bay, off Orford. Finally, on the 30th, she led her little flotilla into Harwich harbour, landing a total of 34 prisoners.[11]

As a consequence of Neerwinden the French fled Ostend on 30th March. British warships, coming down the coast from the Maas, recaptured six British merchant ships in the harbour or leaving it.

And so the southern part of the North Sea was more or less cleansed of enemy raiders within two months of war's outbreak. For a few British warships to have captured or recaptured so many privateers and their prizes, and landed 115 French prisoners in East Anglian ports alone, was rather a striking achievement. Some gloating was understandable. A popular story along the east coast at that time was that when a captured privateer crew were brought ashore at Margate their officers asked not to be locked up in the same place as their men, but that their captors solemnly told them such a privilege would go against the egalitarian decrees of the National Convention in Paris.

The commerce-raiding war was not all in one direction. By March five East Anglian revenue and excise cutters were given letters of marque (privateering licences) so that if they came across enemy merchant or fishing vessels on their North Sea patrols they could capture and sell them. They were the *Hunter* (Captain Thomas Riches) and *Lively* (Matthew Gunthorpe) of Yarmouth, *Argus* (John Saunders) and *Viper* (Robert Adams) of Harwich, and *Repulse* (Haske Munnings) of Colchester. Their captains were as celebrated along the east coast as those of the Harwich packets. Most were to serve throughout the war – that is, for more than two decades. Their vessels, with their fore-and-aft sails on long booms and bowsprits, were fast and manoeuvrable, and each carried at least half a dozen cannon and about 18 crew for dealing with the often well-armed smuggling craft. In March two French fishing doggers came so close to Yarmouth they could be seen from onshore: *Lively* promptly cut her cable, rushed out and captured *L'Isabelle* and her three crew. A few days later the *Hunter* brought in the 40-ton Dunkirk fishing boat *Le Fruit de la Mer*. The same month the *Argus* seized the *Catherine and Ann*, a Hamburg merchantman carrying contraband to Rochefort in France. And in April the *Repulse* retook the captured London collier *Commerce*.[12]

That spring the *Ceres* frigate and *Nimble* cutter were patrolling and convoy-escorting up and down the east coast. On 26th June, off Harwich, the two ships joined up and headed north. Two days later, nine miles east of Orfordness, they intercepted the *Petite Victoire* of Dunkirk (and her prize, the Newcastle collier *Catharine*.) For the next four weeks the trio of frigate, cutter and captured privateer patrolled round the North Sea as far north as the Tyne and almost to the Belgian and Dutch coasts, before coming back up the Suffolk and Essex coasts to the Nore.

While all this was going on absolutely nothing was seen of the enemy regular navy. Not only was nearly all of it based on Atlantic and Mediterranean ports, but it had been plunged into disorder by the purging of politically suspect officers and a crisis in manning and supply. From the outset the British North Sea frigates and sloops had been cruising in total safety and confidence (for they completely outgunned the privateers) all along the Continental coast from Helvoetsluys to the Dover Strait, recording their logbook positions in relation to the church spires in enemy-held Ostend, Dunkirk and Calais. So free of French ships was the North Sea by May that some of the handful of British warships there were heading back to the Channel and on to the Mediterranean or Caribbean.

Temporarily driven away from the east coast, some of the enemy privateers moved over to the Skagerrak, south of Norway, to prey on shipping bound from the Baltic to Britain. A Lynn brig was reported taken there in April. Then a Yarmouth merchantman, the *Helen*, was seized by *Le Patriote* privateer, whereupon a Danish ship came into that port claiming that no fewer than 11 British ships alone had just been taken in the same area. Fox himself raised the issue in the Commons, accusing the Government and the Admiralty of neglect. It soon turned out that the Danish report was false, but the Whig leader argued that so many warships had been sent overseas that home waters were wide open to the raiders. He pointed out that huge merchant convoys, such as those from the Baltic, generally had an escort of just one or two men of war. The Government feebly responded that it had taken care of the risk on the east coast with a single frigate, the *Sheerness*.[13] But it did send *Ceres*, *Nimble* and other ships to Norway, where they exchanged fire with *Le Patriote* but found no other raiders.

The Royal Navy presence in the North Sea for the first two years of war was indeed pretty scant. For instance, there were, properly speaking, no naval bases in eastern England (or, for that matter, anywhere in Britain north of the Thames). Only Plymouth, Portsmouth, Chatham and Sheerness could be so described. This was because only a small part of the French coast faced the North Sea. British warships in the area were too few and scattered to be grouped in fleets and squadrons; mostly operating singly and, reliant on sail, they did not need to berth in harbour to refuel, as 20th century ships did, and could reprovision in the Medway at the end of their cruises. Additionally, since there was no radio for ship-shore communication they could not be directed or plotted from onshore. The Royal Navy men of war running up and down the east coast escorting convoys or hunting privateers might anchor for a few days in offshore roadsteads, such as Yarmouth or Harwich, but seldom came into actual harbours. Because the Nore (Thames-Medway anchorage) was officially counted as a fitting-out and provisioning port, and not a high seas operational station, the ships based there did not at first feature in the Navy Lists under the heading of "North Sea and Downs" (the Downs is the anchorage off Ramsgate). Indeed in 1793 these lists give never more than three (and often zero) British men of war in the North Sea, as opposed to over 100 in the English Channel.[14] However in reality about 15 frigates, sloops and cutters were operating off the east coast that year, not counting the many and often larger ships waiting in the Medway.

This was more or less adequate at the time. The Scheldt and Ostend were back in Allied hands. Only a few French privateers operated in the North Sea. In February 1794 a pair of them captured two colliers near Yarmouth – the *Good Intent* of London and *Friend's Goodwill* of Sunderland. Both were recaptured approaching the French coast and taken to Dover. In April two Harwich vessels were taken off Norway and destroyed by *Le Subtile* – *The Sisters* and the *London*. The same month the Hamburg-bound London-based *Mary* was captured off Yarmouth. At Dunkirk her mate, who was still on board with a French prize crew of four, attacked them with a hammer, smashing in the skulls of three and breaking the arm of a fourth, then sailed her to Margate.[15] Few privateering incidents involved such violence. No privateers or recaptured Allied ships were brought into Yarmouth or Harwich between mid 1793 and late 1794.

The *London Gazette* carried all officially released information, including Orders in Council that dealt both with civil matters and actions required for the war effort, recruitment for the army and navy and rather sycophantic letters of loyalty from cities and boroughs. Intelligence from the war was printed and the regional newspaper of East Anglia would repeat and adapt such information for their readers.

Numb. 13527.   **[389]**

The London Gazette.

Published by Authority.

From Saturday May 11, to Tuesday May 14, 1793.

AT the Court at St. *James's*, the 9th of *May*, 1793,

PRESENT,

The KING's Most Excellent Majesty in Council.

WHEREAS by an Act passed in this present Session of Parliament, intituled, " An Act " for indemnifying all Persons who have been co-u " cerned in advising or carrying into Execution an " Order of Council respecting the Exportation of " Wheat and Wheat Flour ; for preventing Suits in " consequence of the same, and for making further " Provisions relative thereto ; and also for authorizing " His Majesty to prohibit the Exportation of Corn, " Meal, Flour, Bread, Biscuit and Potatoes, and to " permit the Importation of Corn, Meal or Flour " on the Low Duties," it is enacted, that it shall and may be lawful for His Majesty, His Heirs and Successors, and He and They is and are thereby authorized, by and with the Advice of His or Their Privy Council, until the End of the present Session of Parliament, from Time to Time, to prohibit generally, for a limited Time, the Exportation from Great Britain of any Sort of Corn, Meal or Flour, Bread or Biscuit whatsoever, or of Potatoes ; and in like Manner to permit generally the Importation of Corn, Meal or Flour, subject to either of the Low Duties specified in the Table D. contained in an Act passed in the Thirty-first Year of His present Majesty's Reign, intituled, " An Act for regulating the " Importation and Exportation of Corn, and the " Payment of the Duty on Foreign Corn imported, " and of the Bounty on British Corn exported :" His Majesty therefore, by and with the Advice of

this His Majesty's Order in Council, it shall be lawful to import Wheat and Wheat-Meal or Flour upon the lowest Duty specified in the Table marked D. in the said Act passed in the Thirty-first Year of His present Majesty's Reign, until the End of the present Session of Parliament, or until such Time as His Majesty shall think fit to revoke this present Order.—And the Right Honourable the Lords Commissioners of His Majesty's Treasury are to give the necessary Direction herein accordingly.

W. Fawkener.

Extract of a Letter from Colonel Sir James Murray, Bart. Adjutant-General to the Forces under the Command of His Royal Highness the Duke of York, to Mr. Secretary Dundas, dated Tournay, May 10, 1793.

IN consequence of the Movements of the Enemy, which gave Reason to expect an Attack upon the Austrian and Prussian Posts, His Royal Highness determined to march in the Morning of the 8th to their Support. He arrived about Six o'Clock at the Camp of Maulde with the Brigade of Guards, and a Battalion of the 10th Regiment of Hanoverian Infantry. The Prussian General was by this Means enabled to reinforce himself, at St. Amand and the adjoining Wood, with the Troops which had occupied that important Position.

The Attack commenced about Seven o'Clock. It was directed against the Posts occupied by General Clairfait, which extend from the Scheldt to the Abbaye de Vicogne, and the Prussian Corps which defends the Wood in the Front of the high Road, leading from that Place to St. Amand.

To these Points were directed the whole Efforts of the French Army, which had been previously reinforced by all they could bring together from every Quarter. General Knobelsdorf, having been under the Necessity of sending a considerable Part of his Troops to support the Austrians at the Abbaye de Vicogne,

Loyalists & Jacobins   3

For Tories and loyalists the mood in the spring of 1793 was confident (it later transpired overconfident). General James Murray (the Duke of York's adjutant) and Ambassador Auckland shuttled back and forth liaising between Holland and London through Harwich. In April the Norwich and Ipswich press, reprinting the official *London Gazette* "posts", announcing that British, Dutch, Austrian and Prussian leaders had met at Antwerp and agreed on a joint plan to converge on Paris and oust the revolutionaries – and then that the Duke of York's modest army had marched south and joined Coburg's Austrians at Tournai. Similarly, in May, that the Duke of York had been reinforced with a cavalry brigade. These same newspapers also reported each week on every twist and turn of the political events in Paris-- and in some ways, owing to the less populist journalism and looser security in those times, with more accuracy and precision than in more modern wars.

One great and significant difference between 1793 and the 20th century was that in the first case much of Britain's opposition party did not back the government's war. In spite of the French killing their king, invading other countries, and declaring war on *us*, Fox and Coke of Holkham resolutely refused to condemn the Revolution, vote for Pitt's budgets and militia laws, or applaud the British military and naval operations. No one should judge their apparently very disloyal and short-sighted attitude before asking themselves one great question. Were the French Revolution's fundamental ideas so noble and inspiring – at any rate for the oppressed, excluded and idealistic – that they transcended the bloody feuding, revenge and hysteria in which its participants were indulging? Or were its principles in themselves so crazy that they caused its violence? The Whigs and Norwich radicals still took the first view – as did many Americans, Irishmen, Belgians, Dutchmen and others. Burke, of course, had long taken the second – and so by now did disillusioned local folk such as Windham of Norfolk and Young of Suffolk, along with thousands of loyalist Tory gentry, Anglican clergy and the like.

And on balance loyalism was in the ascendant in the East Anglia of 1793, as it was throughout England. Since two months before the war the right-wing backlash movement started by the ultra-loyalist John Reeves had spread to almost every part of the region. In consequence every other town (not excluding Norwich) and rural hundred had its anti-revolutionary "association", the purpose of which was quite explicitly not just to rally patriotic feeling against France but to isolate, spy on and scare the radical and anti-war contingents. At so small and rural a place as Lavenham in Suffolk, it was later recorded…

> Mr (Isaac) Taylor irritated the turbulent loyalty of the mob … who in their loyalty for Church and King had a grudge against him as a leading

member of the Meeting House. These friends of order assembled with flags, drums and pitchforks, vowing to burn his house down.

Taylor, father of Jane the writer, was unrelated to the Norwich family of the same name, but shared their qualified and peaceful sympathy with the French Revolution. He was saved by the local Anglican rector.[1]

The guillotining of King Louis, French territorial aggression, and the fact that British soldiers and sailors were now risking life and limb in war, pushed the "Foxites" and radicals onto shaky ground. Fashionable pro-revolutionary views which authority had at one time tolerated, even to some extent shared, were now to be condemned and if possible suppressed.

At Cambridge University, where once Cromwell and Milton, and more recently Pitt and the anti-slavery campaigners Wilberforce and Clarkson, had studied, and the tradition was left-leaning and Whig, a controversy broke out just as war began. It concerned William Frend, a divinity lecturer at Jesus College, who had not only voiced his doubts about the Church of England and its conventional Trinity but enthusiastically expressed his approval of the French Revolution. He had set out his views in a booklet entitled *Peace and Union Recommended to the Associated Bodies of Republicans and Anti-Republicans*, printed by P C Croft at St Ives. For his distributing this round the university some of his colleagues, mainly a Dr Kipling, subjected him to a kind of trial in the spring of 1793. Many of the university's undergraduates, including the young poet Coleridge and the logician Augustus de Morgan (a romantic and a rationalist!) campaigned in his defence, graffitiing walls, insulting dons and holding noisy meetings. Frend admitted that originally he "did rejoice at the success of the French Revolution", but at the time so had every other decent person, "when tyranny received a fatal blow, when despotism was overthrown … (and) at the time when that horrid dungeon was destroyed, in which had been tormented so many wretched victims of caprice and effeminate cruelty". He added that that had been the feeling of the whole university in 1789, and that, like "every other lover of freedom", he had been shocked by the subsequent (1792-3) bloodshed. He admitted that the recent turmoil in France had left him in a "wretched state of suspense, and not having sufficient grounds for uniting fully in our wishes for the success of any party, we have conceived that silence on French affairs is most advisable". A fair and wise remark! But the Vice-Chancellor, Dr Isaac Milner, who presided at the hearing, found against him and deprived him of his fellowship.[2]

Frend's thinking, even if theologically unorthodox, was no more radical than that of Fox or Coke, and till recently not much more so than Windham's or even William Pitt's, but Cambridge was in part a seminary for the established church and a nursery of statesmen, and, moreover, authority had by now swung behind the alarmism of Edmund Burke. Frend did not have the parliamentary and aristocratic privilege to demean officialdom of a Whig magnate. Smearing him with his earlier comments about the Bastille was rather a dirty trick of Kipling's, but his continued references to "despotism" and "tyranny" were not acceptable to an Anglican, patriotic, traditionalist (and Tory) court in 1793.

A few weeks later (in June) Coke and other Norfolk Whig MPs, and of course the Norwich radicals, supported Fox's demand in the Commons that Pitt negotiate peace with France and thereby end the tax rises, militia-conscripting, naval press gang and other measures which in their opinion endangered civil liberty. Their timing was bad. For some months the press had been reporting that the Jacobins had been gaining ground in France from the more moderate (though still republican and pro-war) Girondins, and that July they seized Paris in a coup. The term "Jacobin" had originally referred to a broad-based "enlightened" Paris club to which even constitutional monarchists had belonged – Arthur Young had briefly been an honorary foreign member! But by 1792 it had been taken over by such Rousseau-inspired leftist fanatics as the Robespierre brothers and Saint Just, who had not only pushed for the death of the King but demanded an ongoing ideological and class war against ex-nobles, clergy, former officials of the old regime, wealthy men in general, and even "dubious" members of the Revolution's own National Convention.

East Anglia's right-wingers, whether longstanding Burkeans or more recent converts to conservatism such as Windham and Young, from now on attached the label "Jacobin" to anyone they disliked, from Tom Paine (who was in fact a Girondin) to Fox and Coke's Whigs. Simply to say the word was to allege treachery, terrorist cruelty, depravity and rabid madness. By the summer of 1793 Frend was being called a Jacobin by Milner, and the Norwich Unitarians, Baptists and Quakers by their Anglican neighbours.

Young in particular was now outburking Burke in his right-wing pronouncements. His *The Example of France a Warning to Britain*, published that spring, not only condemned the French republicans for anarchy, mob rule and territorial aggression, but attacked all ideas of fairer elections and social reform at home. He snarled at "the whole race of reformers and Jacobins". A Whig reviewer rebuked him:

> "We dread anarchy, and we abhor massacre and plunder, as much as Mr Young…but we cannot be convinced that in order to prevent these evils it is necessary to relinquish every idea of representative government and to adopt the despotic sway of self-appointed power, and place the merit of a legislative body precisely in speaking against the will of the people whom they govern; to arm the rich against the poor, and to consign the lower classes of society to perpetual ignorance and slavery".[3]

Young, incidentally, now had a direct vested interest in Pitt's government, since he had been appointed Secretary to Sir John Sinclair, head of the Board of Agriculture. The Board was not a modern executive ministry, but a research institute which supplied the authorities with statistics and advice on food production. Young spent more time at Bradfield than in London. Nevertheless, as in the 20th century world wars, the food supply was to be militarily and politically vital.

That 25th June 1793 the various Norwich radical groups sent a letter to the London Corresponding Society which, when it later became public, lent at least some credence to Young's views. Goff, the Norwich secretary, seemed to exceed London's impatience. Noting that they had listed as proposed tactics for achieving parliamentary democracy petitioning the King, appealing to the MPs themselves, or holding a National Convention of the British people, he summed up the first as "futile", the second as "tolerable", and the third "best of all". He did add "if circumstances permit", but his dismissal of George III in favour of a popular assembly named after the one in Paris obviously struck many as disloyal and unpatriotic.

He and his friends undoubtedly stirred additional controversy by despising Pitt's war effort and the army which Dundas had sent to the Continent to spearhead it. When the Duke of York scored his first victory by capturing the French border town of Valenciennes that August, the mayor and loyalist clubs of Norwich rang the church bells and held a great street party in which free beer and lashings of roast beef were dispensed to the populace. The city's United Societies (as the radical groups now called themselves) glumly boycotted the occasion. They were congratulated by Thomas Hardy, the self-educated, Paine-inspired, leader of the London Corresponding Society, in an exaggerated and overoptimistic letter on 17th October. He declared:

> "The ignorant ... betrayed their imbecility on the occasion; but the taking of a town; the slaughtering of thousands of human beings; the laying waste of whole provinces, or the enslaving of a nation (however evil they may be) can only, for a small space of time, retard the progress of truth and reason: Be not disheartened therefore, pursue your plan, instruct mankind, and constitutionally set your faces against existing abuses: Be assured that many of our friends, who only wait a favourable opportunity to join us, while our enemies have much enfeebled themselves and their cause by arbitrary executions: Despotism is at its last gasp: one or two campaigns more will terminate its existence".[4]

His "favourable opportunity" and "last gasp" do not in themselves spell rebellion, but he did go on to repeat a false rumour that a French invasion of England might soon be attempted. In the New Year Pitt had him and his London colleagues arrested for treason; such letters, they alleged, were incitements to revolution, and revolution in the midst of war. Later Isaac Saint, landlord of the *Pelican* inn in Norwich and secretary of one of the city's many radical clubs, was taken up to London and questioned – by the Privy Council no less. It seemed to bode ill for the prisoners that in the meantime the Jacobin Committee of Public Safety had unleashed their Terror – massacring captured rebels, and guillotining first ex-Queen Marie Antoinette, then various generals (such as Custine), then numerous critics both to their left and right, including Danton, the Parisian orator-hero who had until recently been the scourge of counter-revolutionaries and hero of the crowds, but now advocated moderation and reconciliation. Tom Paine himself had been cast into the Luxembourg prison and sentenced to death for his Girondinism. It seemed that the direst prophecies of Burke, the darkest forebodings of Windham, and the fiercest claims of Young, had come true. The Revolution had gone from bad to worse, and was "devouring its own children". If the Norfolk Foxites and Norwich utopian intellectuals would not give up on France and rally behind Pitt's war effort even now they must be Jacobins themselves.

This was certainly the thinking of most propertied and educated East Anglians (at any rate outside Norwich and some nearby Whig estates), and to us today it is understandable. The blind eye turned to the dictatorship, mass murder and territorial aggression of a hostile foreign regime by its British sympathisers seems so akin to that of the apologists for assorted totalitarians and terrorists 150-200 years later. On the other hand, as the dark side of Robespierre and company became undeniable, Norfolk anti-war Whigs and radicals such as Coke, Gurney, Wilks and the Taylors sincerely claimed that the Revolution and its ideals were greater than their betrayal by the Jacobins, that Britain was not France, and that they themselves were legally campaigning for a free constitution – not plotting bloody revolution and terror. And although modern conservative interpreters of Burke and Young see in them a defence of British liberty against totalitarianism, *Reflections* and *A Warning to Britain* read much more like a defence of British wealth and privilege against liberal democracy.

After Valenciennes, on the orders of Dundas, the Duke of York marched not on Paris but Dunkirk. As a nest of French privateers, and a potential naval base halfway between the Channel and the Scheldt, the British government aspired to hold it, if only as a bargaining counter. The city was only invested on the eastern side and held out – and in September a French relief force defeated the Duke's German contingent at nearby Hondschoote and forced him into retreat. Further south-east the following month the Austrians were pushed out of French territory at Wattignies. The Allies' opportunity to converge on Paris and oust the revolutionaries had been lost.

At Norwich anti-war opinion was further sustained by economic hardship and the unyielding attitude of the government towards electoral reform. The Quaker banker Gurney paid for and signed a handbill which blamed the government for the war and the war for the hardship, said that hostilities could and should be ended, and praised Fox for demanding this. A copy found its way to Edmund Burke himself, who denounced Gurney as a "virulent Jacobin" and exploded: "By the means of this gentleman…one of the most insidious and dangerous handbills that ever was seen, had been circulated at Norwich against the war, drawn up in a hypocritical tone of compassion for the poor".[5]

At the same time he launched a tirade against another of his Norfolk bêtes noires, Coke, who (he declared)…

> "has been lately very busy in spreading a disaffection to this war (which we carry on for our being) in the county in which his property gives him so great an influence. It is truly alarming to see so large a part of the aristocratic interest engaged in the cause of the new species of democracy, which is openly attacking or secretly undermining the system of property by which mankind has hitherto been governed. But we are not to delude ourselves. No man can be connected with a party which professes publicly to admire or may be justly suspected of secretly abetting this French Revolution, who must not be drawn into its vortex, and become the instrument of its designs."[6]

By November there were signs that the wealthy Norwich liberals such as Gurney were losing control over their working class tutees. Another handbill read: "Ninety thousand pounds are taken out of our pockets every week for the expenses of this cruel, unjust and destructive war. Oh, ye sons of liberty, why will you suffer it? Haste and revenge your wrongs. Let us all join and rebel". Still another (though I wonder if this was the product of a Tory smear campaign) proclaimed: "He who wishes well to the cause of liberty, let him repair to Chapel Field at five o'clock this afternoon. There he will meet with hundreds to begin a Glorious Revolution".[7]

For all their extremism it was clear by 1794 that the Jacobins were a military success and that the French Revolution was set to overspill the frontiers of the country as it had for a short time a year earlier. However, when Fox attacked both Pitt and Dundas's participation in the war and their strategic handling of it in a Commons debate on 21st January, he could only find four East Anglian MPs to vote with him (out of around a dozen Whigs), namely, Coke, Burch of Thetford, Western of Maldon, and Crespigny of Sudbury – and his motion was lost.

The Norwich loyalists were beginning to even the odds, or at any rate regroup. On 12th April hundreds of citizens packed the Shire Hall for a county meeting to vote whether Norfolk should raise voluntary subscriptions and form volunteer "Home Guard" companies for the war. J R Dashwood, in the chair, struggled to keep order as the noise swelled. The speakers included Windham, like-minded members of the celebrated Whig Townshend family, Coke, the Thetford lawyer John Mingay, and the Norwich radical Barnard. Coke denounced the resolutions as unconstitutional, and along with them the war itself. Such was the uproar that Dashwood said he could not count the vote, whereupon the right-wingers moved off to another room and passed the resolutions anyway. Oh to have been there that evening![8]

In May news came of another Allied defeat. The Jacobin generals Jourdan and Carnot ("the organiser of victory") had defeated Coburg's Austrians at Fleurus, in Belgium, and forced them back into Germany. The Duke of York, committed to defend Holland and dependent on Dutch ports, had fallen back again to the Maas. The Revolution again bestrode the Scheldt, even though there were momentary celebrations in June when Admiral Lord Howe destroyed a French fleet off Ushant on the Breton coast. For a year and a half William Windham had supported Pitt's war and warned against revolution, but tried to keep his links with Fox and Coke by saying that he was still a Whig concerned to safeguard traditional English civil liberties. He had had private meetings with Pitt and Dundas, and they had gone so far as to promise him a post in government, but he had declined and stayed on the fence, albeit leaning in the Tory direction. He had called his position "Old Whig", or "third party", to distinguish it from the pro-French radicalism of "New Whigs" like Fox. But in July he finally made his move and joined the new coalition government brokered by Pitt and his Whig allies the Duke of Portland and Lord Loughborough. He accepted the post of Secretary at War (minister in charge of army recruitment, supplies and weaponry – as opposed to Secretary of War, i.e. Dundas, in charge of strategy).

Man of honour that he was, Windham immediately submitted himself to a by-election at Norwich. His Foxite Whig challenger was the above mentioned John Mingay. To his high-ranking friends Windham still spoke of regret and moderation, but he allowed his supporters to cart a mock guillotine and bloody headless corpse through the streets, with the banner "This is French liberty".[9] He declared that he represented "not only the cause of this country, but of all the civilised world" – by no means an untoward comment at a time when Robespierre's Terror was reaching its peak.

The by-election result was significant. Windham won by almost a two to one majority, in a constituency which was not some backward "rotten borough" where a handful of voters were controlled by the sitting MP or the Government, but most of the adult male population could vote.

In conceding defeat in a letter to the Norwich sheriffs, Mingay had a final dig at the Government's smear tactics, its military failure, and the "treachery" of his one-time Whig leader:

> "We have lately been so very assiduously reminded of the horrors and iniquities of Jacobinism that we have been in the habits of esteeming it a sort of allegory of all that is cruel, bloody and wicked. But we must begin to suspect that there is something amiable in the system we are taught to abhor, if those persons are Jacobins who oppose the present absurd war, and who reprobate such men as by a dereliction of former principles and sentiments, seek to perpetuate and increase its calamities."[10]

Read carefully, however, his protest goes some way to explain why he had lost.

One of Windham's first tasks as a minister was to go and see the Duke of York in Holland. Their meeting was courteous, but Windham told him that his army was failing and that he no longer enjoyed the confidence of the Government.

Ironically, just a fortnight after the Secretary at War's re-election the *coup d'état* of Thermidor removed the Jacobin leaders from power and sent them to the guillotine. Tom Paine, a moderate by their standards, was freed from the Luxembourg, having just escaped the blade when his guards failed to spot the death sentence chalked on his door because it was open at the time. ("The destroying angel passed by", he wrote). A month later his persecutors' party was expelled from the Committee of Public Safety which effectively ruled France. By the end of the year their club was shut, and many of their laws (including those regulating the market) had been scrapped. The Norwich radicals took heart, believing that a more moderate regime in Paris and the disappearance of the terrorist bogey would improve their chances of peace and reform. In October William Taylor, Amelia Alderson and a young lawyer named Marsh launched the *Cabinet*, a quarterly literary magazine full of enlightened and progressive articles. Pitt and Dundas had suspended Habeas Corpus (the traditional right not to be held without trial) and passed the "Two Acts" making attacks on the Constitution and holding anti-Constitution meetings to be felonies. Instead of praising revolution, which would have antagonised peaceful middle-class dissenters, the Norwich radicals were able to attack the Government for destroying existing civil liberties, which appealed to them. The city's Common Hall was packed for another meeting against Pitt's repression, and well over 5,000 citizens signed a protest petition which Fox read out in Parliament.

That same month the leaders of the London Corresponding Society were tried for high treason. The trial was closely followed at Norwich, because the prosecution cited the earlier correspondence (back to the spring of 1792) between the two cities' radicals. The London jury acquitted all the defendants (it was a Whig town), and on the whole the evidence presented by the prosecution rebounded on them, because it made the accused appear naïve and peaceful rather than sinister and violent. Furthermore the economic hardships, the hopeless prospects of the war, Pitt's repressive laws, and the new political moderation in France once again had Fox, Coke and the Norwich radicals calling for peace negotiations. While Burke thundered against talking to terrorists in his *Letters on a Regicide Peace* Arthur Young also took up his pen to squash this talk.

> "Put an end to so ruinous a war, say other men, and leave the French to themselves, they will quarrel and cut one anothers' throats in a civil war … Suppose a peace concluded with the moderates, our fleets laid up, and our armies disbanded: a new revolution of party takes place: the friends of peace destroyed, and Jacobin fury predominant"[11]

In order to head off the sort of "poor man's arguments" heard so loudly at Norwich, he pointed to the ruthlessness to the lower orders of Carnot's armies, which looted occupied towns, lived off the crops of the peasantry, conscripted men with the "*levée en masse*", and killed those who deserted:

> "But there are men among us in a state of poverty, thrown perhaps out of employment by bankruptcies or the war, who, being in distress, think that no change could to them be worse. Miserable infatuation! Let them also view the French operations in Flanders! What is the language used to the lowest of the people, even to such as were friends? Money they have none, for all was seized, but they have arms and legs – their bodies are in requisition – and the only salute of fraternity – MARCH OR BE HANGED!!!"[12]

The Cabinet put the leftist counter-argument. It lambasted the government as "nefarious and unprincipled", and elaborated:

> "…by the various means of fraud, falsehood, exaggeration and calumny; by dark rumours of insurrection, by dismal warnings and lamentations from the pulpit, and by horrid tales of plots, pikes, knives and poisoned arrows, the nation has been alarmed with imaginary evils, and deluded into fatal insensibility to real danger".[13]

To Young at this juncture a British victory was more a hope (to be brought about by counter-revolution in France) than a prediction. The "war against an armed principle" was going badly, and this was to bring new developments to East Anglia.

The Émigrés 4

Bizarre it may seem, but during the French Revolution some of its most celebrated refugees found their political asylum in that most English of counties, Suffolk.

The first, at the end of 1791, were Madame Stéphanie Félicité du Crest de Genlis (to give the best-known of her many aristocratic names), and her household. She was 45, and possessed of a handsome round face, large eyes, and charisma. Her fame was as a writer on education, one of the mistresses of King Louis XVI's cousin the Duc d'Orléans, and the chief tutor and temporary guardian of his 15-year-old daughter Adélaide. To 2, Angel Hill, Bury St Edmunds, she brought a group of 18 or so, including Adélaide, her own illegitimate daughter Pamela, her niece Mme de Cercey, three science tutors, and her servants. They had left Paris for Bath the previous summer, because Orléans, now known as "Philippe Égalité", had wanted to send his sickly daughter to a place of safety while he played his ill-advised game of allying with the current leftmost French faction so as to preserve his own wealth and prestige, isolate the King and Marie Antoinette, and perhaps eventually become head of state himself.

At Bury de Genlis presided over a busy and cultured household. The three girls had lessons in chemistry and botany from their tutors and went on nature walks. They were driven over to Hengrave Hall to play the harp (de Genlis's favourite recreation) with the children of Sir Thomas Gage. They toured Cambridge University, went to Newmarket Races, and danced through the night at Bury balls. Inevitably de Genlis soon came across Arthur Young and Fanny Burney. Fanny, who had met her before the Revolution and admired her, now found her flashy and frothy.[1] Visiting London, Mrs Young and her daughter narrow-mindedly and jealously gossiped about Angel Hill, and said how scandalised they were by de Genlis living under the same roof as her low-born landlord, dining with her servants and taking them on her walks, and letting her girls dance with strangers.

Hengrave Hall, Suffolk, one of the places favoured by Madame de Genlis and her three girls.

After the republican takeover of September 1792 the new regime ordered all émigrés back to France on pain of the loss of their property and civil rights. Consequently Égalité recalled his self-exiled household, but on arrival in Paris they were immediately banished to Belgium, where Pamela married the Irish revolutionary Lord Edward Fitzgerald, who was to die fighting the British in 1798. Later her estranged husband, Brûlard, Marquis de Sillery, was guillotined by the Jacobins.

There is a plaque at Angel Hill proclaiming that Philippe Égalité's son, Louis Philippe (then known as the Duc de Chartres, and from 1830 till 1848

Madame Stéphanie Félicité
du Crest de Genlis.

François-Alexandre,
Duc de Rochefoucauld-
Liancourt: agricultural
improver, author, adviser
to King Louis XVI and friend
of Arthur Young.

the French king), also stayed there. This visit seems to be a myth. No French historian, nor Mme de Genlis in her own memoirs, nor Arthur Young or Fanny Burney, mention it. No longer de Genlis's child pupil in 1792, Louis Philippe was still in France, and an officer in the revolutionary army. The following spring he deserted to the Allies with Dumouriez, and settled for a time in Germany, where Mme de Genlis and her girls also found refuge. His father, having gone so far as to join the Jacobin Committee of Public Safety, was purged by Robespierre and died under the guillotine.

No sooner had the de Genlis group left Bury than another French aristocrat arrived. François-Alexandre, Duc de Rochefoucauld (until recently Duc de Liancourt), had been a great Norman seigneur, landowner and royal courtier, and like Orléans and de Genlis a person of the liberal and reforming Enlightenment. This was his second stay, because he had first visited back in 1784, thereby befriending Arthur Young, with whom he shared a passion for the modernisation of agriculture. It was with him that Young had stayed during his three tours of France just before the Revolution. In 1789 Liancourt, like Orléans, had pressurised King Louis to ignore the advice of Marie Antoinette, and instead shed his absolute power. Yet, unlike Philippe Égalité, for the next three years he had stood by the King, living with him at the Tuileries Palace and helping to protect him from the Paris mob. In the summer of 1792, when the building was stormed and the royal family seized, he became a marked man. After his cousin, the then Duc de Rochefoucauld, was killed by a slogan-chanting Parisian wielding a stone, he fled to England, adding his kinsman's name to his own.

Liancourt-Rochefoucauld lived in a modest Bury house rented for him by his old friend Young – whether at Angel Hill or not is unclear. They frequently dined together at Bradfield Hall. There Fanny Burney met him, finding him physically imposing, charming, and dignified, and empathising with his fall from grandeur. She was amused by the lively conversation, especially Young's reverting to English when his French ran out.

In March 1793 Liancourt-Rochefoucauld (reported by the *Ipswich Journal* as two different people!), and other French émigrés (names unreported) joined Young at Apheston Church, south of Bradfield, for Sunday service. The rector, Humphrey Smythies (son of a one-time vicar of St Peter's, North Hill, Colchester), preached a sermon lamenting the recent execution of King Louis, which deeply moved the Frenchmen in the congregation. His text, from Proverbs, was:

> "He that said unto the wicked: Thou art righteous: Him shall the people curse, Nations shall abhor him. But to them that rebuke him shall be delight, And a great blessing shall come unto them".[2]

A stern rebuke for the likes of Coke and the Norwich radicals, if ever there was one.

However, as Young worked on his *Warning to Britain*, and Rochefoucauld, whose English was fairly good, widened his social circle among the Suffolk aristocracy, their friendship cooled somewhat. Young believed that his guest had brought misfortune on himself – and on France – by his short-sighted conduct in 1789. In return Rochefoucauld, though he had always found Arthur Young admirably modest and kind, confessed that he had never much liked Mrs Young, whom he dismissed as a swarthy, charmless, bully. He later claimed that his original stay at Bury had been due, not to his admiration for Young, but such contacts as the squire at Hessett (six miles from Bury), the Huguenot Leceup.

Indeed why de Genlis and Rochefoucauld had both come to Bury is something of a mystery. They were far from friends. It may be that the explanation runs as follows. Liancourt-Rochefoucauld's first stay in 1784 was due to his interest in East Anglia's go-ahead farming, and Bury was the market town at the heart of the region. There he inevitably befriended Young, whether he had already studied his writings or not. His account of the visit was read by de Genlis (with her interest in scientific botany). And when Rochefoucauld fled to England in the Revolution it was to the town he best knew and most appreciated. Also, perhaps, both émigrés were almost as much escapees from London as from Paris. This was because the other French refugees in and around the capital – mostly minor nobility and clergy – detested and ostracised them for their "playing with revolution" and blamed them for their own plight. Clearly it would be a mistake to see the French émigrés as a united community!

In 1794 de Genlis and the survivors of the Orleans family were in Switzerland, while Rochefoucauld began a great tour of North America (simultaneously the refuge of the very different Tom Paine and Joseph Priestley). In 1799 Napoleon allowed both back into France, where they ended their days.

The third of our notable Suffolk émigrés was the Breton intellectual Réné de Chateaubriand, another former liberal noble who was to be a prominent figure in post-Napoleonic France. He was an appalled eye witness to the mob violence of 1789 and 1792, but in between travelled in the USA. While fighting as a counter-revolutionary in 1793 he was badly wounded, escaped to Jersey, and finally reached England. Meanwhile half his family were killed by Robespierre. After several dismal months living in poverty in London, in 1794 he moved to Beccles, on the Norfolk border of east Suffolk. In his posthumously-published memoirs (1850) he said that this was to consult its rector, an expert in ancient manuscripts, about some translation work he was doing at the Camden Collection. However, according to his biographer Le Braz, who visited Suffolk over a century later, he had actually been hired to teach French at two local schools, the Fauconberge at Beccles, and Brightley's at nearby Bungay.[3] His employers were two Anglican rectors – Bence Sparrow at the first and Charles Brightley at the second. Outside the classroom, in his Beccles lodging, he began writing *Les Natchez* and *Atala*, poetic stories about the encounter between Indians and Catholic missionaries on the fringes of the United States.

After an interval back in London, the following year he was back in Bungay, where he met John Ives, the rector of another local parish, Ilketshall St Margaret, who lived in Bridge Street. It was Ives who was the scholar (of Greek and mathematics), though apparently also a heavy drinker. After falling from a horse the young exile was invited by Ives to stay in his house and recuperate. There he taught Ives's 15-year-old daughter Charlotte, took her on walks, and fell in love with her. But when Mrs Ives took him aside one day and told him that Charlotte wanted to marry him, he admitted that he had a wife in France, and fled for London, never to return. The girl later wed a

Réné de Chateaubriand, the most famous of the French exiles who stayed in East Anglia, in his case Beccles and Bungay in north-east Suffolk.

Norfolk naval lieutenant named Sutton, eventually a rear-admiral, and settled at Ditchingham just outside Bungay. Chateaubriand himself went on to be one of the most famous men of the age – the great defender of Catholicism and constitutional monarchy against atheism and republicanism, the leading intellectual of the Bourbon Restoration after Napoleon's fall, and (if any one person merits the title) the founder of European cultural Romanticism.

But, according to his memoirs, he never forgot Charlotte. Over a quarter of a century later, while Louis XVIII's ambassador in London, they met again. According to Chateaubriand, she called upon him to ask him to use his influence with Canning, the British Foreign Secretary, to find a job for her eldest son in India. The boy and his ambition disappear into the background as the great man and the middle-aged Mrs Sutton clasp hands and breathlessly keep asking "Do you remember?" [4]

Whether this meeting really happened, at least as Chateaubriand describes, is uncertain. Cynics have suggested that what occurred at Bungay was the selfish seduction of a naïve child, that this was notorious around the Waveney at the time, and that he was sacked for it. More charitably, they have supposed that the author turned his encounters with Charlotte into literary devices to illustrate love and nostalgia. On the other hand, some Suffolk historians, following Le Braz's own theory, have claimed that his local stay was so influential for Chateaubriand that it shaped his Christian and romantic thought and, through that, the wider international outlook of the 19th century. I have to admit that I see more in the first view than the second, admirer of this great Frenchman though I am.

These three celebrated people were by no means the only émigrés to live in the region, and unlike them many of the others stayed. The first refugees from revolutionary France tended to be Catholic clergy, rather than nobles or political dissidents. In 1790 the new regime confiscated most of the land and funds of the Church and used them for state finance and backing the new "assignat" paper currency. In 1791 all clergy were made dependent on the state for their posts and pay, and had to swear an oath of loyalty to it, which meant that they were no longer free to preach their old "superstitions" and social conservatism. In 1792 many clergy were massacred along with other undesirables in the panic triggered by Allied invasion. And in 1793 the Jacobins branded Christianity as counter-revolution, looted and shut the churches, banned religious preaching and teaching, and set up their own quasi-religious "Cult of the Supreme Being".

Eastern England had traditionally been a stronghold of Protestantism, as hostile to Catholicism as Jacobin France. Virtually the only "papist" presence was a few gentry families who had clung to what their neighbours had dismissed as an alien creed since the time of Queen Elizabeth I. But these were new (and for many strange) times. Pitt's government had hit on the principle "My enemy's enemy is my friend", so that instead of being agents of the French enemy and to be persecuted, Catholics were its victims and to be rescued. In 1793 the Rev. Hayward of Copford, near Colchester, preached sympathy for the exiled French clergy and asked parishioners to offer them financial help. His sermon was published as a one-shilling booklet. [5]

That January, during the first French advance across Belgium, 140 French émigrés landed from the Helvoetsluys-Harwich packets. The Harwich Customs were ordered to write down the identity, place of origin and occupation of each, search their baggage, and disarm any that carried weapons. The following year, during the second French invasion, more refugees arrived. Many were Belgian and English, hitherto safe under Austrian rule. A particularly interesting group to settle in East Anglia were the English Catholic nuns from the Belgian cities. Sir Thomas Gage, who two years earlier had hosted Mme de Genlis's harp-playing, welcomed the very different Augustinian nuns from French-occupied Bruges, mostly daughters of old North Country recusant families. Their prioress, Mary More, was a direct descendant of the Sir Thomas More beheaded by Henry VIII.[6] The English Canonesses of the Holy Sepulchre at Liége settled in New Hall, at Boreham just outside Chelmsford, thereby founding the school which still exists there.[7] At Bodney, in west Norfolk, the Tasburgh family loaned their manor house to the French nuns from Montagris, who had escaped their homeland via Flanders.[8] As these exiled nuns died off during the course of the war they were buried on the north sides of the local Anglican parish churches, not far from suicides, criminals and Protestant Dissenters.

Meanwhile the French refugee priest Louis Simon lodged with Mrs Margaret Wood, one of the extremely few Catholics in Ipswich, and in her Silent Street parlour celebrated the first mass to be held in the town for 235 years, thereby re-founding the Church which has since continuously existed there. His first congregation mostly consisted of Irish soldiers and their families from the local army garrison. [9]

One of the youngest émigrés to pass through East Anglia was a French boy of 14, who came ashore at Aldeburgh from Rotterdam, probably with a group of Dutchmen, when the French finally overran Holland in the winter of 1794/5. His refugee diary, narrating his journey from Dunkirk through Belgium, Germany and the Netherlands, was published in London as a two-column bilingual text – part educational, part propagandist.[10] What became of him is unknown.

Defeats & Discontents 5

We left Britain's under-strength expeditionary force recoiling from Flanders into Holland in the middle of 1794, and Windham conveying Pitt and Dundas's disapproval to its commander, the Duke of York. For the rest of the year it took part in no major battles, but was worn down and demoralised by having to man the line of the River Waal against frequent French raids, coping with supply shortages, and neglectful and incompetent officers. Some of the reinforcements Dundas had sent it (via Ostend) earlier in the year were diverted to operations against the French sugar islands in the West Indies, where, incidentally, most died of disease. Illness also hit the remainder of the force in Holland. The sick were evacuated to Harwich, and in July temporary wooden-hut hospitals were installed there and at Ipswich by the Admiralty Transport Board official Jeremiah Fitzpatrick. In December the Duke of York himself returned home on the *Fly* frigate via Harwich.

On the morning of 19th January 1795 a Dutch warship put into Yarmouth Haven and landed Princess Wilhelmina of Orange, her daughter-in-law Princess Louisa of Hesse-Darmstadt and Louisa's infant son. Wilhelmina was the wife of Prince Willem of Orange, the Dutch Stadtholder or head of state. She was a sister of King Friedrich Wilhelm II of Prussia, nephew of the late King Frederick the Great. Louisa was a daughter of the British king George III and therefore sister of the Duke of York. The Orange family – since the Netherlands was a republic technically not royalty but very close to it – were fleeing from the French. That very day the French army, after a rapid advance across frozen rivers, had entered Amsterdam and The Hague.

The two princesses and the little prince were, according to the *Gentleman's Magazine*, greeted "with that generous sympathy which characterises Englishmen". The garrison lined the market square, where the public unhitched the refugees' carriage from its horses and pulled it twice round. The Mayor laid on a meal at his house.[1]

Later that day a letter reached Rayner Cox, the Mayor of Harwich, from the Home Secretary, Lord Portland, telling him of the imminent arrival of the Stadtholder himself.[2] Next morning dawned with snow and gales, and the North Sea off the harbour was churned into white foam. But three small open-decked Dutch fishing boats came in round Landguard Point, having crossed from "Scheveling" (as the English then called Scheveningen), just outside the Hague. On board one, accompanied only by four crew, one a boy, and feeling understandably queasy, was the Stadtholder. On the others were his son and heir Prince Willem (known as the "Hereditary Prince"), his younger son the

Prince of Hesse-Darmstadt, General Bylandt, two officers named Bentinck, and a secretary. The Stadtholder was King George III's first cousin. Having quickly recovered from their seasickness in the way that people do once on dry land, the Dutchmen were given breakfast and later lunch at the *White Hart*. Then the Hereditary Prince went ahead with the baggage to Colchester, where accommodation for Orange himself awaited at the best inn in town, also called the *White Hart*. Then he immediately set off for Yarmouth to fetch the other half of the family. The Stadtholder arrived at Colchester in the evening. Next day the Hereditary Prince and the Yarmouth group came down to join him. Somehow they were unwittingly passed on the road by the Duke of York, the Dutch ambassador Baron Nagel, and Pitt's young envoy Hugh Elliott, who arrived at Yarmouth and found them gone.

Finally, at midnight on the 22nd, the Orange family were reunited at the Colchester *White Hart*, outside which we should picture a military guard and a large crowd. The next morning the Mayor, garrison commander Colonel Sloper and all the Corporation, greeted the Stadtholder at the Town Hall, where Town Clerk Francis Smythies read a message of sympathy and lunch was provided. Outside it was still snowing and blowing a gale.

Next day the guests were moved to the High Street house of textile manufacturer Isaac Boggis, today the Minories art gallery. Fortunately Boggis had bought a dinner set in expectation of hosting Princess Caroline of Brunswick during her proposed journey from Germany via Harwich to London to marry the Prince of Wales, though in the event she had landed at Greenwich. The Orange men, accompanied by Count Bentinck, took a walk around town, visiting local shops and chatting to onlookers. The weather had improved.[3]

The house which was once the home of Colchester merchant Isaac Boggis – the Dutch Stadtholder stayed here in January 1795, in quarters Boggis had intended for Princess Caroline.

Only 11 years before Holland and Britain had been at war, since the former had joined France and Spain in support of the rebel Americans. To be fair, William Prince of Orange had gone along with this reluctantly, since at the time he had been little more than a figurehead, in spite of descending from his namesake William the Silent, the first Stadtholder and leader of the 16th century war of liberation against Spain. In 1787 Pitt and Friedrich Wilhelm of Prussia had ousted the Republican or Patriot Party who had been gaining control of the country, and reinstated the Orange dynasty in full power. But now France, having disposed of her own ruling family, had overrun Holland and reinstalled the Patriots. The French revolutionaries had toppled their first foreign ruler, and the country for whose independence Pitt had long been struggling had fallen.

There had not been enough transport at Harwich to bring the Dutch army officers, so they stayed one night at the house of one of the town's MPs, the fortunately-Tory John Robinson. The same shortage existed at Colchester, so the Mayor had to hire farm wagons to carry the Orange family's baggage to London. Standing orders on the coast were to detain all Dutch fishing boats, but Dundas wrote to Cox to allow the three Scheveningen ones back home.

On 31st January, the Dutch ports having fallen to the French, the North Sea packet run was moved north to Yarmouth-Cuxhaven, almost tripling the length of the crossing.

The fall of Holland triggered fresh demands for peace from leftist circles in England. On 5th February Henry Hobart, one of the Norwich MPs, presented to the Commons another 5,000-signature petition to this effect from that city. Britain, it said, should desist from all interference in French internal affairs, contrary to the Burkean position that she should support counter-revolution there. Coke said that the petition represented the unanimous feeling of Norwich, and accused the Government of dictatorship, corruption and being deluded. Fox said that the economic hardship in the city was partly due to its loss of overseas markets due to the war. Hobart, heading off the Tory argument that the local (and national) economy were in fact holding up quite well after two years of war, said that general business confidence was low and (rightly) predicted a bad year. The Whigs joined in another attack on the renegade Windham, claiming that the "ruinous situation" was caused by his "pernicious councils". The Secretary at War had given his critics ammunition by sneering "Perish commerce!" (in today's parlance "Damn the economy!") in response to those he saw as short-sightedly putting profits ahead of national security.[4]

Merchants and small traders in other towns also wanted their local corporations to send in protests to London, but at Tory strongholds such as Colchester and Ipswich the mayors and aldermen refused.

The petition debate was of course won by the Government, but concern about the economy, and with it social and political discontent, grew. East Anglia was as badly hit as any part of the country. Half the population of Norwich, and several thousand more people in north Essex, had long been employed in woollen manufacture. As Fox himself admitted, they were in trouble even before the war, owing to competition from the mechanised cotton factories in the North. But the war had cut them off from their nearest overseas markets in the Low Countries, and exporting further afield was hampered by privateers and rising insurance rates. On the agricultural front, business-minded landowners (prominent among them Coke in Norfolk), were not renewing leases of tenant farms when these expired, but incorporating them in their own "home farms" and thereby dispensing with much of their labour. The unemployment caused by these two trends was offset by men joining Army, Navy and Militia, but only partially. And to pay its additional armed forces the Government was increasing taxes on business, which passed them on to the wider public with price increases and wage freezes. To feed the unemployed parish rates (the equivalent of modern Council Tax) were generally rising – steeply in some places.

The main expenditure of the "lower classes" was on bread baked from wheat flour. The 1794 harvest had been a fairly good one, and for most of that year the per-quarter (ton) price of wheat had been around 60 shillings (£3). In December, however, it had started a steady climb, rising above 70 shillings in January 1795, 80 in May, and 100 in July. In August it approached 120 in some places, fell sharply back to 70 in September, then rose steadily through the autumn and winter to over 100 again.[5]

The associated disorder started as early as January 1795. In April attacks on bakeries, flour mills and markets flared up in dozens of small towns and villages, mainly in the area of north-central Essex and west Suffolk between Chelmsford, Saffron Walden, Bury St Edmunds and Hadleigh. It mostly took the form of people seizing control of provisions (not just bread, but also meat and dairy) and selling them off at what they considered "fair" old prices. The Riot Act was read at some places, while Militia and mounted Yeomanry (the latter mostly local farmers) stood guard or patrolled the streets. On 12th August the hungry mob at Halstead were so formidable that they held off a party of Surrey Fencible Cavalry sent to disperse them from Lexden camp, and a sizeable infantry force had to come from Danbury to rescue them. One of the cavalrymen was pulled from his horse and gravely injured with a pitchfork.[6]

For a whole year a greater controversy raged over the wheat crisis than British military strategy or political ideology. Everyone from the great expert Arthur Young to the illiterate labourer had an explanation. In December 1795 an "Ipswich farmer" wrote to the *Gentleman's Magazine* in defence of the yeoman, while a complete idiot sent another letter blaming the overpopulation caused by floods of foreign refugees (who numbered, in truth, not more than one in a thousand). The farmers, and many of the consumers, blamed the corn dealers. "No such trade is as much exposed to popular odium", the great economist and Pitt-mentor Adam Smith had written 20 years before.[7] He had argued that high corn prices were always due to bad weather, because by its nature production was so widespread that it was impossible to monopolise, meaning that no one could sell the crop for more than the supplier next door. But was the war a factor, as some radicals alleged? It had cut Britain off from possible wheat imports from France and the Low Countries, and made ones from the Baltic and America more expensive, but this was not the late 19th or 20th century, when half the nation's flour was milled from foreign grain – the proportion in 1795 was no more than about 5%. Similarly, the theory that the price had been inflated by the armed forces (including Militia) buying up bread might be true if it cost more near the coast, where all sailors and most troops were based, but this was not the case.

The Government rightly claimed that production of the other, hardier, cereals (barley, rye, oats) was only slightly down, and their prices only marginally up – and that nutritious bread could be made from them. 200 years ahead of time they blamed consumers for turning their noses up at coarse, dark, bread through a fussy addiction to the fine, white, variety, and for not eating enough vegetables!

The actual causes of the problem were far from clear-cut, and still defy textbook analysis. The rise in wheat prices, and the discontent, started when the 1794 stocks were still plentiful and no one could have predicted the 1795 harvest. Most authorities, whatever their political bias, agreed that the 1795 harvest was only about 20-25% below that of 1794's. As Young pointed out, the weather of 1795 was better than that of 1788, 1789 and 1790, when the price rises had been far less. The winter had been shorter, the spring and summer neither unusually wet nor dry. Nevertheless, others said, the snow which had greeted the House of Orange in January had quickly thawed and then the ground had frozen hard again round the vulnerable young roots.[8] It might be surmised that, sensing that their sales and profits would be down as a result, farmers and dealers had raised prices at that point to offset the poor returns they foresaw later in the year. When the shortfall was confirmed at harvest time, the second price surge occurred.

Considering that East Anglia was the granary of England – or at any rate one of its granaries – one might expect that its wheat, flour and bread prices would have been some of the country's lowest. In fact they were, both before and after the 1795 harvest, the highest apart from those in the immediate London area, and the wet and cold north-west and north Wales.[9] The notion that Essex, Suffolk and Norfolk people were being overcharged and starved, so that the lion's share of the crop could be sold in London, therefore spread among the local poor.

Many other factors in the bread crisis were suggested, and taken into account by a parliamentary inquiry on the subject. Wheat flour, with its ability to yield a fine, white, paste, was widely used to make starch for wig powder (in an age when wigs were worn, not just by lawyers and gentlemen, but by all middle-class men and even by soldiers). It was used to thicken soups, for making cakes and biscuits, and for distilling. Where there was a local surplus around a seaport, such as at Yarmouth, some was exported. Above all it was fed to cattle, pigs and poultry.[10]

After its inquiry the Government banned the exports and the use of wheat for wig starch and distilling, authorised bakers to sell a mixed wheat-barley loaf with a stamp indicating ingredients, and directly bought scores of shiploads of north German wheat and paid for it to be stored at ports such as Yarmouth and Lynn. It also removed import duties on wheat which its wholesale buyers agreed to sell for under 70/- (£34.10s) per quarter. Later the dealers, such as those at Lynn, were to protest – and demand compensation – when prices fell back below that level and saddled them with stocks they could only sell at a loss.[11]

As for the rioting, I must add that it is too mechanical an explanation merely to plot this against the average, published, monthly corn dealers' prices. It may well be that the bakers disproportionately upped their prices too, without this being recorded. And also that the increases drove many to desperate action in the Chelmsford-Bury area because they were jobless owing to the depression in the local textile industry. (Norwich woollens also suffered, but there an efficient, though costly, poor relief system operated). Pitt himself paid a visit to Gosfield Hall, at the centre of the distressed area, and is said to have walked through nearby Halstead after its riot, and been shocked by the visible hunger and misery of the townsfolk.[12]

Meanwhile the army sent to Holland by Pitt and Dundas in 1793 had retreated to Bremen in north-west Germany, and in March and April 1795 landed at Yarmouth and Harwich. Most of the troops were ragged, hungry and sick. Colonel Arthur Wellesley (later Duke of Wellington) came into Harwich with his 33rd Foot Regiment, which then marched on through Colchester and Chelmsford to London. He later said that his year and a half on the Continent had taught him how an army should *not* be led. Prussia made peace with France in April 1795, Spain in September.

The authorities were still sufficiently worried about Norwich to station 2nd Dragoon Guards and 53rd and 88th Foot (the Connaught Rangers) there after their return from the Continent. According to James McGrigor, the 88th's surgeon, their officers were regularly insulted and even attacked in the street. Up to 30 men deserted per day, some allegedly helped by radicals who provided funds and safe houses.

From France Paine published a new edition of his *Rights of Man*, via a London printer, and surprisingly without interference from Pitt and Dundas. In the preface he rhapsodised:

"It is now very evident that the despots of the world are beginning to totter, and the foundations of the thrones to shake. There is also a tremendous storm approaching, the thunders roll nearer and more near, the whirlwinds sweep the surface of the deep, and the vessels of Monarchy and Aristocracy already blaze amid the fury of the lightnings – a moment more and the tempest shall overtake them, and they shall founder forever and ever."

In October the poor's discontent with their lot flared up in the capital. Readers of the eastern counties newspapers learned that the mob had stoned the windows of the King's coach and Downing Street. This outrage against the monarch brought the predictable breathless declarations of shocked loyalty from the Tory town Corporations of Norwich, Ipswich, Bury, Colchester and so on.[13]

In the spring of 1796 an abundant wheat crop sprouted, the price dropped back to 1794 levels, and the rioting ceased. Following the practice at Speenhamland (Berkshire) many East Anglian parishes began to pay the unemployed a weekly dole linked to the current bread price. Pitt and many major landowners backed this idea, though his attempt to persuade Parliament to enforce it universally was defeated. Among the keenest advocates of the scheme in Eastern England was Tory Suffolk MP T C Bunbury.[14] He, Young and the Essex Whig Montagu Burgoyne also called for allotments for the poor, but few landowners of either political party ever parted with the necessary land.

In late May Pitt held another general election. Such was his grip on the electorate, corrupt and uncorrupted, that his government kept its large majority. In East Anglia many Tory and Old Whig loyalists were returned: one Cornwallis at Eye (the third to win that seat since 1790), another in the adjacent Suffolk county, a Seymour at Orford, Lord Charles Fitzroy and Lord Hervey at Bury, Sir John Vanneck at Dunwich and Robinson at Harwich. There were, though, two rather alarming upsets. At Norwich Bartlett Gurney, of the radical Quaker family, challenged Windham and narrowly lost only because the absentee voters supported the sitting MP. When Lord Charles Townshend, of the famous Norfolk Old Whig dynasty, travelled back to London by private coach after retaining one of the Yarmouth seats, he argued with his brother and fellow passenger, Lord Frederick. After passing through the noisy election crowd in Colchester High Street Frederick became hysterically excited. The driver ignored the commotion below, but when the coach drew up in London the MP was found dead from a pistol bullet wound in the head.[15]

John Thelwall, minor author and member of the London Corresponding Society, had been one of the defendants acquitted in the celebrated 1794 treason trials. In 1796 he was at Norwich supporting Mingay against Windham. After the election he toured East Anglia, lecturing on the struggle between rulers and populace in Ancient Rome. His real theme was of course political. In August he showed up at Yarmouth. Local shipowner-merchant Samuel Hurry loaned him a warehouse for his meetings. On Wednesday the 17th, in addition to the left-leaning middle-class audience, several soldiers from the town garrison turned up and heckled. On Friday the 19th there was a much more serious disturbance. During the talk several dozen Royal Navy seamen from the *Espiegle* sloop and a cutter invaded the room, roared out the national anthem, put out the lamps and set about the audience with clubs. Among those injured were Yorkshire MP Christopher Atkinson, Yarmouth Customs Collector John Bell, *Dolphin* packet captain Matthew Flynn, and several women, one pregnant. Two young men suffered fractured skulls. Hurry had his hat and wig torn off and pocket book and money stolen. The sailors tried to grab Thelwall himself, threatening to press him for the Navy and take him to the Kamchatka. (They can only have known about that Siberian prison land from the Russian sailors then at Yarmouth). He made them back off by waving a pistol, and was then pulled away by the young Palmer brothers and safely locked in a nearby house. Some of the audience went off and appealed to the Mayor to send the Militia, but he declined. The violence ended when a signal gun sounded out in the Roads and the attackers headed back to their ships.

Evidently the sailors were angered by an "enemy sympathiser" undermining public belief in the war they were fighting, though Thelwall and his audience were avowed peaceful reformers and constitutional monarchists, not revolutionary republicans – closer to Fox and Coke than Tom Paine.

Thelwall published his own account of the riot, accusing naval officers of planning it with the collusion of the Government. "Never was the name of the British sailor more disgraced…deluded by their officer…the most cowardly attack on the unarmed, the helpless and the feeble".[16] The Whiggish *Monthly Magazine* called for "a rigorous inquiry, and the officers of the vessels called to a most severe account". On the other hand the Tory *Gentleman's Magazine*, while disapproving of the violence, said that "natural opinion will not suffer itself to be insulted by insidious demagogues". Asked about the incident in the Commons, Windham himself shared this view.

Thelwall and his friends laid charges against the alleged chief instigator of the attack, Captain Roberts of *Espiegle*, at the Court of King's Bench in London. Their chief witnesses were a local blind fiddler and his son, who had been on board that warship when Roberts sent off his men on the raid. It seems that no actual trial occurred. Roberts remained on his ship till promoted to a ship of the line and sent to the West Indies the following year

John Thelwall, the London radical who fell foul of irate soldiers and sailors on his speaking tours of Norfolk.

– though Thelwall claimed that the authorities had arranged this to prevent justice taking its course.[17]

Just before the end of 1796 a French fleet reached south-west Ireland and was only prevented from landing an invading army by a great storm. In February 1797 there was another failed attempt, in which one small French force actually made shore in Wales before being captured. Throughout the country bank customers, fearing seizure of their deposits of golden guineas by invaders and mobs, withdrew them. Private bankers hurried to the Bank of England to cash in their notes for gold, so as to meet these demands. On the 25th Pitt ordered the Bank to suspend this gold issue. When John Gurney, the famously trustworthy Norwich banker, came up to Threadneedle Street to exchange £40,000 of notes he was refused. Traditionally, though notes were prolifically printed and issued by all banks, and widely used by business and the well-off, they were regarded like modern cheques or credit cards – that is, as promises of future payment rather than "hard cash". The smaller local banks were most vulnerable. Within a fortnight three in Bury St Edmunds, including the well-respected Spink and Carss, with their fine new building on Cornhill, failed – so much coin withdrawn, and so little deposited, that they simply ran out of funds and shut.[18]

In Parliament Coke, seconded by the Unitarian Sudbury MP William Smith, accused Pitt of mismanagement, blaming him for running down the national gold reserve with his war expenditure, and leaving businessmen and employers unable to pay their creditors and workers.

But, as with the corn shortages, the economy rallied. Bankers and merchants, already often of Whig-radical persuasion, might well agree that Pitt's economic genius had been debunked, but the lower classes used neither golden guineas nor banknotes, nor had bank deposits or wage bills to worry about, and were therefore largely unaffected. It also says something for the confidence, patriotism, or perhaps self-interested shrewdness, of business communities that instead of panicking they met to issue joint public declarations that they would leave their gold in their local banks and instead accept paper money. Two meetings were held by the Mayor of Norwich to this effect as soon as news of Pitt's Order in Council to the Bank of England had reached the city. At Bury James Oakes' new bank survived by putting on a brave face and continuing to exchange its customers' notes for gold and silver coin till confidence returned. It helped that his main customer was the town corporation.

Meanwhile Thelwall was continuing his controversial lecture tour. In May 1797 it sparked another ugly episode, this time at Norwich. Someone threw a radical leaflet over the wall of the Inniskilling Dragoons's barracks, causing them and the Oxfordshire Militia to offer sizeable rewards for anyone identifying the culprit. When Thelwall turned up a few days later some of the Inniskillings invaded his lecture room in the *Shakespeare* inn, beat members of the audience, and yelled horrible death threats. In pursuit of the publican they went on to terrify his pregnant wife and wreck his premises and the adjoining house. The Whig mayor, John Crowe, came and told them to desist, but later their whole regiment massed in the street and attacked another pub, knocking down many civilians including what the local press described as "an amiable young lady of 16". The Norwich citizenry and the Oxfordshires played no part in the attacks. But Thelwall slipped away to London and ended his lecture tours for good.[19]

As the socialist historian E P Thompson observed, such events were almost an English version of the bloody "White Terror" which had occurred in France after Thermidor, though I am also reminded of the fascist Blackshirts and Nazi Stormtroops

Anti-government and anti-war feeling were still high in Norwich at that time, notwithstanding (or was it because of?) fear of invasion. The admittedly Whig *Monthly Magazine* reported that a county meeting had, with one dissenting voice only, called on the King to sack Pitt and his cabinet. The appeal ran:

> "... our ministers have so exposed and degraded their own character in the eyes of all Europe, that it is impossible for them to remedy the evils they have occasioned, by a secure and honourable peace. They are objects of contempt to your enemies, and of distrust to your faithful subjects".[20]

The magazine conceded that loyalists had responded with a counter-meeting on Castle Hill, but said its supporters had shown "little vigour".

There is little doubt that after all the crises in the first half of 1797 Pitt had lost much of the credibility that had won him the election the year before – and not just locally. In May a plot was hatched at Westminster to oust him. A group of Foxite Whigs and disillusioned Tories hoped to get the Anglo-Irish Whig ex-soldier Lord Moira appointed by the King, and then to join his cabinet. An elderly East Anglian, Lord Thurlow, was involved in this. Born in Norfolk, and resident at Great Ashfield in Suffolk, he had already intrigued with Fox to make the Prince of Wales regent when the King suffered his first madness just before the French Revolution.[21] Pitt had sacked him from the Lord Chancellorship in 1792 for opposing his budget. However the King snubbed Moira when he approached him with the proposal, and the Prime Minister survived in office.

From the Quota Act to Camperdown   6

On 18 February 1795 there came from Westminster an Order in Council (government decree), one month later regularised as the Quota Act:

> "Whereas it is expedient for the Public Service, at the present Conjuncture, that the most effectual measures should be adopted for providing a speedy Supply of Men to serve in his Majesty's Navy..."[1]

So far the local civilian authorities had been under no obligation to help the press gangs – and their recruits had to be merchant mariners. Now at every seaport a stipulated number of men (whether sailors or landsmen) was to be found by local mayors and magistrates, and none of the British merchant ships in harbour were to leave till this had happened. The number to be recruited was to be equivalent to one in five of the locally-based merchant seamen. No east coast port was exempted. Yarmouth's quota was 506, Lynn's 193, Harwich's 144, Maldon's 94, Colchester's 84, Ipswich's 58, Wells's 50. Little Aldeburgh and Wisbech had to find 19 each, Blakeney 26, Southwold 21, and Woodbridge 18.[2] Officials failing to identify the recruits for the Impressment Officers at Lynn, Yarmouth and Harwich, and merchant ship captains leaving harbour before the quotas were filled, faced hefty fines – and, if these were unpaid, confiscation of their property or ships. This draconian measure came in the wake of the fall of the Low Countries, though it is unclear whether this was because of the resultant actual threat from the Batavian navy, or because that navy gave Pitt a justification for another erosion of civil liberty in order to make up an existing shortfall in naval manpower. The Batavian Republic was not quite the puppet state of British propaganda, being the creation of the numerous native Patriots who included much of the Netherlands' educated and middle classes. However, one of its treaty arrangements with France was that it would supply the best part of its navy for a common war effort.

In addition to its arbitrary conscription, the Government advertised for more volunteers in the local press, offering "bounties" (inducements) of £20-£25 to individuals coming forward from these same eastern ports but also nearby inland villages.[3]

It was also the Dutch situation which brought the Navy to Great Yarmouth, or "Yarmouth North" as they often called it to distinguish it from Yarmouth Isle of Wight. The Roads which lay between the town and the offshore shoals had always been used as a temporary anchorage by warships escorting convoys, hunting privateers, or in transit down the coast. They now became a permanent base for a squadron guarding against the Batavian fleet at the Texel, some 110 miles east off the port of Den Helder. In June 1795 Vice-Admiral MacBride arrived with a force of 13 British and three Russian ships[4] – the latter provided by Tsarina Catherine the Great, who had denounced the Revolution at an early date but so far made no armed intervention. MacBride's flagship was the 3rd-Rate (74-gun) *Russell*. Later additional ships joined. One, the 3rd Rate *Director*, was captained by William Bligh, of mutiny on the *Bounty* notoriety.

Yarmouth did not offer an enclosed harbour for large vessels but there was a certain amount of shelter for them in the 'Roads', the area inside the sand banks. Gigs and jolly boats could access the harbour but pictures show that the jetty was a principal means of transhipping men and goods. Tall lookout towers enabled sigtnals from vessels offshore to be read.

The Navy was to base itself in Yarmouth Roads for the next 18 years. It so dominated the North Sea from henceforth it could fill the rest of this narrative. As a matter of fact (as implied earlier) it was less tied to the town than one might assume. Most of it was too deep-draught to get into the actual harbour. Its command centre was the admiral's flagship, though he also rented a residence in the town. It took over the local prison and converted a warehouse into a hospital. Repairing timber, canvas and rope, spare anchors, and the like were kept in a yard on the quay. The small sloops, gun brigs and supply tenders could moor there, but the larger men of war anchored about two miles offshore, where they could receive signals and visitors from land, and had some shelter from rough seas from Scroby Sands. Initially their food, drink, powder, shot – and the livestock they took out with them to slaughter on board – were brought up from Chatham and Deptford in tenders, but in 1796 MacBride's successor Duncan protested that even in moderate seas cargo was being dropped into the water and his ships damaged by grinding hull to hull. So henceforth most supplies were stored in town and then taken out to the ships by local boats. The Admiralty's Agent Victuallers increasingly relied on a young local man, Samuel Padget, who arranged for the purchasing, storage and delivery of bread, beer, live animals, meat, vegetables and water purchased from far inland. He had started this business with modest funds which his mother had raised from neighbours. Initially Whiggish and anti-war, their scruples were overcome by their considerable profits – Samuel became one of the richest and most influential men in Yarmouth, its second largest shipowner, and after the war its mayor.[5]

The North Sea fleet lies offshore at Yarmouth; around the jetty is a hive of activity. There is a crane in action at the end of the jetty.

Great Yarmouth was by no means a bad place for shore leave (while ships were weather-bound or out of action). Though crammed into a narrow rectangle of 32 acres, around one long street, and hemmed in by ancient walls, it had many shops and taverns, and a civilian population of 15,000. Its quay, one and half miles long and up to 100 yards wide, was famed. With its 200 fishing craft it offered a change of diet from beef and biscuit. A contemporary guide book recommended the theatre for relieving the "dull vacuity attendant upon lounging at a watering place". It was famed for its novelty shows. In 1797 it put on a display of war-dancing and tomahawk-fighting by "Cataweaw" Indians, followed by a Highland reel. Later in the war there was a visit by "the spotted Indian … born of black parents in Jamaica, his head covered with black and white wool, his body spotted with white and resembling a beautiful leopard", "the Patagonian youth", and a gymnastic dwarf called "the sporting little man".[6]

The strategic role of the Yarmouth Roads fleet was dual – to protect the East Anglian coast against raiders and privateers, including any coming up from France to the south, and to blockade the main Dutch fleet at the Texel. It was therefore split into two sections – one in the Roads, or cruising along the coast to north-west and south, and one within sight of Den Helder, each under a rear- or vice-admiral. Cutters and tenders shuttled between the two with messages, provisions and people. Ships from the forward division came back to the Roads for repairs, or in stormy weather.

Apart from some encounters with privateers, the first action fought by a Yarmouth ship was not with the Dutch, but with a group of eight Frenchmen (six of them frigates), who had come up from the English Channel into the Scheldt, off Flushing. On 21st July 1795 they were about 30 miles north of this anchorage, and 15 miles off Helvoetsluys, when the large Yarmouth frigate *Glatton* (a 56 gun ship and therefore almost a "ship of the line") sighted them while en route to join Captain Savage's detached squadron then off Flushing. Captain Henry Trollope headed straight at the third ship in the French line, and a fierce gun action lasted for 20 minutes, as other French frigates closed on her from all directions. In spite of her being almost spar to spar with one opponent, and having one of her masts and some of her sails torn down, *Glatton* had only two marines wounded (one fatally) before the enemy broke away and headed inshore. Trollope believed that in firing when his ship tipped on her downward roll, instead of upwards at the enemy's rigging, he had done serious damage. He paid tribute to his officers, such as Alexander Schomberg, one of a remarkable family of learned London Jews.[7] It says something about the tempo of this war, and the strategy of the French, that this was the first time opposing warships had gone into action in the North Sea.

Admiral Adam Duncan would become the Viscount of Camperdown, an honour some thought was less than he deserved as a result of his naval service and particularly his victory at the battle of Camperdown.

In February 1796 Admiral Duncan took over the Yarmouth command from MacBride. He was a son of the Dundee burgh elite, a physical near-giant (both in height and girth), in his mid-sixties, and had been in the Navy on and off for almost 50 years. He had the conventional "good officer's" reputation for being tough but fair and asking his subordinates to take no risk he would not face himself.

Not for the better part of a year after the *Glatton* encounter was there an action with the Dutch Navy – or any other battle in the North Sea. While off the Texel with three ships early on 12th May 1796 one of Duncan's ablest captains, Halsted, ran into five Dutch vessels returning from Norway. He took his frigate, the *Phoenix*, close to the windward side of the enemy frigate *Argo*, and after another 20-minute gun duel forced her to "strike" (surrender). Six Dutchmen had been killed, and 267 captured, 28 of whom were wounded. Three Dutch brigs fled the scene, leaving behind a cutter which turned out to be the Yarmouth-Cuxhaven packet *Duke of York*, taken by them the previous day.[8]

On 23rd February 1797 several Batavian ships broke out of the Texel and headed north-west. Though this was not yet known in the North Sea, the previous day the small French amphibious force had been rounded up on the Welsh coast. Because of storms and contrary winds Duncan and his bigger ships were then back in Yarmouth Roads, but Thelwall's enemy Captain Roberts was near the Dutch coast on the *Espiegle*, and he shadowed the enemy for some distance, having sent a cutter back down to Deal in Kent with news of the sortie. The Dutchmen were probably either bound for Ireland, or trying to decoy the British eastwards away from that objective, but the whole operation was soon called off and they returned to harbour before Duncan came across.

That spring his fleet was plunged into chaos by the celebrated mutiny in which underpaid, underfed and otherwise maltreated seamen seized control of most of the ships of the Channel and then North Sea fleets. By the end of April the crews at Spithead, off Portsmouth, had already made their demands, been appeased, and gone back to duty. Their North Sea comrades now issued a very similar manifesto, mainly concerning food, treatment of the sick, bullying officers, prize money and shore leave – though not, perhaps surprisingly, flogging, press-ganging or politics. On the 26th news reached Yarmouth Roads that Admiral Howe had just negotiated a return to duty at Spithead in return for a settlement of the grievances just listed. However the Spithead fleet had demanded that Parliament pass an act to give this agreement legal force. That same day sailors met on Duncan's ships and gave a vote of thanks to the Admiralty – adding assurances of loyalty and a desire to give battle to the enemy most of them had so far hardly seen. But three days later men on the *Venerable* and *Adamant*, flagships of Duncan and his deputy Onslow, massed on deck and shouted. When Duncan sent for five of the instigators they told him that they wanted an assurance from him that the Spithead concessions would also apply at Yarmouth. He gave this

The *Espiegle*, a captured French vessel. Whilst based in Yarmouth Roads she did her best to reconnoitre the Dutch fleet and intimidate disloyal civilians on shore.

– or, more exactly – said that he trusted that it would turn out to be the case.[9]

Ship by ship and step by step, between 6th and 20th May, most of the fleet anchored round the Nore, at the mouths of the Thames and Medway, elected delegates, refused orders, issued demands, detained their officers or put them ashore, raised red flags and blockaded the London River. The awaited Act of Parliament ratifying the Spithead agreement was passed on the 9th, and the Admiralty and mutineers met and negotiated, but the mutiny continued. On the 12th the Admiralty entrusted (ironically but perhaps aptly) William Bligh, captain of the *Director*, with a message for Duncan when he returned to Yarmouth from a visit to London. This asked Duncan if he believed that his men would support him in sailing south and suppressing the mutiny. Having already told them that his crews were loyal and contented, he repeated this claim, but tactfully implied that, if asked to attack their Nore comrades, they might refuse.

On 26 May the Nore mutineers, who had elected as their leader the former disgraced midshipman and Quota Act re-enlister Richard Parker, sent the cutter *Cygnet* up to Yarmouth to recruit Duncan's crews to their cause. As the contemporary ditty had it: "Go tell your brothers, near Yarmouth they lie". Duncan headed her off, detaining all of her crew except for three men who got ashore in a boat and later claimed that their mission had been to advise moderation, not mutiny. Next morning he signalled all of his ships to follow him out to sea. Though he gave blockading Dutch would-be invaders as their mission, in reality his aim was probably to get his men away from malign influences from the Nore or the shore, because there was no wind to take them east to Holland and they stood becalmed just beyond Scroby Sands. Most of his crews refused to join him. No one has been able to pin down how the mutiny spread from the Nore to Yarmouth, and broke out there at this point. But I think it likely that the sailors' demands and talk of taking action had been spreading all round the Navy for many weeks, as ships shuttled between harbours and ferried supplies and reinforcements – and that by ordering his men to sea on the 27th without his earlier promise being kept Duncan effectively triggered it. Refusing an order to put to sea and seek the enemy is obviously the best (if most provocative) moment for mutineers to strike.

Two days of standoff followed, in which his vessels stood idle, though undoubtedly with tremendous tension and grim threats and counter-threats. Then, on the 29th, starting with the 4th rate *Montague*, his ships began to

William Bligh of the *Bounty*, and at the Nore mutiny, of the *Director*.

haul up red flags, weigh anchor, and head – not for Holland – but to join the mutineers at the Nore. Vice-Admiral Pasley came from the Admiralty on the 30th and boarded several ships to implore their crews to stay loyal and go off and confront the Dutch, but was heard in stony silence on some and rudely interrupted on others – especially the 5th rate *Leopard*. The deserters included the *Agamemnon*, until just a few months earlier Nelson's ship, and with its partly east coast crew. By 6th June, when the *Ranger* sloop was the last to flee, Duncan had only five ships left out of 14, and three of these had seemed likely to abandon him until he clapped objectors in irons on his own *Venerable*, trained his guns on the *Trent*, and famously dragged an *Adamant* seaman to the gunwale and dangled him overboard. Only Trollope's *Glatton* and the *Circe* were totally loyal.

The French and Dutch had for ideological and propaganda reasons long claimed that British sailors hated their government and their officers, so that when actual evidence of this reached them were slow to respond – such as by resurrecting the previous winter's invasion plans. Since Duncan's previous blockade had consisted in holding his bigger ships back out of sight of the Texel while observing it from a few smaller craft, the Dutch did not realise that most of his fleet was absent. He sustained their ignorance by flying fictitious signals.

Reinforced by the Yarmouth ships, the Nore mutineers became more confident and overtly political. They hanged effigies of Pitt and Dundas from their yardarms. Parker said that Pitt must re-open peace negotiations, and that if all of his demands were not met he would lead his ships to a neutral port. Though the phrase "Floating Republic" was a civilian radical's[10], and not the mutineers', with its democratic meetings and total defiance of the government this is almost what the North Sea Fleet had become.

Yet it took just one more week for the mutiny to collapse. The Government had cut off the ships from all supplies and communication from shore, declared the ringleaders traitors, and was sufficiently back in control of the much larger Channel fleet, with its many 1st and 2nd rate ships, to threaten battle should the defiance continue. Two ships had already made a run for it. The 9th May Act acceding to the Spithead demands had already become known to every crew and presumably seemed a better prospect to many than going into exile or fighting against their own countrymen. One by one they sailed out, replaced red with white flags, and let themselves be boarded and taken over by officers. On 13th June Parker himself was captured on the *Sandwich*, the biggest, oldest and most crowded North Sea ship, when the loyalists came back on board. By then all of the Yarmouth ships were back under control.

The East Anglian press gave close attention to the trials, presided over by Pasley, which quickly followed. Parker was of course hanged. True to form the *Norfolk Chronicle* was sympathetic to the accused, blaming the Pitt-Dundas regime for driving the men to mutiny and distinguishing between treason and helping the enemy, which it rejected, and legitimate protest, which it endorsed. Equally predictably the Tory *Ipswich Journal* stuck to the Government line, though it did express sympathy for Mrs Parker and admit that her husband had died bravely.

Official retribution fell heavily on the Yarmouth ships. Of the 29 men hanged, 11 were from Duncan's ships – seven from the *Leopard* (four executed on board) and four from the *Monmouth*. Two *Leopard* men were capitally convicted but reprieved. None of those condemned had been from the east of England, however.[11] The executions, in the second week of July, were solemn and dreadful occasions. All the ships were drawn up together at the Nore, with all their crews on deck. When signal guns boomed out, the condemned were led up onto the forecastles by chaplains, swallowed wine, joined in the singing of Psalm 104, had nooses lowered over their heads, and were hauled up onto the yardarms. Richard Brown, one of the *Monmouth* prisoners, apologised to his captain, the Earl of Northesk, whom he had detained on board, and begged his forgiveness, which was granted. He confessed to his guilt and implored his listeners not to heed agitators in future. Another condemned man tried to do the same but his voice faltered. All meat and drink to authority and its loyalists.[12]

What was the root cause? Tories predictably blamed Jacobinism – not so much actual enemy agents, but its insidious influence on simple minds. Since several of the mutiny leaders were Irish the United Irishmen nationalist movement was also accused. Whigs pointed to the government's unjust war and general contempt for liberty. Admiral Jervis, then Nelson's superior, thought "the Quota men are at the bottom of it".[13] Many shared his view that rot in the crews had arrived with the ex-convicts, vagrants and undisciplined "landsmen" recruited over the previous two years. Yet the trial reports show that many ringleaders were long-serving sailors, holding positions of (lesser) responsibility on their ships, and with good conduct records.[14]

Left-wing modern writers like E P Thompson have argued that the 1797 mutinies – the greatest in British naval history – were part of the same radical political movement as the Norwich anti-war and parliamentary-reform radicalism, Corresponding Societies, Tom Paine, and 1795 food riots. By contrast, it has always been the conservative, "patriotic", and official Admiralty, line that the average mutineer was loyal at heart and apolitical, and had been temporarily misled by a few ringleaders.

The evidence is ambiguous. Were the mutineers merely seeking their stated practical demands, or using these as a springboard to end impressment, flogging and the war itself? Had they picked up the onshore civilian political and social radicalism? Was there any connection between the naval mutinies and some scattered ones that happened in army militia regiments, including one that had recently been at Yarmouth and moved to the south coast (the Oxfordshires)? On these questions there is only space for a few suggestions, and I will take what might be called the middle ground. Seamen cooped up in very close proximity on warships which are almost never in action, spend long periods at anchor, and are subject to delayed wages and poor rations, can become more bitterly discontented than soldiers in bloody battle on land. The Russian Revolutions of 1905 and 1917, the German Revolution of 1918, and indeed the French Revolution, illustrate this. On the one hand the 1797 British mutineer almost certainly did not share the full-blown democratic thinking of Paine or the libertarian pacifism of the Norfolk Whigs and radicals. And he seldom went ashore and mixed with militiamen. He was essentially concerned with his own day-to-day life as a sailor. On the other hand he certainly knew of the landsmens' disaffection. After all he had not been born and brought up on a warship, but originated from an onshore community where food, wages, and class tensions were common concerns – not least in seaport towns. Quite likely he had brothers or friends who had been pressed into the militia. Going onto a warship does not turn a man into a super-patriot and unquestioning lover of authority.

Duncan's role is also controversial. In playing down his men's discontent till the last moment was he perilously naïve and out of touch, or judiciously trying to calm the tension between them and the Admiralty? Was he one of the causes of the trouble? It seems that, though a courageous and charismatic leader, he had been no more in sympathy with his men's longstanding grievances than other admirals, nor ready to take on himself responsibility for rectifying them. His crews were for the most part just as neglected and harshly treated as those elsewhere. On one ship (the *Nassau*) the men had not been paid for a year and a half!

Would the sailors have taken Duncan's orders and fought had the enemy shown up? All the trial defendants denied any intention to betray the country to the French. Had the enemy gone onto the offensive they presumably would have fought them, though perhaps only after demanding a government guarantee of pardon and implementation of the Spithead concessions.

During the mutiny the French were again planning an invasion of the British Isles, in which they were to attack Ireland while their Dutch subordinates staged a diversion in Western Scotland. The British Admiralty and Duncan were aware of this by 5th June, and therefore especially angry with the more truculent attitude Parker was taking. Luckily for them the French only secured Batavian agreement to participate on the 21st, by which time the trouble was over and Duncan was again blockading the Texel in full force.

What the Government and the Admiralty needed was a great naval victory to restore the confidence and loyalty of sailors and public, and foster the idea that the mutinies had been only a passing malady. The Dutch eventually obliged. In September Duncan gave up his close blockade of the Texel and pulled back to Yarmouth in the face of autumn gales. At that moment the Batavian government reluctantly agreed to attempt its Scottish expedition. On 9th October Duncan got news from Trollope's forward light patrol that they were leaving the Texel. Two days later they rendezvoused about six miles off Camperduin ("Camperdown"), a small coastal village close to Alkmaar in North Holland, 100 miles due east of Yarmouth.

Both sides had 16 ships. It was a cloudy, dark, morning, with a brisk north-west wind. Duncan closed diagonally on the straggling Dutch line

A lithograph illustrating the cutter *Active* signalling to Admiral Duncan that the Dutch fleet had left the Texel and was at sea. Duncan lead his fleet back across the North Sea to confront it.

from seaward and windward, then signalled each of his ships to go through a gap between enemy vessels, get alongside the landward side of an opponent, and thereby force a general action. These tactics were only semi-Nelsonian, because he planned a ship-to-ship, broadside encounter, not a concentration against one part of the enemy line. But a comparable situation accidentally ensued. In the poor visibility and with signal flags blowing end on half his ships turned east too early. So while he led the less heavily-armed half of his ships up against the Dutch van, Vice-Admiral Onslow, on the *Monarch*, took the stronger half onto their rear, and their centre was left unguarded. *Ardent* and Duncan's own *Venerable* therefore had a hard time dealing with most of the enemy force until Onslow finished off the others and moved up to reinforce him. Yet the British had advantages. In slightly more inshore and shallow water, and being mostly larger, their ships rolled less and scored more hits on the enemy gun decks and gunners. Their total weight of metal was in any case about 12% greater. Their more-practised gun crews reloaded more rapidly. It has also been suggested that their courage and determination was superior because of a desire to wipe out the shame of the mutinies, while the Dutch had little will to sacrifice themselves for the sake of French ambitions. Neither claim is susceptible to solid proof.

The two British ships under Duncan's immediate control were battered, burned, almost motionless and barely still afloat when the rest came to their aid. In mid-afternoon, after more than four hours of close-quarters firing, some of the Dutch ceased fire and "struck their colours", and others fled inshore. After a most valiant defence their flagship, the *Vrijheid* ("Liberty"), surrendered to Captain Bligh's *Director*. Their admiral, de Winter, was brought aboard *Venerable*, where he surrendered his sword to Duncan. In all nine Dutch ships were captured.[15]

The subsequent struggle to stop the leaking and demasted ships of both sides from running onto the Dutch coast before the gales was nearly as arduous as the battle itself. All were eventually saved. Of the British ships *Venerable* and four more got back to Orfordness, three to the adjacent Hollesley Bay, and three to the Kentish Knock. And eventually all the prizes reached Yarmouth or the Nore.

A contemporary illustration of the Dutch flagship *Vrijheid* and Captain Bligh's *Director* after the engagement.

The British battle casualties totalled 203 dead and 533 wounded. The worst damage had been on the *Ardent* (41 killed – including her captain, 107 wounded), *Monarch* (36 and 100), *Bedford* (30 and 41), *Triumph* (29 and 35), and *Belliqueux* (26 and 78). 15 were killed and 62 wounded on the *Venerable*.[16] Most of the ships involved in the action had been mutinous just four months earlier, including the *Monmouth* and *Belliqueux*, although *Leopard* and *Nassau* were not present. The Dutch officially put their own casualties as 1,160, excluding several thousand prisoners. Small craft ferried many hundred wounded to Yarmouth, where, at the barracks, they were as well cared for as the crude medicine of the day allowed. The Scots surgeon John Bell, elder brother of Sir Charles Bell, later famed for his medical work at Waterloo, was one of the doctors, and used the occasion to make a pioneering sketchbook of wounds and treatments. One casualty he could not save was Captain Van Rysoort of the Dutch *Hercules*, who was buried at St Nicholas's church.[17]

De Winter was treated as an honoured guest at Yarmouth. Duncan gave him back his sword and took him on a walk round town. The Dutch admiral, though a Patriot republican, had no enmity against the British, and only put to sea to help the French on the insistence of his own government.

To hail this important victory bells were rung, bonfires lit, and flags flown all over East Anglia. Duncan was made Viscount Camperdown, given the Russian Order of Alexander Nevsky, and got a bounty of £3000 a year. Onslow was knighted. The loyal citizenry of Yarmouth raised money for the wounded, gave the freedom of their borough to Duncan, and bought 30 barrels of beer and sent them by cutter for the crews of the *Venerable* and *Ardent*. Camperdown was the third of the six great British naval victories of the 1793-1815 wars. Not only had it eclipsed the recent mutinies but also lifted any invasion threat from the Dutch.

Dutch and British sailors were brought ashore at Great Yarmouth jetty after the battle of Camperdown. They were taken to the naval hospital in the town.

Corsairs of the Republic 7

From Louis XIV to Hitler Britain's Continental enemies lacked the sea-power to invade her but believed that her existence depended on overseas trade which they could choke off by means of continual raiding with small craft. All of them were convinced, in truth excessively, that her wealth, her propertied classes, and therefore also her government, owed almost everything to this buying and selling abroad and little to her own resources, industry, and financial system. The French Revolutionaries, and their successor Napoleon, therefore fell almost automatically into the "*guerre de course*", or "hunting war" against the merchant shipping of the British and her trading partners. Their campaign was not usually waged by their navy, but took the traditional form of privateering – that is to say, the capture and sale of ships and cargoes by civilian-owned and crewed vessels licensed by the French state. They called these commerce raiders the "corsairs".

The French had privateered against the British in every one of their wars during the previous 100 years. Some of their raiders sailed from the Mediterranean and Atlantic coasts, and the Breton port of Saint Malo was a major base, but their principal home was the northern ports of Boulogne, Calais and Dunkirk, since they were ideally placed for intercepting shipping bound to and from London through the narrowest waters between England and the Continent. 189 privateers were fitted out at Dunkirk alone between 1793-1801, during the first phase of the war. That city had the greatest privateering tradition of all, having been the home town and the raiding base of Jean Bart, ironically in temporary official oblivion because of his service to King Louis XIV.

Privateering was by 20th century standards a peculiar form of warfare – as much a state-regulated commercial business as a ruthless naval strategy. The raiders generally sailed under false Allied or neutral flags, for which there was no penalty. Most were converted lugger fishing craft of only 20 to 60 tons, just a fraction the size of an average merchantman – and therefore hoped to be mistaken for fishermen. Apart from muskets and cutlasses they generally carried only a few light (2, 3, 4 or 6-pdr) cannon, firing shot about the size of tennis balls, and swivel guns. But they had relatively large crews of between 20 and 100, so as to sail captured vessels (standardly five or six men to each) back to base. They were fitted out and armed by private shipyards, captained by local men who had been in charge of merchantmen or fishing boats in peacetime, and manned by hired civilians – all of whom would take a share of the prize money when captured vessels and cargoes were sold. So capture,

Corsairs seizing British
merchantmen.

Corsairs being built in
Dunkirk, 1797.

A captured privateer crew
list of 1796.

Opposite: A chart of the
North Sea published by
William Faden in 1796.

not sinking, was the aim. Accordingly they used only limited violence – shots across the bows – and, if chased down and threatened with capture themselves, were usually ready to surrender to the same level of force. Serious casualties were rare both on them and their prey. Their captains bought licences from the Ministry of Marine and the Colonies via the officials of their local départements and ports, called "*lettres de marque*". Headed with beautifully engraved emblems of the Revolution (and later the Napoleonic regime), and footed with official seals and signatures, these were for presenting to those concerned on either side (British naval officers, merchant ship captains, port authorities, and lawyers, French officials), to show that they were operating legally and were not pirates. Without his letter, a captured raider could legally be put to death. With it he would merely be kept prisoner. Without it his own government might detain him on suspicion of his not paying them, or going off to smuggle or trade illegally. With it they would allow him on his way and

if he was especially successful give him extra reward. The corsairs' captured cargoes were sold off, partly at public auctions advertised in the newspapers as far inland as Lille, Arras and Ghent.

If captured, a privateer captain and sometimes other officers were interrogated by the chief naval officer, mayor, JP, or chief customs officer at the British port where they were landed, via an interpreter. They were asked 32 prescribed questions, concerning the names, nationalities and shipboard status of each of their crew, their port of origin, the date they had sailed, and how many vessels they had taken. Usually these questions were freely and fully answered. Again odd from a modern standpoint, where a war prisoner would only be required to give name, rank and number, and though he might be tricked or pressurised into saying more, would not do so if he could help it. Significantly, both *lettres de marque* and interrogation reports were written in legal rather than military language, with prize courts as much in mind as the needs of naval intelligence.

The corsair crews were primarily but by no means exclusively French. They included many Flemings (apart from the many native Dunkirk men of Flemish surname), Germans, Scandinavians, Americans, Portuguese and Italians. The officers used the titles "capitaine", "deuxième capitaine" or "lieutenant" at sea, but on shore were known, in revolutionary style, as "citoyen". Some fought for patriotic and political motives: Dunkirk had been a republican and for a time a Jacobin city, and had repeatedly faced English attack, most recently in

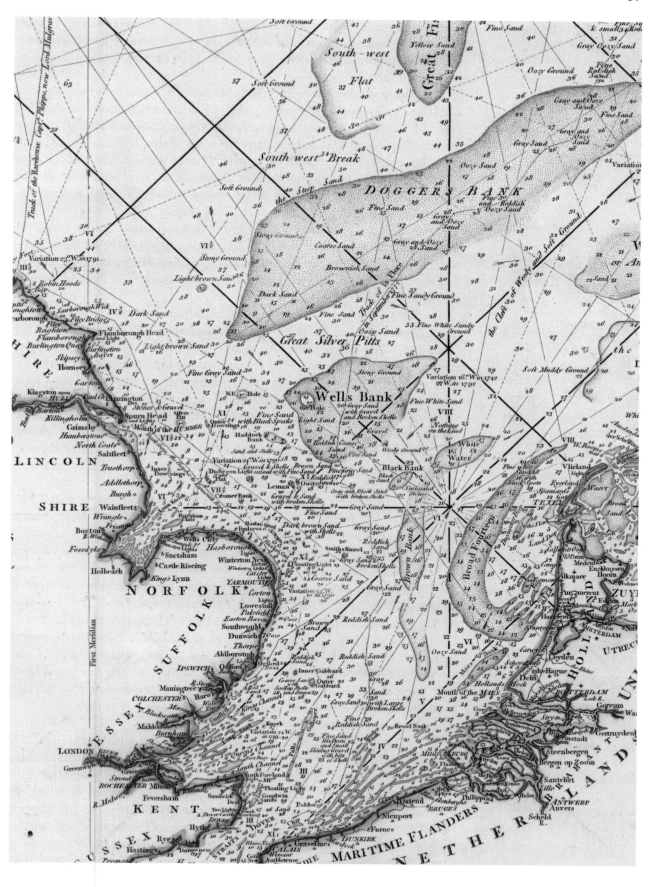

1793. However it seems safe to assume that for the ordinary sailors at least, French and foreign, it was all about making a lucrative, if decidedly risky, living – especially as the British blockade had put many Continental seamen out of their jobs.

A very extensive seaborne trade, indispensable to Britain both commercially and strategically, ran down the east coast of England to and from London and other southern ports. Apart from coal, the other crucial southbound cargoes were timber, hemp and flax (needed for naval masts, ropes and sails), and corn (imported in large quantities especially after the bad domestic harvests of 1795 and 1800). In addition to these, the privateers were also happy to take lighter consumer goods such as coffee, spices, tobacco, alcohol, and textiles which they could sell for rich profits back in port.

After their early flurry of activity in the first few weeks of war, very little was seen of them on the east coast of England until the fall of Holland in the winter of 1794/95, when the withdrawal of the Royal Navy from Dutch ports, and the ability of the French to use those same harbours, opened up new prospects for them.

On 22nd December 1794 a very small French privateer called *La Victorieuse*, from Dunkirk, seized a small Flemish commercial brig (originally from Ostend) off the Norfolk coast.[1] An easterly gale drove the prize and the prize crew of two Frenchmen who had re-manned her onto the beach at Blakeney, near Wells. Eight days later the privateer and her six remaining men were forced ashore nearby. Militia marched the captives to Yarmouth, where they were recorded as naval prisoners 224-231 at the Gothic-windowed Tolhouse Gaol in Middlegate Street.[2] Low-ranking captives generally stayed behind lock and key. But the system soon developed of releasing privateer captains and seconds-in-command landed at Yarmouth on parole at Beccles, ten miles inland, where they lodged in a hostel, fed and clothed themselves with small living allowances, and periodically reported to the local mayor or magistrate – yet another inconceivable practice from a modern standpoint. Occasionally a few would break their promise and abscond.

On 15th June 1795 the French *Republicain* captured and then sank Anthony Deane's packet *Princess of Orange* on her Yarmouth-Cuxhaven run. Deane and his crew were detained at Flushing, but well treated and later repatriated on an American ship.[3] That July a French raider seized two large Harwich fishing smacks, the *Sally* and the *Gleaner*, along with the Southwold pilot boat *Princess*. In October Dutchmen equipped the two smacks at Flushing and sent them out to raid. However, it was on the whole another very quiet and safe year for Allied merchantmen sailing the North Sea. Only one Royal Navy ship, the *Weazle* sloop, was assigned to Yarmouth to cruise the whole Norfolk coast on privateer patrol, and seldom came across any.

1796 saw more activity.

On 29th January the small French *La Nayade* was driven onshore at Pakefield, just south of Lowestoft. Her six crew were captured by the Oxfordshire Militia (who included a brother of the author Jane Austen), then held at Yarmouth. In February Capitaine Léveillé's Dunkirk-based *La Vengeance* pulled off a remarkable coup by boarding three large merchantmen, the *Coldstream*, *Chancellor* and *Duchess of York*, in plain view of Yarmouth, and within cannon-shot of British men of war. She got all three back to Ostend, along with 130 prisoners, including troops who were on board *Duchess of York*.[4] On

20th March the *Poisson Volant* and another privateer took two more ships near Harwich, one of which, the *Amity* from that port, sank.[5]

Two months later in May the Yarmouth *Dolphin* naval cutter retook the *Mary Bark*, a British merchantman manned by French "prize master" Réné Geffroy and seven more privateer men. In June the *Ann and Mary*, flying the American flag, was boarded and brought into Yarmouth, apparently on suspicion of privateering. The senior man on board, Lieutenant-Colonel Blanchet, was held but then paroled at Beccles. Eleven weeks later he fled to Gorleston, presumably in the hope of getting out of the country on a neutral ship, but was recaptured there and then held till November.[6]

The first major success of the Yarmouth navy came on 20th August, when the sloop *Dispatch* captured *La Augustine*, Captain Hippolite Deschermes, and his 32 crew.

With their manoeuvrability and speed, guns, experience of handling tough smuggling gangs, and familiarity with local waters, the Yarmouth, Harwich and "Colchester" (Wivenhoe) revenue and excise cutters were also up to the task of hunting the privateers. On 13th September 1796 the Harwich revenue cutter *Argus* (Captain Saunders) seized and brought back the small Dunkirk privateer *Marander*, which, complete with false name-board and nets, had been masquerading as the fishing boat *Sally of Blakeney*, and taken several merchantmen. Her crew were Captain Dollatriou and 17 others. They were held in the little gaol under the Harwich guildhall before being sent up to Yarmouth.

On 16th October the Yarmouth naval cutter *Phoenix* took the small Dunkirk privateer *Le Hardi Mendicant* and 23 crew after she had attacked two coal brigs off Southwold and captured one.

1797 turned out to be the peak year of enemy privateering, both in the North Sea and beyond. The Royal Navy was very stretched that year blockading and fighting the Dutch and Spanish fleets as well as the French, and was disrupted by mutinies. The French authorities issued an unprecedented number of *lettres de marque* and many raiding craft were fitted out. Aware of how many British warships now came and went from Yarmouth Roads, they ventured away from their previous haunts off east Norfolk and towards Harwich and the Wash. Without radio, radar, regular coastal patrols, and even (as yet) a system of ship-shore signalling, and with convoy still only voluntary, the British were relatively slow to respond.

On 29th January that year the Yarmouth naval cutter *Griffin* and Harwich revenue cutter *Argus* each took a privateer and brought her into their harbour. The captures were named *La Liberté* and *L'Enflame* respectively. The prisoners totalled 31. The same day another Harwich anti-smuggling craft, the Excise cutter *Viper*, seized a large French fishing smack named *Happy*. Though it turned out that she was not a privateer, her 12 occupants were all sent on to Yarmouth prison. Captured merchant seamen and fishermen were indefinitely detained by both sides along with naval and privateer prisoners, on the grounds that they were serving the enemy war effort and were potential enemy naval recruits. The number of Frenchmen checked into Yarmouth Prison reached 1,000 by the spring of 1798 and not far short of 2,000 by the first suspension of hostilities in autumn 1801.[7]

This antique building only housed about 50 inmates. So from 1797 onwards, perhaps after a few weeks at Yarmouth, the enemy prisoners were

The monument at Norman Cross and the field where the prison camp once stood.

marched 60 miles to the recently-opened prisoner-of-war camp at Norman Cross, near Yaxley in Huntingdonshire, which held privateers, naval seamen and soldiers alike.[8]

Norman Cross was controversial. Late in 1799 France refused to go on paying for the prisoners' food and this became the responsibility of the British Admiralty Transport Board, which may have caused shortages. By then there were some 4,000 men in the 40-acre camp, so it must certainly have been very crowded. Napoleon's press denounced it as a hell-hole, and, writing just after the war in 1815 General Pillet, a onetime inmate, wrote that it had been a death trap where 30,000 of his compatriots had perished of starvation and disease. He alleged that Lord Moira, who investigated conditions there in 1806, was packed off to an overseas posting by the Government so that the truth should not emerge.

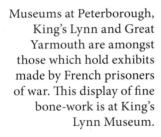

Museums at Peterborough, King's Lynn and Great Yarmouth are amongst those which hold exhibits made by French prisoners of war. This display of fine bone-work is at King's Lynn Museum.

However an American magazine (and the USA had recently also been at war with Britain and had men in the camp) rejected this as "an infamous and impudent libel". In 1914 the Anglo-French "*Entente Cordiale* Society" put up a monument near the site (it still stands) giving the total death toll as 1,770, which there seems no reason to question: if the figure is correct it would mean the camp was far healthier than those of the much later American Civil and Boer Wars. Charles Aldiss, its doctor from 1797 to 1799, was a tender-hearted Yarmouth Quaker who said that he missed its "sunny" atmosphere after moving on to private practice at nearby Chatteris, and was the sort of person whose conscience would have moved him to complain had there been cause. The camp was built on dry ground overlooking the Fens, and its inmates lived in large two-storey wooden barrack huts with stoves and chimneys, where they were supplied with clothes, coal, and food which they cooked themselves. They were not required to work for the British war effort. On Sundays they had visitors, who bought toys, ornaments and boxes they

The Guildhall at Harwich. Captain Dollatriou and his crew were held on this site, in a small cell under the building.

had crafted from straw or meat bones – some of them lovingly intricate. Not all of them were as tame as this suggests. Two army battalions at a time guarded the camp – quite a high ratio of guards to prisoners. In the middle stood a wooden tower with a loaded cannon poking from each of its eight sides. The regulations stipulated that would-be escapers be banished to a "black hole", go on half rations, and lose any officer status they might have. Escape attempts there certainly were, but I will describe these in a later chapter. It should not be forgotten that most of the British merchant seamen captured by the corsairs were imprisoned in worse conditions in France and Flanders, such as in the dark citadels of Calais, Arras, Lille and Verdun. This included several hundred from east coast ports.

On 14th February, 1797, the *Espion* and *Martin* sloops brought back into Yarmouth the most impressive privateer capture so far. She was the *Buonaparte*, of 17 guns and with 82 crew headed by Jean Mulenaer. From Cherbourg, she had cruised round the top of Scotland, hoisted Danish colours, captured but freed one ship in ballast, and reached a position 30 miles north-west of the Texel before being taken. She was, of course, named after the young Corsican general then conquering northern Italy, and within three years dictator of France. His victories were already being narrated in the British press, including newspapers read at Yarmouth.

On 4th April civilians onshore at Cromer spotted the British merchant ship *Dunbar* suspiciously skirting inshore. Militiamen rowed a boat out to her and found that she was manned by a four-man prize crew from the privateer *Voltigeur*, headed by one calling himself Jean Bart (no less!)

At the top and bottom of the page, photos of the Tolhouse which can be visited in Great Yarmouth. Below is a bone model of a ship of the line, made by a prisoner in the Tolhouse. It is now on display at the *Time and Tide* museum in the town.

On 13th June a French privateer seized Matthew Flyn's Yarmouth-Cuxhaven packet *Dolphin* about halfway along her route. Flyn dumped his register and papers in the weighted bag. An Emden merchant bought the vessel, and then Flyn bought her back on behalf of the Post Office. She was sailed back to her original Harwich base to be refitted at the dockyard there. More silliness by the standards of modern war.

Further south the task of hunting the corsairs fell on the armed Customs vessels. On the morning of 24th June Robert Adams' Excise cutter *Viper* found *L'Espoir* ("Hope") just half a mile south of the Naze Tower on the Essex coast. She boarded and sailed her into Harwich. There three of the crew were interrogated at the *Three Cups* inn by Mayor James Pulham, Navy (civilian) Commissioner Robert Culpack, innkeeper-cum-actuary William Bull, and interpreter Thomas Warboys. The French captain was Pierre François Codderin and his second-in-command was called Langlois. Codderin inaccurately said that his crew consisted of nine Frenchmen, three Danes, three Americans and one Italian. The third interviewee was already a doomed man, for, contrary

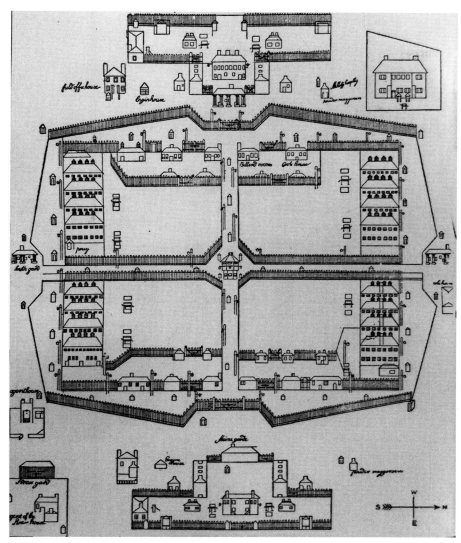

At Norman Cross. Below, the central gun tower, and beneath, prisoners sell artefacts they have made. To the left, a plan of the camp. Today only the commandant's house still stands.

to his captain's account, he was a renegade Englishman, George Jay of Hull and Yarmouth. He not only admitted his nationality, but explained how he had been captured by the French off Newhaven while a merchant seaman on a ship bound from Ipswich to Plymouth, been imprisoned at Boulogne and Calais, hospitalised, and then gone of his own accord to Dunkirk and served on various vessels there. He added that he had joined *L'Espoir* eight or nine days before she sailed. Surprisingly he was almost 60 years old. After a few days at Harwich he was separated from the other prisoners, who went on to Norman Cross via Ipswich and Yarmouth, and was sent to Chelmsford Gaol and later Newgate. In 1798 he was tried next door at the Old Bailey by Sir James Marriott's Admiralty court, as a traitor and pirate. He was hanged in front of a huge crowd at Execution Dock, Wapping. Throughout he seems to have shown a calm fatalism.

On 27th June 1797 Captain Bowater's sloop *Trent*, one of Duncan's blockading fleet, chased and captured the lugger privateer *Poisson Volant* ("Flying Fish"), Captain Lanbonne and her other 21 occupants 30 miles east of Yarmouth. In order to lighten herself her quarry dumped all of her 14 cannon into the sea during the chase. The Frenchman, originally from Le Havre, had

This painting by Butcher may not be precisely contemporary with Napoleonic times but illustrates the busy shipping traffic in the Yarmouth Roads.

taken two prizes off north-eastern Scotland and then come down with them to the Norfolk coast. Another boat went out from Cromer and retook one of these captures, with her six French crew.

That same afternoon G G H Munnings' Colchester Revenue Cutter *Repulse* conducted a three-hour chase after *Le Tigre*, from off Orfordness to almost within sight of the corsair's base at Ostend. The 30-ton raider, which carried two 2-pdrs, two swivels and small arms, was captured and sailed back to Wivenhoe. Her captain, Louis Augustin Buen Chatening, and his 27 men, were marched up to Colchester by Northumberland Militia and held in the borough gaol in the Castle. Munnings, incidentally, lived at Thorpe-le-Soken.

Three days later the *Lady Neville* lobster boat returned to Harwich after a lengthy ordeal. She had been captured by a French privateer off Norway, and then retaken by one of Admiral Duncan's ships while being taken back to France. Only two of her crew were on board: the rest were still with the enemy. The three Frenchmen who had been in charge of her had been landed at Yarmouth.[9]

Late on the morning of 2nd July, just ten days after her previous success, Adams' *Viper* caught another privateer, *Les Graces*, off her Harwich station. After a two-hour chase, in which they dumped their three little cannon, the French beached their lugger at Clacton, and ran ashore with their muskets, pistols and cutlasses.[10] The whole neighbourhood, including the militia camp nearby at Little Holland, was roused. The "invaders" headed inland, presumably hoping to hide till nightfall, then steal a boat. From Colchester Sir William Howe, the Eastern District commander-in-chief himself, sent out a horsed artillery battery, and the Warwickshire light infantry militia from Holland also pursued.[11] But it was Adams' own men who quickly caught Captain Guilliame Gaspard Malo and 21 of his crew. Five others seem to have given them the slip, because the Harwich prisoner book records that one was brought in the next day – by the local Impress Officer, Lt Silver, one on 5th July by the Hamford Water Revenue officer Brotherton, and three on 13th September – again by Silver. Had these last three really managed to conceal themselves for ten weeks – or were they held by the militia and then handed over? Again one prisoner was sent to Chelmsford Gaol, but what became of him is unknown.[12] Malo had commanded a previous raider off Norway. By a bizarre coincidence his wife was from Hitcham, Suffolk: they can only have met before the war, when, as a merchant seaman, he had visited an English port such as Ipswich. After his postwar repatriation to Dunkirk they invested his extensive raiding profits in a shipyard. Their son inherited this, set up a building firm, bought up most of the land east of the city, and there built the seaside resort of Malo-les-Bains. He was also elected to the French National Assembly.[13]

The contest between the Yarmouth navy and the corsairs continued, but then slackened. On 22nd July the *Tisiphone* and *Rambler* sloops captured *Le Prospère* and 40 men near the Dogger Bank. On 12th August the sloop *Swan* captured a Dutchman, the *Goede Verwagteng*, 18 miles north-east of Vlieland (called by the British "Fly Island"), one of the Dutch Frisian islands. The *Swan* was going to Denmark with a convoy, so her 28 prisoners did not reach Yarmouth for almost a month, which was not unusual. Her rather unusual prize had left Amsterdam 15 weeks before, and taken three British ships. Meanwhile on 23rd August *Espiegle*, now captained by J Boorder in place of Roberts, took the French *Le Prodigé* and 84 men (a local record so far). One month later, close to the spot where the previous Dutchman had been taken, Boorder came across another one, a very fast schooner named *D'Ondeilbaarlaid* ("The Invincible"). She fled inshore into the shallows, but *Espiegle's* master, Stephenson, was familiar with the area, so she followed, constantly firing round and grape shot, till she got close enough to board. The privateer's second lieutenant was killed, 33 men were taken, and the remaining 13 managed to flee ashore in a boat. Enemy troops were clearly seen bringing up two artillery pieces, but the two ships got away and reached Yarmouth four days later. The privateer, based at Amsterdam, had only put to sea from Vlieland a few hours earlier.[14]

The *Viper* excise cutter passing the Gunfleet beacon, drawn by William Wallace. The fore and aft rig of the cutters made them handy vessels for the chase.

That summer long columns of corsair prisoners, flanked by local militia, were seen tramping the roads of East Anglia en route to Norman Cross, some entirely overland, others from staging ports at Lynn and Wisbech. The system at Yarmouth was to gather up a number of captured crews, then send them off together. For example, the prisoners from the *Augustine, Marander, Hardi Mendicant* and *Buonaparte* marched out as one group on 17th June, and those from the *Poisson Volant, Tigre, Argo, Les Graces* and *L'Espoir* on 14th July.

Incredibly, so far no one seems to have been killed in action in the North Sea privateering war. On 26th February 1798 there was a dramatic exception. Lt Webb's Yarmouth-based *Prince Cobourg* cutter intercepted *La Révanche*, the largest Calais lugger so far seen, about 35 miles north of her base. She chased the French south-eastwards all night and for a hundred miles till dawn, and then closed in for a gun battle which lasted two hours. Sixty-two Frenchmen were captured, after seven had been killed and eight wounded and the privateer sank from her underwater damage. *Cobourg* had only two slightly injured men. Webb generously praised his whole crew for their skill in "knotting, splicing, and shifting sail in variable weather ... having been exposed to a sharp and well-directed fire from the stern chasers and musquetry (of the enemy)".[15]

The captures by Yarmouth Roads warships were not restricted to privateers. What was left of the enemy's own seaborne trade was also snapped up. On 4th and 5th May 1798 Duncan's fleet seized a flotilla of 12 Dutch whaling ships sailing past for Greenland, along with two American vessels homeward-bound from Amsterdam. The captors included the once-mutinous *Monmouth* and *Director*, the heroic *Ardent* of Camperdown, the veteran *Glatton*, the *Cruizer*, *Jalouse* and *Prince Cobourg*, and the ill-fated *Lutine*. It took almost two more years for a gathering to take place at Yarmouth in which prize money was distributed to their crews.[16]

In May 1798 Pitt, against predictable objections from the Whigs and some leading merchants, compelled all merchant ships to sail in escorted convoys. Undoubtedly a modest fall in the rate of shipping losses to privateers resulted – nationally and off the east coast. But this should not be exaggerated. The system was for one vast convoy – and by 1800 some had 400 or 500 ships – to gather off the Tyne each month and then head south about five to ten miles off the coast. However, it was likely to have only two or three naval escorts. Precise steering and distance-keeping were impossible in the age of sail, and in any case at night. In consequence the ships could soon be so widely scattered many were out of sight of the escorts, meaning that privateers still reached them. By the way, "convoy" in 1790s parlance meant "naval escort" rather than "group of merchant ships".

Notwithstanding their civilian status and mercenary motives some of the corsair captains achieved the same kind of fame as the German U-Boat "aces" of the world wars, grudgingly admired in England as well as lionised in France. Their tallies of captures, daring approaches to the English coast, and narrow escapes were lauded in the French press. By the time Napoleon had taken power the best-known were the Fourmentins, four Boulogne brothers who mainly sailed the Channel but sometimes the North Sea, and Étienne Jean Blanckeman, a Dunkirker of Flemish ancestry. Blanckeman was twice captured (first in the Revolutionary, then the Napoleonic, phase of the war), and landed at Yarmouth. On 23rd June 1799 the British *Champion* intercepted his *Anachreon* lurking near the Dudgeon shoal, about 25 miles north of Wells in Norfolk, chased her for three days back towards France, and finally captured her far out from the Roads. On 30th November the same year, 30 miles north-west of the Texel, Captain Dunbar's Yarmouth sloop *Driver* boarded *Le Barras*, a 14-gun Dunkirk schooner privateer four days out from Ostend, which had on board ten British prisoners from a Hull collier, and her own 57 crew – mainly Danes and Swedes but including Denis Fourmentin. Barras, after whom his prize was named, was the French government Director to whom Napoleon owed much of his early career. Captors and captives came into Yarmouth on 3rd December. Having forwarded Dunbar's report to the Admiralty, next day Admiral Duncan sent another one from Captain Temple of the *Jalouse*, which had brought in the Dunkirk *La Fantasie*, her 44 crew, and 39 Britons she had taken from four laden colliers close to Flamborough Head in Yorkshire. "saved from the horrors of a French prison", he observed of the rescued merchant seamen.[17]

The *Cruizer* sloop was the most successful east coast privateer-hunter of the war. At this period her captain was Charles Wollaston, son of the Rector of Woolverstone in Suffolk. On May Day 1798 she captured the 36-man lugger privateer *Jupiter*, a fortnight out of Boulogne, after a three-hour chase. On 21st May 1799 she landed 50 prisoners from the Calais corsair *Deux Fréres*, which she had chased down near Scarborough, while "convoying" down from Leith. Within two days in March 1800 she took the cutter *Pérséverant* and brig *Flibustier*, with 100 crew between them, and sent them back into Yarmouth. The first of these, commanded by Delattre, had made a huge number of North Sea captures.

Within two days in November 1799 two French privateers approached the English east coast. On the 21st Lt Searle's Yarmouth-based cutter *Courier* fought a 50-minute action with *Le Geurier* off Lowestoft. Her master was killed but she finally captured the raider and 44 men. On the 23rd a Sunderland merchant vessel was taken near the Kentish Knock. While her master, Urwin, was being rowed across to the privateer he wrested a sword from one of his captors, forced the Frenchmen to take him back to his ship, jumped on board, and made her prize crew jump overboard and swim away!

On 5th April 1800 two privateers were taken – *Inattendu* (25 crew) by Captain Temple's *Jalouse* and *La Virginie* (50) by Sotheron's *Latona* – all captives to Yarmouth as usual.

Towards the end of that June the packet *Dolphin*, normally captained by Flyn of Harwich, left Yarmouth for Cuxhaven under Captain March. About halfway she was attacked by Capitaine Pollet's 12-gun Boulogne privateer *Le Napoléon*, and, after a lengthy gun fight, captured for the second time and taken into the Texel. One of her crew was wounded, and had to have an arm amputated, and some of Pollet's men were also injured. March and his crew

The French press recorded the triumphs of the country's corsairs, in the same way that the *London Gazette* reported on British successes. Here Blan(c)keman's capture of *L'Ami* is related.

MINISTERE DE LA MARINE.

Le corsaire l'Anacréon, de Dunkerque, capitaine Blankeman, s'est emparé sur les côtes d'Angleterre, du sloop l'Ami, de Londres. Il a combattu pendant près de trois heures un cutter anglais, qui cherchoit à lui enlever cette prise. Il l'eût abordé, et, probablement, capturé à son tour, si dans l'action il n'avoit été désemparé de ses principales manœuvres.

Le corsaire l'Adèle, de Calais, capitaine Malo, a conduit à Berghen deux sloops anglais, ainsi qu'une goëlette chargée d'orge, de lin, habillement de troupes, etc.; et à Stavanger, un brick de la même nation, chargé d'orge.

Le même corsaire a envoyé à Ostende le sloop la Liberté, pris à trente lieues à l'ouest du Texel, et chargé de poissons frais.

Le corsaire la Virginie, de Calais, capitaine Mulard, a fait entrer à Ostende le cutter le Fox, allant de Douvres à Flessingue, sur son lest.

were imprisoned in Amsterdam. The captured passengers included Sir Robert Barclay, two Swiss, two English women, and a Jew. On shore Barclay protested firmly to the French commissioner about the boarding party beating the British crew, insulting the women, and robbing the passengers. As a result the ship was ransomed back to Yarmouth, and its 15 crew were put onto a Dutch brig and taken to Dover.[18]

The names the privateer owners and captains gave their ships is a small study in itself. *Inattendu* means "unexpected" – ideal for such a raider. Just as the aristocratic generals of 1792 disappeared from the *lettres de marque* under the Jacobins, the mob orators and terrorists vanished after Thermidor, and Bonaparte and his officers began to feature from 1797. *Le Napoléon* speaks for itself. As late as April 1801, only a few months before he mended fences with the Catholic Church in his Concordat, a corsair captured by one of the Yarmouth Roads fleet was called *L'Antichrist.*[19] If Windham and Young spotted this all their fear of France must have been confirmed!

Part of the first page of Blanckermann's crew list. It refers to the "*Contre Amiral Magon*, going commerce raiding, built at Dunkirk, equipped at Ostend, commanded by Citizen E-J Blanckemann ...".

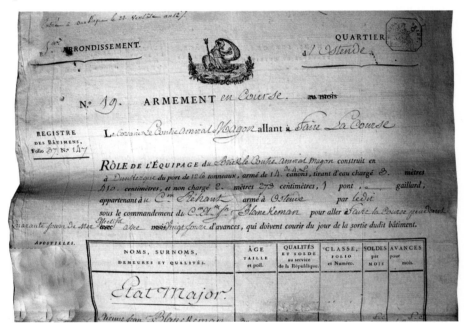

In response to enemy privateering some East Anglian shipowners and captains armed their vessels with cannon and obtained their own letters of marque. The most enterprising were the owners of the Aldeburgh-based *Daphne*, who included Orford farmer George Cullum and Norwich tobacconist Phineas Jacobs, and her captain Thomas Abbott of Aldeburgh. In October 1795 she captured two large Dutch doggers, bound from Iceland to Rotterdam with cargoes of cod and fish oil, and sent them back to Orford. However she was more smuggler than privateer. The following January she took another Dutch vessel, the *Clarissa*, into Woodbridge. En route she secretly anchored overnight in the River Deben off Ramsholt, where she handed over the *Clarissa*'s tobacco to the notorious local smuggler Richard Arnold, alias "Little Dick". That September she seized two more Dutch doggers, in spite of the cancellation of her letter of marque. The Admiralty Prize Court in London confiscated the proceeds from the public sale of her captured cargoes. A warrant was issued for the arrest of some of her owners and crew, though Cullum avoided this by accidentally falling from a coach and killing himself early in 1797.[20] Jacobs and the *Daphne* somehow stayed in business, till she captured the French merchantman *Circe* in 1799 without first registering her own crew's names as the law demanded – presumably because they included known smugglers. Jacobs was ruined because the Court again confiscated his profit and fined him into the bargain. Those testifying against him had included Robert Thatcher

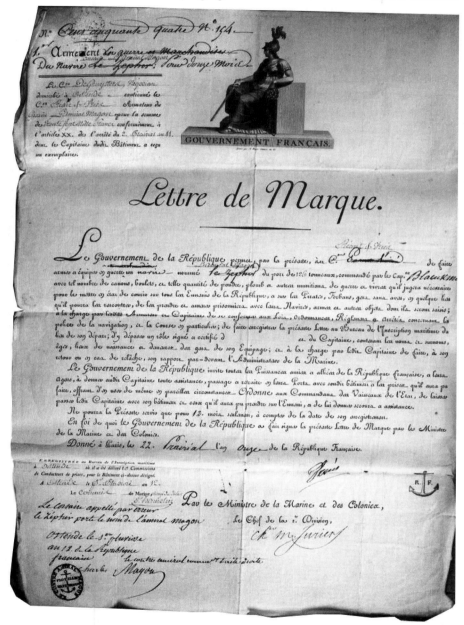

Blanckemann's *lettre de marque*. The vessel was captured by the sloop *Cruizer* and taken into Yarmouth.

of Woodbridge, *Daphne*'s mate, who had been on board during her earlier captures. The case became nationally famous, and there is still a Daphne Road in Orford. "Little Dick" carried on unmolested till killed in a riding accident in 1807. There seems little doubt that, often behind patriotic talk, many east coast men of rank and property protected and patronised such rogues, though it was the radical journalist William Cobbett, an outspoken critic of official corruption, who later defended Jacobs in print.[21]

Occasionally privateering and smuggling even merged with treachery. In September 1801, after smugglers were arrested at Burnham-on-Crouch, one of them, William Pooley, was taken off to London by a Bow Street officer to face the terrible charge of high treason. Did he share the fate of George Jay? – this I have not been able to discover. He had, presumably, been in French pay, for Napoleon later claimed that smugglers were his main source of intelligence about naval and troop deployments in England.[22]

The *London Gazette* – this extract from the edition published to cover 3rd-10th December 1799 – regularly carried the reports submitted after the capture of enemy privateers in various area of the North Sea and Channel. The French captains clearly report their names with the title 'Citoyen'.

[1256]

Captain Temple, of His Majesty's Sloop Jalouse, giving an Account of his having captured the French Lugger Privateer the Fantaisie, belonging to Dunkirk, which I had sent him in quest of on the 24th of last Month, and have no Doubt the uniform Zeal and Exertion of this Officer will meet with due Attention from their Lordships.

I am, &c.   DUNCAN.

His Majesty's Sloop Jalouse, at
MY LORD,   *Sea, Nov. 30, 1799.*

Yesterday I had the good Luck to fall in with the Privateer your Lordship sent me in quest of, and after a Chace of Five Hours I captured her; she is a new Copper-bottomed Lugger, of Fourteen Guns and Sixty Men, called the Fantaisie, of Dunkirk, and had the Day before taken Four laden Colliers, close in with Flambro' Head; I determined to get towards Ostend, and this Day I retook the Sally of Lynn, one of her Prizes, the others I have great Hopes of falling in with; I feel great Pleasure in having rescued Four Masters and Thirty-five British Seamen from the Horrors of a French Prison. The Lugger is just refitted, well stored, cost Two Thousand Six Hundred Pounds Sterling, and I think well calculated for His Majesty's Service.

I have the Honor to be, &c. &c. &c.
J. TEMPLE.

Right Honorable Lord Viscount Duncan, Commander in Chief, &c. &c. &c.

Admiralty-Office, December 7, 1799.

Copy of a Letter from Vice-Admiral Lutwidge, Commander in Chief of His Majesty's Ships and Vessels in the Downes, to Evan Nepean, Esq; dated the 3d Instant.

SIR,

Herewith transmit, for the Information of my Lords Commissioners of the Admiralty, a Letter I have received from Captain Lloyd, of His Majesty's Sloop Racoon, giving an Account of his having captured a French Lugger Privateer of Fourteen Guns and Four Swivels.

I am, Sir, &c. &c. &c.
S. LUTWIDGE.

His Majesty's Sloop Racoon, Downes,
SIR,   *December 3, 1799.*

Beg Leave to acquaint you, that Yesterday Morning at Daylight, Portee E. S. E. I fell in with a French Lugger Privateer, to which I immediately gave Chace, and an Hour after I had the Satisfaction to capture her; she proves to be Le Vrai Decide, of Fourteen Guns, Four Swivels, and Fifty Men, (Nine of whom had been left on Shore when she sailed,) commanded by Citizen Desgardri, belongs to Boulogne, out Thirty Hours, in Company with Three others, and had not taken any Thing. His Majesty's Ship Cormorant was in Sight, and joined in the Chace.

I have the Honor to be, &c. &c. &c.
ROBERT LLOYD.

Skeffington Lutwidge, Esq; Vice-Admiral of the Red, &c. &c. &c.

Admiralty-Office, December 7, 1799.

Copy of a Letter from Vice-Admiral Lutwidge, Commander in Chief of His Majesty's Ships and Vessels in the Downes, to Evan Nepean, Esq; dated the 5th Instant.

SIR,

I Have the Pleasure of transmitting, for the Information of my Lords Commissioners of the Admiralty, a Letter which I have received from Captain Lloyd, of His Majesty's Sloop Racoon, giving an Account of his having captured on the 3d Instant L'Intrepide French Privateer, of Sixteen Guns and Sixty Men, belonging to Calais. The Racoon anchored in the Downes this Morning; and I have the Satisfaction of learning from Lieutenant Coxwell, that the Wound which Captain Lloyd has received in the Head from a Half-Pike is not dangerous. He also informs me, that soon after the Action the Stag Cutter joined, and went in Pursuit of the Brig mentioned in Captain Lloyd's Letter.

His Majesty's Sloop Racoon, Dover-
SIR,   *Roads, December 4, 1799.*

I Beg Leave to acquaint you, that Yesterday at Ten P. M. Dover North about Five or Six Miles, I observed a Lugger board a Brig; I soon discovered her to be an Enemy, and made all Sail in Chace; after a running Fire of about Forty Minutes I laid her alongside, when we were received with a smart Fire from the Cannon and small Arms, which was immediately returned with Success; finding themselves unable to make any further Resistance, Bowsprit and Foremast gone, they thought it fit to strike. She proves to be L'Intrepide, of Calais, mounting Sixteen Guns and Sixty Men, quite new, commanded by Citizen Saillard, sailed from Boulogne Four o'Clock Yesterday Evening.

I feel myself much indebted to Lieutenant Coxwell (the only Commissioned Officer I had on board) for the great Assistance I received from him, as well as the other Officers and Men for their Attention in obeying my Orders. It is with Satisfaction I have to state (through Providence) that there is only One Man wounded, and myself slightly. The Privateer has lost Thirteen in Killed and Wounded. I am sorry to state that the Brig captured was the Welcombe, from London to Plymouth with Malt; and it was out of my Power to pursue her as I must have lost my Foremast, all my Foreshrouds being gone on the Starboard Side. It gives me particular Pleasure to have deprived the Enemy of a Vessel which they considered the largest and best Sailer from Calais; and have the Honor to be, &c.
ROBERT LLOYD.

To Skeffington Lutwidge, Esq; Vice-Admiral of the Red, &c. &c. &c. Downes.

Admiralty-Office, December 7, 1799.

Copy of a Letter from Vice-Admiral Lutwidge, Commander in Chief of His Majesty's Ships and Vessels in the Downes, to Evan Nepean, Esq; dated the 6th Instant.

SIR,

INclosed I transmit, for the Information of my Lords Commissioners of the Admiralty, a Letter which I have received from Captain Griffiths, of

The First Invasion Scare 8

In the course of 1796 and 1797 General Napoleon Bonaparte conquered northern Italy and forced Austria to make peace. Hervey, Earl of Bristol, of Ickworth, Suffolk, fell foul of his troops when they entered Rome and dragged him off along with his beloved art collection. In October of that second year, just a fortnight after Camperdown, Bonaparte returned to France to command the would-be invasion force called "the Army of England". He met Tom Paine, who advised him to swamp the British defences with landings from a mass of small boats.[1] Bonaparte lauded Paine as a political inspiration, but did not believe that he had taught him any military lessons. Like Hitler 143 years later he was in any case much fonder of threatening the British, and gloating about their supposed eventual collapse, than planning an actual invasion. Though he was assigned some 40,000 troops, he was based in Paris and did not visit the main proposed embarkation ports at Calais, Dunkirk and Ostend until February. Thereupon he immediately reported to his government that a combination of enemy naval superiority, French lack of shipping, and impossibility of surprise, ruled out any attempt in the short term. He suggested the more glamorous alternative of invading Egypt.

Napoleone di Buonaparte, Napoléon Bonaparte, grew swiftly into one of France's most respected military authorities during the Revolution. His political skill and mastery of propaganda led him to be appointed Consul and then Emperor.

However this was not known in England, and while he was supposedly based just across the Dover Strait with the best of the battle-hardened and victorious French Army a state of alarm prevailed along our south-eastern shores, not least because he and his Italy veterans had a reputation of being Jacobin-inclined and ruthless.

The British army and navy in the area were reinforced accordingly. However, there had been a concern with the vulnerability to enemy attack of eastern ports and harbours ever since the French seized the mouth of the Scheldt back at the end of 1792 – it had been one reason for the outbreak of war.

At that time the British Army theoretically numbered under 50,000 men, and, subtracting sick and pensioners, in reality less than 40,000. The French were mobilising hundreds of thousands. There was already a precedent for using the existing Regular Army for service overseas, and the defence of London and the key naval bases, and defending the rest of the coastline with the Militia regiments which existed on paper in every county. Legally militiamen were not required to serve overseas. Their regiments, last "embodied" (called up) in the American War, consisted of gentleman officers, whose names, ranks and units were already registered, and labourer, tradesman and servant other ranks who had yet to be recruited. Their enlistment consisted of picking out one in ten young adult men in each parish by ballot (e.g. drawing a short straw). Enlisted men could pay "substitutes" to stand in for them. Men had already formed clubs – or even taken out commercial insurance – which, by pooling individuals' contributions, provided enough money for this purpose. Later, when follow-up Militia Acts demanded the balloting of those who had escaped the first time round, many evaded this by joining the local "Home Guard" style Volunteers, who met only part-time and did not leave their localities. Later militiamen were incentivised to transfer to the regulars. All this made for lack of cohesion, numbers and fighting spirit.

Not that the regulars were vastly better: most of their officers had obtained their commissions through purchase or family influence and had attended no military academy. And as for the overall planning and direction of the land war, throughout his time in office Pitt presided over a system of divided and illogical command whereby the Army's Master-General of Ordnance, not its Commander-in-Chief, controlled its artillery, engineers, and supply of guns, ammunition, uniforms and maps, and its transport and the supply of food and forage was farmed out to profit-making civilian commissaries.[2]

Though a handful of militia officers were retired regulars, predictably most were men of local social standing rather than military prowess. Of the seven East Anglian Militia regiments six were commanded by MPs and six by men with aristocratic titles. Sir William Smyth, MP for adjacent Cambridgeshire, was colonel of the West Essex. Elderly Essex MP Sir John Bullock commanded the East Essex. Francis Rigby, the main landowner at Mistley, whose house and twin-towered neo-classical church Harwich-bound travellers all admired, later took over from him. The Earl of Euston, one of the great aristocrats of West Suffolk, commanded its militia. His father, the Duke of Grafton, had been prime minister in the 1760s. West Norfolk's colonel Horatio Walpole, otherwise MP for King's Lynn, was a cousin of the writer Horace and also of Nelson's wife Fanny, and a descendant of Sir Robert Walpole, Britain's first prime minister. He was succeeded by the young William Keppel, Earl of Albemarle, of Quidenham Hall near Diss, a descendant of King William III's courtier Van Keppel. Sir John Wodehouse, local MP, led the East Norfolks. For the first year or so these officers did not hold formal army ranks, but in March 1794 they were granted, which legally authorised them to command in battle.[3]

Having old men, MPs and even government ministers as military field officers was of course not ideal. They were bound to be semi-absentee, as likely to be in London or on their estates when the enemy invaded as with their regiments. In reality they were akin to the honorary colonels of modern times, while their second-in-command majors ran their units. In May 1795 the Marquess Townshend, then commanding Eastern District, reported that, having allowed the Pembrokeshire's colonel to attend to some private business, he had not heard from him for over six months. Another officer from the same regiment was in prison for debt! In the West Kent, at Bury, half the officers were off sick.[4]

For all their undoubted shortcomings production and stockpiling of "Brown Bess" flintlock muskets and uniforms from previous wars meant that by February 1793 these militia regiments were on the march to the coast. On 15th February the East Kent were deployed between Chelmsford, Maldon and Rochford, the West Norfolk was heading for Harwich and Landguard

Fort, the East Essex were at Ipswich, the East Suffolk at Yarmouth, and the West Suffolk down near Portsmouth. By June the Hertfordshires were at Woodbridge and the Royal South Lincolnshires at Aldeburgh, while Harwich was garrisoned by the Bedfordshires, West Kents and East Suffolks, who shared a camp outside the town at the harbour entrance. Wealthy civilian travellers delighted in stopping to sight-see what they described as "lively" and "beautiful" camp scenes set against "the ocean".[5]

However, some of the inmates of these places were less delighted. The *Ipswich Journal* was soon regularly printing the names, homes and descriptions of deserters and the rewards offered to those who shopped them. The resulting penalties could be severe. In April 1793 an East Essex private got 300 lashes for desertion – and theft. After 25 strokes he escaped across a field, only to be found in a ditch and given the rest of the punishment.[6]

Among the Regulars, seven foot (infantry) regiments had East Anglian names – though most of their recruits, both officers and men, had come from further afield. 12th Foot were East Suffolk, 30th Cambridgeshire, 44th East Essex, 54th West Norfolk, 56th West Essex, and 63rd West Suffolk. In 1794 12th joined the Duke of York in Flanders, returning from Bremen to Harwich the following year after the debacle in Holland. 30th, 60th and 11th successively garrisoned Colchester between then and early 1797. 60th, the "Royal Americans", had originally been raised from British North American colonists during the Seven Years War, but by this time consisted almost wholly of native Englishmen.

From the spring of 1794 a few regiments of "Fencible" infantry and cavalry appeared in the region – differing from the Militia in that, though restricted to the home defence of Great Britain, they were volunteers. The first was Colonel Harbord's Norfolk Fencible Cavalry. This was followed six months later by the Suffolk and Loyal Essex Fencible Infantries. On 1st January 1795 Windham reported that there were nearly 4500 militia and fencibles (i.e, full-time but "hostilities-only" troops) in East Anglia.[7]

It so happened that Britain's most experienced general, the Marquess of Cornwallis, owned the estate at Culford, in West Suffolk, and in 1794 he returned from India to be Master-General of the Ordnance. He was a cousin of the ill-fated Yarmouth MP Lord Charles Townshend. He was certainly of mixed repute, having surrendered to the French and Americans at Yorktown but since then defeated Tipoo Sultan, "the Tiger of Mysore", in India. He moved to London and exercised command from an office next door to Pitt's. In 1795 the post of "Field-Marshal on the Staff" (i.e. commander-in-chief) was taken by the Duke of York, recently back from Holland. Surprisingly he turned out to be much better at organising and reforming the wider army than he had at leading a field force.

Within the first year of war tented troop camps had been set up on at least five sites in Essex alone. Apart from Harwich, these were Warley, near Brentwood, Danbury Hill (with its view down the River Blackwater), Lexden Heath west of Colchester, and Little Holland, on the coast near Great Clacton.[8] By now, in addition to their tents and training grounds, and billets in houses and inns, garrisons were acquiring brick and wooden barracks. Colchester already had one for a thousand men between the town and the Hythe Quay a mile east. (The area still has a Barrack Street and Military Road, some distance from today's garrison district south of town). Chelmsford and Ipswich each housed another 500. The Chelmsford site was at Moulsham, the Ipswich on the Woodbridge road. In February 1796 Parliament voted additional funds to house another 2,600 infantry at Colchester and 1750 at Chelmsford. These were the largest barrack plans in the country at the time.[9] That spring Colchester accommodated three militia battalions in addition to 30th Foot.

As we know, Arthur Young was so alarmed by the French Revolution and its would-be English imitators that he was one of the first to call for an additional, paramilitary, force which would mobilise in the event of invasion or revolt. In the spring of 1794, when the French Jacobins had gained the upper hand in Belgium, Pitt authorised local "men of substance" throughout the country to recruit and lead Volunteer (infantry) and equivalent (mounted) Yeomanry, which would train on Sundays and mobilise to meet emergencies. Of course these emergencies meant domestic riots and rebellions as well as foreign invasions.

It would be wrong to say that there was an immediate scramble to form or join these voluntary "corps". The first, the "Suffolk Gentlemen and Volunteers", headed by Lord Rous, was set up on 9th April of that year. It took another year before there were Loyal Essex and Cambridgeshire Yeomanries (Colonels Burgoyne and Adams). Each of these units was only about one to 200 strong.[10] They were part police, part invasion home guard, part social clubs. They were essentially of and for the wealthy and their dependent tenants and servants, because they had to provide their own horses, uniforms and weaponry. Most met up and drilled on the estates of their colonels. Throughout the war they never saw an invader, but sometimes turned out to patrol towns and villages threatened by hungry rioters. Though they had a reputation for being right-wing and anti-radical, this was not always deserved: Montagu Burgoyne was a Foxite Whig, for example.

The French victories in Belgium in 1794, followed by their overrunning also of Holland, naturally caused alarm in the region, especially as there was at that time little more naval presence along its coast than the odd sloop escorting a convoy. However in 1795 the squadron in Yarmouth Roads, and the distinctly passive posture of the Batavian fleet, were reassuring. Invasion fear only returned towards the end of 1796, when the French general Hoche planned – and gathered troops for – a descent on Ireland which seemed also to mean simultaneous secondary landings on the east coast of England. That November Cornwallis visited the garrison at Colchester to discuss this possibility. He had heard that the French were concentrating at Dunkirk for landings a mere ten or so miles away, at Tillingham, Bradwell, Mersea and St Osyth, so as to secure the deep water Blackwater Estuary for their navy and then march on London, just forty miles distant. Coast artillery batteries had already been installed at Walton, Holland, Clacton, St Osyth and Bradwell to forestall such an attempt. Each had a furnace for heating shot so as to cause fires and explosions on enemy ships.[11]

For most of the war this part of the east coast was to cause strategic concern. The many estuaries and creeks between the Crouch and Alde were only between 70 and 100 miles from the enemy's ports, could have accommodated any number of warships and transport vessels, and were flanked by shorelines, which, although cliff or marsh in some places, were mostly easy to land on. Although numerous sandbanks ran along off the coast as far north-east as the Naze, they were crossable by shallow-draft invasion

WE, whose Names are hereunto subscribed, do hereby acknowledge to have received of *Lieut Acton Marsh* the Sums against each respectively expressed, for attending at *Wivenhoe & Rowhedge* to be exercised as Sea Fencibles, under the Command of *Henth Capt Johm B. N*

No.	Names.	On what Days exercised.			Number of Days.	Sum.			When paid	Received by
						£.	s.	d.		
0	John Pretty	do	do		2		5		do	John + Pretty
1	Abr. Ham	do	do		2		2			Abr + Ham
2	Edwd. Bacon	do	do		2		2			Edw + Bacon
3	Geo. Lawrence	do			1		1			George + Lawrence
4	Wm. Chiswick	do	do		2		2			Wm + Chiswick
5	John Mills	do	do		2		2			John Mills
6	Sam. Cole	do	do		2		2			Sam Cole
7	Joseph Daughty	do	do		2		2			Joseph + Daughty
13	Stepn Reynolds	do	do		2		2			Stn Reynolds
9	John Kent	do	do		2		2			John + Kent
10	Wm Taylor	do			1		1			Wm + Taylor
11	Robt Willis	do	do		2		2			Rob + Willis
12	Wm Barnard	do	do		2		2			Wm + Barnard
13	Jas. Arnold	do	do		2		2			James + Arnold
14	Sam. Watts	do	do		2		2			Samuel Watt
15	John Coppin	do	do		2		2			John Coppin
16	Joseph Mills	do	do		2		2			Joseph + Mills
17	Wm Marshall	do	do		2		2			Wm + Marshall
18	Rich Ham		do		1		1			Rich + Ham
19	Thos Ham		do		1		1			Thos + Ham
20	Wm Bligh		do		1		1			William Bligh
21	Wm Sadler		do		1		1			Wm Sadler
22	Edwd Bacont		do		1		1			Edw + Bacon
						2	2	0		

W. Keymer, Printer, Colchester.

A volunteers list for Sea Fencibles at Wivenhoe.

craft at high tide – but not by major British warships. The local waterways also divided up the defenders along the coast, preventing them from quickly concentrating against a landing at a given spot.

It was, incidentally, mostly a lonely and open shore that had to be guarded. The seaside towns of Clacton, Frinton, Walton, Dovercourt and Felixstowe, with their esplanades, hotels and piers, did not yet exist. Even the few coastal towns that there were – (King's) Lynn, Yarmouth, Lowestoft, Harwich – faced inland onto rivers, not seawards.

In September 1796 Pitt secured an act of parliament for a Supplementary Militia – that is, the conscription of some of the civilians who had not been called up four years earlier, so as to form additional home-defence battalions. In November another act obliged every owner of ten or more horses to supply one, with a rider, for a new Provisional Cavalry (home defence) regiment. Norfolk raised 1781 men for the first requirement and 337 for the second.[12] However the Norwich Whigs and radicals were fiercely opposed, and when the county's Lord Lieutenant, Field Marshal Lord Townshend, chaired an enlistment meeting at the Shire Hall he faced what the local press called a "tumult".[13] There were still many who thought Pitt's armed forces and other war measures unjustified, and invasion a mere Government-contrived fiction.

But between February and June 1797 the French reactivated their back door invasion plan and actually got a small detachment ashore in Wales, the financial system almost collapsed, the Navy mutinied, and the Dutch agreed to join an attack. Though all these threats were dealt with, anxiety intensified. Camperdown was won, but then Bonaparte reappeared in Paris. Britain remained without major allies (except for a distant and inactive Russia), and discontent came to a head in Ireland.

In these circumstances the East Anglian Volunteer movement took on a second wind. At the time of the Dutch invasion alarm, in February 1797, Norwich loyalists formed their Light Horse Volunteers and Loyal Military Association, under Captains Harvey and Patteson, two city aldermen well-known for their war of words with the likes of Coke, the Gurneys, and Wilks. Soon each Norwich parish had its own additional volunteer company. Local loyalist morale was boosted by news of Nelson's exploits against the Spaniards in the Battle of Cape St Vincent (which had happened the same day) and his gift to the city of a captured Spanish admiral's sword. The *Norfolk Chronicle* declared:

> "... to defend our country against the common enemy is now the only measure left to us, and no man, whatever his political opinions, will hesitate to take his share of danger and fatigue".

Two Yarmouth volunteer companies were also formed – one headed by the naval contractor Samuel Padget.

The Army's most notable invasion expert was another son of Norfolk, Colonel John Money. He had enlisted at the age of ten and fought in the American War until captured, in the process learning much about the part irregular forces and civilians could play in war. One of the very earliest aeronauts, he had gone up in hot-air balloons and once had to be rescued 20 miles out to sea by the revenue cutter *Argus*. Whig-radical politically, he had joined the Belgian Patriots rebelling against Austria, and, after their defeat in 1789, emigrated to revolutionary France and enrolled in her army. When the Paris mob massacred the Swiss Guard in front of the Tuileries Palace, he rushed there to help guard King Louis. With the French anti-Jacobin general Dumouriez he deserted to the Allies and so returned to England.

Politically suspect to King George III, Pitt and Dundas, he nevertheless caught the attention of the Duke of York when he became commander-in-chief in 1795. He toured the whole coastline facing the enemy and wrote reports on how best to defend it. In 1797 he influenced the Duke to move Eastern District HQ from Norwich to its more central location near Colchester. He called for the flogging of deserters and mutineers to be replaced by the more humane, and also less debilitating, branding on the shoulder. In June 1799 he wrote a notable letter to Windham, calling for military reforms of American and French inspiration. Troops were to be trained as sharpshooters, firing accurate rifles singly or in small groups from woods and hedges, instead of lining up on open ground so as to blast off saturation volleys with inaccurate muskets, yet be cut down in droves. Artillery was to be light and mobile, so that it could be rushed to invasion beaches in the minimum time. He argued that the regular emplaced artillery battery at Cromer should be replaced by mobile light guns manned by the Volunteers and supplied with shot by hired farm wagons – a proposal endorsed by Lynn and Yarmouth naval officers, shipowners and Sea Fencibles.[14]

Although Money was not the first or only officer to promote these ideas his influence was considerable, and he deserves to be better known than he is.

Civilians added their less useful suggestions. Arthur Young wrote a booklet entitled *National Defence and the Means of Safety*, in which he had little to offer about tactics but harped on his usual theme of ferreting out sedition. He exhorted the complacent to remember what the French would do to their wives, children and religion. He also deplored the many folk he saw "languishing" around and enjoying themselves instead of taking the situation seriously. Bury magistrate Capel Lofft proposed a corps armed with England's ancient victory weapon the longbow.

A pencil sketch of Cromer from 1809 shows – on the left – two towers and a wall that probably housed the artillery battery, reinforced in 1804. The towers overlooked the Gangway in the cliff which gave access from the beach to the town.

Until the spring of 1797 Eastern District had covered only Norfolk and Suffolk, been manned mainly by militia, and been commanded by the Marquess Townshend and then the Duke of Gloucester, one of the King's less talented brothers. Essex and Cambridgeshire were now added. More regular regiments arrived. And General Sir William Howe, brother of Admiral Lord Howe of Ushant fame, and commander-in-chief of the British army in the first part of the American War, took over. He was already pushing 70. He moved the headquarters to Wivenhoe Park, just across the river from the Colchester Barracks, so as to be more centrally located. His considerable staff included two lieutenant-generals, seven major-generals, and a Quartermaster-General. The troops quartered at Colchester then included the 11th Foot and

A landscape view of
Landguard fort and
common from the painting
by Thomas Gainsboroguh ,
painted about 1753.

Northumberland Militia – one of the latter was the recent recruit later famous as the author "Rifleman Harris". 44th (East Essex) and subsequently 49th Foot were at Chelmsford.

These arrivals seem to have sparked off a panic along the Ipswich-Colchester coast which threatened to disrupt work and what the authorities called "public tranquillity". Magistrates were told to punish people for spreading false rumours. A militia sergeant who had predicted an imminent enemy arrival in Ipswich was made by his colonel to sit in a north-east Essex church porch and apologise to the congregation.[15]

In October Brigadier-General Sir John Moore and Major Hay (Royal Engineers) toured the area, and then drafted a meticulous geographical survey, down to the direction of the slopes, firmness of the ground, point-to-point visibility, quality of the roads, and fordability of rivers. It included detailed descriptions of possible battlefields, with a defence plan of proposed British troop dispositions.[16]

Moore did not underestimate the enemy. He based his proposals on 100,000 invaders coming from Dutch ports on a moderate easterly wind, and in summer, when storms were unlikely and the ground was dry. He thought it just possible that they might head for the coast between Yarmouth and Bawdsey. He doubted if the Navy would ever be driven from the former, but also thought the generous allotment of artillery along the coast there badly sited. The many guns between Caister and Lowestoft pointed straight out to sea instead of enfilading along the beaches, and in any case lacked the range to hit ships in the eastern half of the Roads. Hollesley Bay concerned him because it was an anchorage but also a firm dry landfall. However he reckoned that landings in north-east Essex were much more probable and dangerous. His likeliest scenario was that 10,000 enemy troops would land on the Landguard Peninsula, 10,000 in "Walton Gap" (i.e. Hamford Water), 30,000 at Clacton, and 15,000 on the north shore of the Blackwater between West Mersea and Virley.

His greatest concern was Harwich Harbour. He thought that the invader would be drawn to this, not only as a large calm anchorage, but because

The haven entrance at Yarmouth. The fort is seen on the north side of the entrance.

it would give him water routes into Essex and Suffolk and interior lines of communication against British defenders who were split by those same rivers. From Harwich he and Hay travelled via Thorpe (where they stayed overnight) to Clacton beach. They judged this the prime danger spot. Not only was "every part of the cliff there accessible to troops", but the Tendring Hundred, immediately inland, was "for an enclosed country the most passable one in all England. The nature of the roads is particularly favourable to military movements. Both the leading and cross roads are remarkably broad".

Unlike in the Second World War there was to be no front line along the coast: the defenders were too few. Moore assumed that – unless the Navy had sunk them, of course – the invaders would get ashore, then be first confronted about five miles inland. His proposed forward interception line ran from Narborough via Aylsham, North Walsham, Acle, Beccles, Mutford, Saxmundham, Snape Bridge, Wickham Market, Woodbridge, Martlesham, Ramsey, Weeley, East Donyland, Maldon, Purleigh and Rayleigh to Hadleigh (Essex). The enemy would push beyond this line, but then be brought to battle about another five miles back, short of Norwich, Framlingham, Ipswich, Colchester or Chelmsford.

He said that in the event of his north-east Essex invasion, the three Colchester-based battalions should march to Clacton, and fight a series of delaying actions as they fell back for five days. This fighting retreat, he thought, should culminate in 30,000 British lining up for decisive battle against 50,000 French and Dutch across the neck of land between the River Stour at Dedham and the Colne near Greenstead, apart from 5,000 "rangers" who were to raid the enemy rear from the woods. He proposed to put most of the British, including the bulk of the cavalry, on the left so as to counter-attack towards Harwich. To cover Colchester from the south, and prevent the main British army from being attacked from the rear, he recommended that up to 6,000 men be gathered at Abberton, from whose high ground they could watch and guard both the Blackwater to the south and Colne to the east.

A strangely diagrammatic
view of Harwich harbour
issued in the early
18th century, with the
Landguard fort of 1626
on the right , the Orwell
straight ahead and the
Stour coming in on the left.

His plan was detailed, with remarks such as…

"Two Battalions formed into a Brigade to move forward on Route No.3
to Great Clackton, where leaving a small Reserve in the Church Yard, the
remainder in two Divisions are to advance to the Support of the Batteries
at k and n by the Roads that branch off to these Points … the Reserve to
take post in the Fields adjoining Langham Woods and lying on the left of
the Ipswich Road between Ardley Green and the 55-Mile Stone".[17]

In case the invader tried to get across the River Colne in either direction,
he suggested making it unfordable between Lexden and the Hythe by
heightening and shutting the existing sluices so as to trap the flow.

In order to bring all the proposed troops into north-east Essex, some from
as far away as Yarmouth and the south coast, he wanted them to have as much
warning as possible. He believed that the invader could first be spotted from
the one-hundred foot lighthouse on the Naze, whence the alarm could be
relayed via St Osyth and Aldeburgh church towers and the North Foreland to
Colchester, Danbury, Norfolk and Kent. Since these places were anything up
to 38 miles apart this seems rather optimistic. He suggested that on a sunny
day the signals be smoke, in dull weather fires, and at night clusters of white
lights. He made no mention of what to do in the event of fog.

At the end of that year the Duke of York and Dundas devised a huge
logistical scheme whereby army and civilians would both be fed, and the
invading enemy starved. The duke wrote:

"If an enemy should land it will no doubt be desirable to distress him
as much as possible by driving away the livestock, and consuming or
destroying all other means of subsistence"[18]

The farmers along the east coast were to drive their wagons and animals
far inland to deny them to the invaders. Ones further back were to lend the
British commissaries their horses and carts for towing cannon and shifting
ammunition, and supply men to drive them. Water and windmills, stocks of
corn and flour, barns and bakeries, were to be requisitioned for military use.

Landguard fort as rebuilt in 1716. From major J.H.Leslie's history of the fort. Both illustrations on this spread are from earlier in the 18th century but illustrate the importance attached to the defence of Harwich and the estuary over the decades.

The Mutiny Act was to be the legal authority for this remarkable interference with private property. The gentry and farmers providing the transport had to sign a pompous legal declaration saying:

> "... we hereby declare our entire approbation of the same, and our thankfulness for the opportunity held out to us of manifesting our loyalty, and earnest disposition to contribute to the Defence of our Country. We do therefore most readily and faithfully promise ...."[19]

The duke, fearing chaos and the blocking of roads needed by the army if the farmers and wagon drivers were unsupervised, wanted them enlisted into a "Voluntary Corps of Pioneers". This was not done, but periodic meetings were held in every town and large village at which tasks and routes were allotted. Eastern District Commissary-General Motz at Chelmsford was in charge of all this. He and the Duke were confident about the food stocks, but worried about the transport.

On 1st March 1798 the Duke asked Howe to report on a host of anti-invasion measures. Had marshy areas along the coast been flooded? Could roads leading to London be blocked? Were the evacuation plans for horses and cattle ready? Was there enough field artillery and were artillerymen able to spike their guns if they were about to be captured? Did the troops have a standard tactic for meeting a landing? Did they know they might have to retreat initially, and to dump cumbersome gear such as tents in order to fight light? The Duke fiercely concluded that their goal must be:

> "... deliverance from a Savage and implacable enemy who has the insolence to aim at the slavery of our Persons, the extinction of our Religion, the Destruction of our Navy, our Constitution, our Laws and Customs, so long the enemy and abomination of the world".[20]

In April 1798, having also toured the whole Eastern District shore, Major Thomas Vincent Reynolds (Royal Artillery) wrote a report on the coast defences, recommending the building of numerous forts of varying sizes. As concerned about Harwich as Moore, he wanted Landguard Fort upgraded, and another small fort built on the Altar, a gravel shoal in the harbour mouth. His next biggest priorities were the Blackwater and Clacton, where he recommended several "towers". He thought there should be two more at Hollesley Bay and a third at Aldeburgh.

By now the Eastern District held 30,000 regular troops and militia. Howe wanted 80,000, but this would have swallowed up most of the home-based army. 22nd Regiment of Foot, and the West Suffolk, North York, Northumberland and Royal South Lincolnshire Militias, were at Colchester. Most of 9th Foot were in mid-Suffolk. Most of the Oxfordshire Militia was at Ipswich, the Cambridgeshire and East Essex at Harwich, and the Royal Buckinghamshire at Chelmsford. Both Norfolk militias were at Norwich and the Durham Militia at Yarmouth. Little Holland camp held two troops of horse, an artillery detachment, the rest of 9th Foot, and ten companies from as many separate militia regiments. On the Duke of York's instructions, Howe had formed them into a Light Brigade, a "rapid reaction force" (in today's terms), unencumbered with supply wagons, tents and the heavier types of cannon.[21]

Now that a French Essex coast landing seemed likelier than a Dutch one in Norfolk, volunteer fever spread south. In April 1798 such a company was founded at Chelmsford. In June they paraded in front of the Shire Hall, received their colours from Lord-Lieutenant de Walden, applauded patriotic and unashamedly right-wing speeches, mingled with the ladies, dined and enjoyed a theatre show.[22] Colchester set up an equivalent force in October. Back in Norfolk almost every major landowner, New Whig as well as Old, felt obliged to head such a unit. Even Coke agreed, and formed his tenants into a Holkham Yeomanry. Membership and turnout were highest in that northern part of the county, especially in and around Lynn. Local Anglican clergy were prominent in recruiting, using their pulpits to persuade parishioners into joining so as to resist the atheism and sedition said to emanate from within the region as well as from the Continent. Some even enlisted themselves, on Lord's Day afternoons donning surplices over the red coats and spurred riding boots they had put on for morning drills.

What manner of men were the various coast defenders? For the army abundant evidence went into the local newspapers, law court and parish records. That many of the rank and file fought each other in the pubs is no surprise. But, to the shock and alarm of civilians, both loyalist and radical, their violence sometimes escalated into huge riots on the streets. In January 1796 the Northumberland and Warwickshire Militias clashed *en masse* at Bishop's Bridge, Norwich. Bayonets were used as well as fists. Four men were killed and two hundred injured! It was by no means the last such affair.

But officers could be equally irresponsible. In January 1797 a lieutenant of the Horse Guards and an ensign from the West Suffolk Militia fought a pistol duel at Ipswich. After missing each other with six shots each from only ten paces, they shook hands and honour was satisfied. More tragic was another encounter on Lexden Heath, near Colchester, that May. Lt John Elliott of 22nd Foot and Assistant Surgeon William Cowan of 11th shot each other, and the first officer died of his head wound next morning. Cowan and both seconds then absconded. Colchester borough magistrate-coroners Thomas Hedge and William Mason examined the body and various witnesses and a jury declared the three missing officers guilty of "Wilful Murder". What became of the culprits I have not been able to discover, but in spite of their depriving the army of a fellow officer at a time of national emergency I cannot imagine them suffering worse than demotions. In April 1800 two more officers, this time from 4th Foot at Colchester, shot each other in the leg and side. All three duels had arisen from accusations of cheating at billiards![23]

Nor did such "gentlemen" confine their violence to each other. In May 1797 four Colchester-based officers pleaded guilty to assaulting civilians from the town, and were fined a total of £106. The (Whig-leaning) *Monthly Magazine* commented:

> "These men had, in many instances of unprovoked rudeness, rendered themselves justly obnoxious to a great number of respectable inhabitants".[24]

That summer there was an even more notorious case. Two privates of 49th Foot stole from their comrades and then deserted Chelmsford Barracks. Soon afterwards they waylaid a young brother and sister at Springfield, just outside town. For two hours they took turns holding down the boy and raping the girl. Retribution duly followed: the men were caught and given 400 lashes each by their regiment, then handed over to the local civilian authorities.[25]

In happy contrast, at all military and social ranks there were numerous marriages between the resident soldiers and local girls. At Colchester in 1796 Isaac Boggis, who had recently entertained the Dutch Stadtholder, married his daughter Charlotte to the brigade major of 30th (Cambridgeshire) Foot. The following year Rebow of Wivenhoe Park married his to Captain Slater of 60th Foot.[26] Slater, who later joined the Life Guards, renamed himself Slater-Rebow and inherited his father-in-law's estate.

Meanwhile the Navy had been setting up a major defence scheme of their own. Duncan's deputy Onslow was in charge of it.[27] By April, in order to deny the enemy access to the whole Thames Estuary from Orfordness to the North Foreland, warships were anchored at fixed positions off the coast. The gunboats *Bruizer* and *Contest* guarded Wells and Yarmouth respectively. The 64-gun ships of the line *Agamemnon* (of Nelson and mutiny fame), and two more gunboats stood in Hollesley Bay, off the Deben and Ore. The 54-gun *Braakel* was anchored at the north-eastern tip of the Gunfleet, off the Naze. The 64-gun *Repulse* and two gunboats stood across the Swin Channel, which leads up parallel to the Essex coast towards the London River. The gunboat *Wasp* moored in the River Crouch. And other ships guarded the north Kent coast. In November the *Acute*, a gun boat with a sliding keel which enabled her to cross shallows, was anchored between Mersea and Bradwell to guard the Blackwater. The first task of these ships in the event of invasion was to pull up all the Trinity House buoys so that the enemy grounded on the maze of estuary shoals. Each vessel was equipped with grappling hooks and boarding netting. Some were later fitted with "firebrooms" for setting fire to invasion craft.[28]

Onslow sent a chart of the ship positions to the Duke of York, and he and Howe were told to keep each other informed of new orders and intelligence via shore signal stations. A chain of these posts, using the remarkable French invention of the shutter telegraph (spelling out numbered words and phrases) had already been built through the southern counties, linking Portsmouth and

Deal to the Admiralty in London. Another was now started for the east coast, connecting the Nore to Yarmouth, points in between, and also warships at sea and troops on land. It initially consisted, of balls and flags hoisted in different combinations from spars projecting from staffs. In the event of the enemy nearing the Essex or Suffolk coast Duncan would in theory know and be able to bring his main force down to Hollesley Bay, and with a threat to Kent, to the Downs anchorage between Deal and the Goodwin Sands. The signal posts were spaced about six miles apart on average.[29] At each one man needed to be on constant watch with a telescope. Coloured lights were tried for night signalling, but caused so much confusion their use was suspended. Each post was manned by a naval lieutenant, a midshipman and two seamen. They were provided with a small wooden shelter complete with fireplace and stock of coal.

Harwich became a naval base for the first time in support of the men of war defending the vulnerable northern part of the Thames Estuary. That year about a dozen small warships were to be found there at any one time – fitting out or repairing at the dockyard, taking on food, water and ballast, picking up or dropping off men, or sheltering from storms. Crews were allowed shore leave. The officers from the different ships met up in the local inns for dinners, drinks and cards. During one such party (in 1799) Captain Renton of the *Martin* sloop, who had served on Admiral Duncan's flagship at Camperdown, suddenly stood up, went outside, and shot himself dead – for reasons unknown.[30]

Months of being anchored within sight of home shores was bad for the morale of the inshore navy – not least because much of it had been pressed from the merchantmen passing to and from London. The *Braakel* in particular seems to have been an unhappy ship. In March 1799 her captain, Lt Walker, ordered 36 lashes for a seaman who had tried to desert, and 24 for two more for what he described as "violence". While she was anchored at Harwich a few days later five men took her cutter and fled ashore. They included two Marines, normally the captain's policemen. They were captured at Colchester by the Middlesex Militia and taken back to the ship in irons. When she visited the Nore in May they were court-martialled: Thomas Creemer was hanged, the two marines were given 500 lashes each, and the other two seamen 100.[31] On the Blackwater Lt Leaver, commander of the *Acute*, cannot have been much more popular. Eventually he was charged for embezzling ship's funds and selling off his crew's food to civilians: he was cleared of the first charge and reprimanded for the second. He had already been punished, because while shooting wildfowl on Tillingham Marshes he was badly injured when his gun exploded in his face.[32]

In May 1798 Pitt issued an Order in Council for enrolling the Sea Fencibles – fishermen and other coast-dwellers who were to enlist and train on the same part-time and local basis as the land Volunteers and go into action against invaders. Each unit was to provide its own boats, and was supplied with muskets, pikes and later cannon. The pay for each "drill" was one shilling – 1s 2½d for the sergeants (later renamed petty officers). Attendance was voluntary, and varied with the fishing seasons. The volunteers were "protected" from the naval press gangs, and so 1200 men were soon signed up along the Essex coast alone, more than any other county except Devon.

The coast was split into districts with a Royal Navy captain in charge of each: Lord Falkland at Lynn commanding from there to Cromer, William

Bentinck at Yarmouth in charge from there to Cromer, Edward Killiwick at Southwold for Suffolk, Thomas Miles at Maldon and later Colchester for Essex. In 1799 the Suffolk and Essex districts were sub-divided. Eliab Harvey, based at Maldon, took over between the Blackwater and Thames, and George Harrison, at Harwich, from there to Clacton. William Edge was given Stour to Orford and Edward Williams Lowestoft-Yarmouth. In 1800 Edward O'Brien succeeded Harvey, but had to retire sick. Contrary to ones first thought, most of these officers were not superannuated, but had recently commanded seagoing warships and in some cases later returned to them. Harvey, a famously irascible former and future MP from Chigwell, Essex, was to command a ship at Trafalgar and reach admiral's rank. The Schomberg brothers, who successively led the North East Essex Sea Fencibles in 1801, were two of the most intellectual officers in the Navy.[33]

The history of innumerable countries and wars suggests that the value of Pitt's various part-time volunteers, whether under army or naval command, might have been dubious. It was – and is – very easy to boast about courage and prowess which are never put to the test. Many professional officers who had to deal with them found them pretty unreliable. Pitt, Dundas, Young, Money and even Nelson claimed to believe in them, but in the case of the landward units much of this was due to their wanting a paramilitary police to intimidate revolutionaries. Since any invasion must have involved full-time and battle-experienced troops pushing rapidly inland many such defenders would have been overrun or by-passed. On the other hand they obviously knew their areas far better than an invader.

In May 1798 revolt broke out in Ireland and the French belatedly sent a few thousand troops round by sea to support it. Arthur Young wrote of

"... an attempt at separation: a combined and bloody effort, of French and Irish Jacobins, which may harass the entire empire, and make this unhappy country a theatre of war".[34]

Pamela de Genlis and her husband Lord Edward Fitzgerald had recently travelled out to the Continent from Yarmouth on the *Prince of Wales* packet. Returning to Dublin to lead the insurrection, he was fatally wounded by the troops who came to arrest him. A large majority of the men in the east coast regular and militia regiments volunteered to go and help put down the rebels. At Little Holland Camp every regiment and company spontaneously cheered in approval as soon as it was suggested. In the event the uprising was soon totally and bloodily crushed without their help. Meanwhile Bonaparte had invaded Egypt, but lost his support fleet to Nelson.

News of Burnham Thorpe's famous son's Nile victory (on the night of 1st-2nd August 1798) reached the country in October. Again there were spectacular rejoicings. On 1st November a grand celebration ball was staged at Ipswich, with the admiral's elderly father and his wife Fanny (neither of whom I can imagine dancing) putting in an appearance, since they now lived nearby at Roundwood Park. On the 29th a festive thanksgiving was ordered by Pitt for all three of the major naval victories of the last two years. At Norwich the enthusiasm was electric. The Spanish sword was paraded through the streets, the Volunteers marched, and an ox was roasted, and beer poured, for the crowd.[35]

Oddly, the idea that British command of the seas made enemy invasion unlikely appealed not only to admirers of the government but also to Whigs and radicals who claimed that Pitt was using fear of it to justify his conscription, taxes and infringements of civil liberty. Montagu Burgoyne of Mark's Hall, near Harlow in Essex, was both Colonel of the Loyal Essex Volunteers and a leading Whig-radical. When his wife presented the colours she and her daughter had embroidered to new Loyal Essex companies from his area, he dismissed enemy invasion preparations as "feeble" and domestic unrest as only a marginal concern.[36] Early in 1799, perhaps in the same spirit, a citizen of Norwich wrote to the *Monthly Magazine* in praise of what he believed to be its warlike spirit, and to mock the claim that it had been disloyal:

> "Norwich a disloyal city! Sir, every other man you meet is decked in regimentals".

He too alluded to the invasion threat as if it had been seen off.

Nevertheless Pitt intended neither to make peace nor reinstate the civil liberties he had taken away since 1792. He did not share the facile complacency that the war was won and that the masses could be trusted. Before 1798 was out he introduced his Income Tax. Those earning more than £65 a year were to pay a 1% rate, those on £200 up to 10%. This lower rate fell on the small shopkeeper, craftsman, and non-commissioned army or naval officer (i.e. the lower middle class), the higher on the wealthy. The labouring classes, servants, and ordinary soldiers and sailors were below the threshold. The tax has a distinctly modern ring, with its five "schedules" (on incomes from land sales, rents, business profits and professional fees, investments, and salaries), numerous regional and local offices (set up in every town of any size) and penalties for evasion. The Foxite Whigs condemned it as a revival of Charles I's hated "ship money", a "vile impost", and an "odious intrusion". What seems to have most outraged them was that the local "commissioners" (i.e. inspectors) would be their neighbours, and sometimes ones of lower social rank. But loyalists grudgingly accepted the tax as the temporary war necessity Pitt said it was.

In spite of their continuing distaste for the government, the New Whigs had by now given up the idea that the French were to be admired and that the war against them could be unilaterally called off from our side. Some, such as the playwright-MP Sheridan, coped with this impasse by backing the Government on condition that it avoided further restrictions of freedom and renounced the idea of "regime change" in Paris and The Hague. Fox and Coke, on the other hand, refused to give Pitt any credit but gave up active opposition and virtually retired to their estates – Fox to his books and garden, Coke to his farming. Many radical intellectuals of a few years before had grown even more disillusioned. Few had admired France more than the Norwich Baptist minister Joseph Kinghorn, but he now brought himself sadly to write:

> "All those notions of liberty which the French Revolution very generally raised a few years ago are at an end ... they (the French) are the tyrants not the deliverers of men".[37]

Like many Christian intellectuals he hated the war but was disturbed by the continuing, indeed recently reasserted, secularism and atheism in

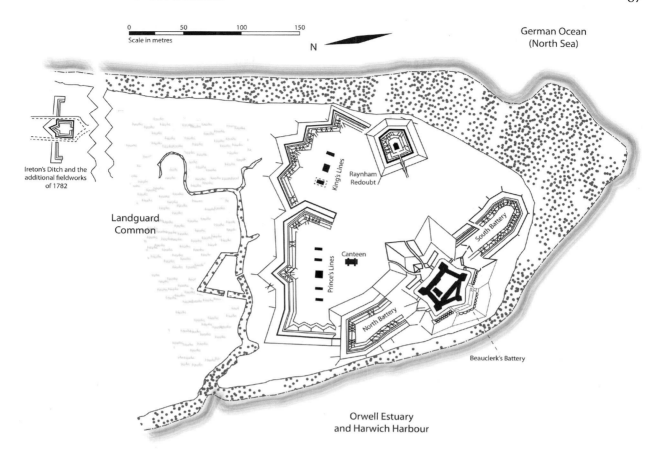

Defences of Landguard fort at the end of the 18th century, in a map based on that of J.H.Leslie in his history of the fort, with additions after Peter Kent in *Fortifications of East Anglia*.

France – the closure of churches, the banishment of priests (albeit Catholic ones), and the official promotion of humanism in place of religion. He was especially shocked by what he called "strumpets drawn in procession as Goddesses" (that is, under-dressed women symbolising "liberty" or "reason" in republican parades). The exiled Tom Paine had recently fed such disgust by coming out with the proto-Marxist claim that religion itself (and not just establishment religion) was a lie concocted to brainwash the masses.[38] Other radicals had begun to feel the emotional pull of naval glory and resistance to the foreign bully.

So though the Army of England, now led by General Kilmaine, remained just across the North Sea, by 1799 there were few who either expected or wanted their arrival. British war believers greatly cheered up. Pitt's Foreign Secretary and cousin Lord Grenville was negotiating a Second Coalition against France, including Austria, Naples and Turkey as well as Britain and Russia. Once again, there was talk of the Duke of York's army and the Navy returning to the offensive against the Batavian Republic.

Turn of the Century Travail   9

Before taking action abroad the Government sorted out some longstanding concerns at home. In mid-July 1799 there came from Westminster to the Lord Lieutenants and magistrates two legal declarations, in the same packages, which began…

> "Whereas a traitorous Conspiracy has long been carried on, in conjunction with the Persons from Time to Time exercising the Powers of Government in France … Whereas great Numbers of Journeymen Manufacturers and Workmen, in Various Parts of the Kingdom, have by unlawful Meetings and Combinations endeavoured to obtain Advance of their Wages …"[1]

Pitt had obtained from Parliament one Act "for the effectual Suppression of Societies established for Seditious and Treasonable Purposes", and another "to prevent the illegal combination of Workmen". Among other organisations, these "Combination Acts" banned the corresponding societies and other republican groups, and what were later called trades unions. Officiating in societies with secret memberships, pledging on oath to take part in revolutionary plots, holding large political meetings not licensed by magistrates, and strike meetings, agreements and funds, were among the activities formally made illegal. Seven years transportation, together with fines and confiscation of personal possessions, was to be the penalty. There was opposition in Parliament by Foxite Whigs and the odd tolerant Tory, who lodged protest petitions sent them from all over the country. But the Government and its loyalists hoped that the old danger of a British Revolution had at last been buried. And so the final blow was dealt to the kinds of radical agitator who had once so stirred up the poor of Norwich and parts of Essex and Suffolk.

Meanwhile Great Britain, Russia and the exiled Dutch Orange family agreed to mount an invasion of north Holland, near the Texel, seize what had been left of the enemy fleet there since Camperdown, rally the Orangists, and march south to topple the Batavian Republic. The first division of British troops, under General Abercrombie, left Yarmouth under escort by Vice-Admiral Mitchell's squadron on 12th August, in a great convoy of 200 ships. For a whole fortnight they struggled to tack round easterly gales until, no doubt horribly seasick, they reached their destination. At that juncture the second division left from Kent, with the expedition's overall commander the Duke of York. Arthur Young joined Sir Henry and Lady Jane Dundas to see him off. He felt awestruck as the Duke's launch was saluted by guns fired from 200 men of war and transport ships.[2] They included the Essex and Yarmouth revenue cutters, which were to serve as despatch and coastal patrol boats. Things began to go well. Not only was Den Helder taken, but the Texel Batavian squadron retreated into a nearby side channel and surrendered without another sea battle. In September 7,000 troops from the Russian contingent put into Yarmouth Roads after a long and stormy voyage across the Baltic and North Seas. They did not land, but set off for Holland after two days.

It says something about the military inability of Pitt and Dundas that they waited till now, when their expedition was going ashore, to put a bill through Parliament whereby the men in the home-service militia regiments could (for higher pay) transfer to the regular army and fight overseas. 25,000 militiamen volunteered to do so and made it possible to form second and even third battalions for several of the existing "line" regiments. Of course none of these reached Holland before the French intervened there.

In spite of its promising start the Allied invasion had not reached as far south as Amsterdam when it was decisively counter-attacked by the French army of General Brune at Bergen, ironically the village next to Camperdown. It hung on for another two months, but suffered further checks and by November was on the brink of capture – notwithstanding British support from the sea. By October a steady stream of wounded and sick Allied troops were coming back into Yarmouth, Harwich and even the River Colne. Their uniforms were tattered and filthy, their bandages bloody, their boots often missing. A dead Guards colonel was laid out in Harwich's *Three Cups* inn. On 1st November the Duke of York called it a day and signed an armistice with Brune under which all the Allied troops, minus those already captured, left in peace. In a typical gesture, which even then jarred with the hardships of his men, he presented his personal horses to the Frenchman – presumably as his sword was not demanded. He stepped ashore on Yarmouth's long wooden jetty from the *Juno* frigate a few days later. As in 1793, he had "marched ten thousand men to the top of a hill" (actually a ridge of sand dunes) "and marched them down again", but remained Commander in Chief of the British Army.

Over the next three weeks some 25,000 Allied troops of three nationalities also landed at Yarmouth – certainly the largest military movement in its history. After burial services were conducted at St Nicholas's, most marched on to Norwich, Swaffham, Ipswich, or Colchester, barracking at one or the other while the government figured out what to do with them. The Russians were shipped round to the Channel Islands, in need of a temporary garrison at the time.

Throughout the war British warships sailed from Yarmouth and Harwich to northern Continental ports carrying gold and silver bullion. Some of this was "subsidies" (financial aid) for our allies, some of it payments for our imports of corn and naval supplies. Coincidentally one of these ships sank almost within sight of the Texel expedition. On 6th October 1799 the *Lutine*, a frigate captured from the French, and commanded by Captain Skynner, left Yarmouth with £300,000 in gold for the Hamburg merchants. She had another frigate, Captain Porlock's *Arrow*, in company.[3] It is said that a fishing smack saw her pass close by, lights blazing and officers drinking in her cabins. A north-north-westerly gale sprang up, so the two frigates went through the Vlie Passage, between the Dutch coast and the Frisian Islands. Apparently compensating for the wind by tacking to "larboard" (port), at midnight on the 9th the *Lutine* grounded on the Vlieland shoals. While the *Arrow* and some local Dutch boats were looking for her she broke up and sank with her whole cargo and all hands but two, one of whom later died of exposure. Some 200 bodies were washed ashore: Skynner's and two others were buried in Vlieland Churchyard, the rest in a mass grave on Terschelling. One of the dead was a Lieutenant Aufrere, from Hoveton Hall, about 12 miles north-west of Yarmouth. Two months later the Batavian government rather remarkably allowed Porlock to join in their attempt to salvage the gold, but most of it remained forever hidden in the Frisian mud. There were at least 15 separate ventures to locate it over the next two centuries, which between them did recover perhaps one third. Ship and cargo had been insured by Lloyd's of London, and long after the war her bell was recovered and sent to their headquarters, where it is still famously rung for important announcements. Timber from the wreck was also used to make the company chairman's chair. Only a few historians now remember the Texel campaign, but the lost treasure of the *Lutine* lives on in legend.

The same week the Duke of York surrendered at Alkmaar General Napoleon Bonaparte returned to Paris after nearly a year and half in the eastern Mediterranean. Although his own great expedition there had on balance failed, his star was in the ascendant. He had conquered Italy and Egypt, and while he was taking the latter the Directory had lost the former. While France seethed with royalist and Jacobin plots, was shaken annually by a coup, and governed by an ever-shifting and faceless committee, he was known as the man of vision and decision. The emergence of such a new Julius Caesar or Cromwell had been uncannily prophesied by Burke nine years before. Most Frenchmen were, with some propagandist encouragement, ready to square their political circle with a leader who was both defender of the Revolution and military autocrat. And anyway Bonaparte had friends on the inside, short-sightedly scheming to use him for their own ends. In the same issues of the *Ipswich Journal* and *Norfolk Chronicle* as they read about the withdrawal of the last British regiments to Yarmouth, literate East Anglians discovered that Bonaparte had led his troops against the French Directory, Council of Five Hundred, and Council of Ancients, and proclaimed himself "First Consul" of the Republic.

As usual the government was "behind the curve". Only a few weeks earlier its propaganda organ, the *Anti-Jacobin*, had published a review (of a Whiggish book advocating peace talks) which declared:

> "the cloven foot of Jacobinism will, occasionally, peep forth from under a covering that fits so awkwardly upon its reluctant wearers".[4]

It was not entirely an absurd claim, since Bonaparte and his allies in Paris had at one time been Jacobin supporters, and had violently purged the city's royalists and anti-war moderates at least twice since. But Bonaparte wanted an authoritarian state of progressive but apolitical meritocrats, not plebeian mobs and utopian ideology. Some clever folk, both foreign and British, began to recognise this and approve, as I will explain later.

But Pitt, Dundas and Windham were most certainly not among them, and in March 1800 gathered their forces for another overseas operation. This was announced in the press, who called it the "Secret Expedition" – not the contradiction in terms it sounds, because it was the army's objective, not its existence, which was undisclosed. Later the term "Northern Expedition" was used, as if to suggest that the force would land in north-west Germany and attack the French across the Rhine. Transport ships went to Yarmouth, Sir John Moore's infantry brigade to Chelmsford, and the Earl of Chatham's to Colchester. (Chatham was Pitt's elder brother). In April the expedition left, not for Germany, but the Mediterranean, where it eventually reversed Bonaparte's 1798 victories by taking Malta and Egypt. Meanwhile the Duke of York was proving to be a much better army organiser than he had been a field commander. In addition to forming a rifle regiment and curbing the promotion of young incompetents, he concerned himself with the soldiers' health. In May he got Edward Jenner, the inventor of vaccination, to go to Colchester and inoculate every man in 85th Foot against smallpox, together with the wives and children some had with them. Apparently not one caught the disease subsequently.[5]

General Sir John Moore. Before achieving fame and an heroic death in Spain he wrote a comprehensive defence plan for East Anglia which focused mainly on a great anti-invasion battle in north-east Essex.

However by now Pitt was again less preoccupied by the French war than the British economy. For three years (1796-98), harvests had been tolerably good, the cost of living had been kept in check, and the Speenhamland and other poor relief systems had coped. For the government, that was a godsend during all the troubles of the period. But the 1799 crop was, if not disastrous, very disappointing, and over the succeeding year the wheat price climbed uninterruptedly and steadily from 56 shilling a quarter to 141 shillings, to take the Essex average figures. When the 1800 harvest was gathered in August, so that the barns partly refilled, it dropped to 90/- (£4.10s), still higher than at any time since 1796, but then leapt back up to 149/5 (£7.9s 5d). (The Norfolk figure was slightly lower, those for Suffolk and Cambridgeshire even higher). Whereas the 1795 shortfall over the previous year's yield had been about 25%, this decline was around 40%.

According to Arthur Young (and there is no reason to doubt him), the disaster had been caused by the scanty 1799 crop being almost all used by the time the 1800 was cut, a scorching early summer, a full week's torrential rain which then turned the fields into "a hotbed", and the withdrawal of 10% of the resulting low yield for future sowing.[6] Nevertheless, as in 1795, the price rise had begun long before the crop deficiency had shown up, and was out of proportion to the shortage. No doubt there was some passing on to the consumer of the Income Tax, so the war was not blameless.

The wealthy, and those lucky farm labourers who had gardens where they could raise poultry, vegetables, fruit and that favourite of the government, potatoes, were not too affected. It was the landless labourer and the poorer town dweller who bore the brunt. As for the manufacturing middle class, and those farmers who grew crops other than corn, once again bread-price inflation ate into the spending money of their customers and harmed their businesses.

In November 1799 the government had for the first time prosecuted a London corn dealer for "engrossing and forestalling", that is, buying up large stocks, withholding them from the market so as to force up the price, and then selling. The judge, citing Pitt's own free market hero the recently-deceased Adam Smith, influenced the jury to convict him, and a mob had then gone and set fire to his house. Few East Anglians of any social class sympathised with him. The poor shared the hungry outrage of the mob, of course. But the middle class perused the escalating wheat prices in the press and related them to their own shrinking profits. And even some of the great landowners and richer tenant farmers were angry that the middleman was getting away with so much, and turning the labourers against their employers. Feeling against the dealers was so great in the region that, in addition to appeals at town council meetings and letters to the press, a society was founded at Ipswich to fund more court cases against them.[7] Arthur Young disagreed, however. Not only did he believe in the free market, but insisted that inciting hatred of the dealers would "disseminate the firebrand of sedition".[8]

A disorderly summer followed.

On the marshy Dengie peninsula, between the Rivers Blackwater and Crouch and the sea, few of the farm labourers had the back-garden smallholdings referred to above. Moreover its cornfields had been giving way to sheep pastures. On their mutton and wool the local landowners had made windfall profits, using them to build or furnish new houses. One of these was the Rev. Bate Dudley, a controversial mixture of corrupt career clergyman, local JP, amateur musician, and "agricultural improver". Recently the Norfolk-born farm labourer John Little, alias Wakeling, had come to the area, and been elected "Captain" of what was in effect the first trade union of Essex farm workers. That June, with the harvest and sheep-shearing season imminent, he toured the area enlisting participants in a strike aimed at raising wages and/or reducing the unprecedented food prices. By all accounts he was very successful. But somewhere there was a spy or informer (the authorities heavily depended on them, as John Thelwall had complained). When Little gathered one hundred supporters at Southminster (just north of Burnham-on-Crouch) Bate Dudley appeared with a company of Loyal Essex Volunteers. The ringleaders were marched to Chelmsford, but managed to escape. Dudley reported to Lord Lieutenant Braybrooke (of Audley End) and Home Secretary Lord Portland, and the resulting manhunt soon had the escapers back in custody.[9]

The East Anglian, and national, press called it an "intended insurrection" and "dangerous conspiracy". It was, of course, a violation of the recent second Combination Act. Men of property across Essex shared the cost of the manhunt and prosecution at Chelmsford Assizes. This little clash between an impoverished (and voteless) majority and a wealthy and influential minority cannot but remind us how utterly undemocratic and class-divided the society of Pitt, Young and Windham was. Whatever may be (justly) said against Napoleon, his France was one where most peasants owned their own farms, and clergymen, judges and landowners were not the same people. Nonetheless the British government was capable of tactical moderation. Had they seen the Dengie "rebels" as political they could, and would, have had them transported to New South Wales, but instead Little, Crisp, Perry and the three other defendants each got off with one year in prison and a pledge of good behaviour for another seven. Soon afterwards Dudley's enemies exalted when an ecclesiastical court ejected him from his living for unlawfully buying it four years earlier. Most of the major office-holders and landowners of Essex wrote to the government reminding it of its debt to him and asking that he be compensated. The signatories included Braybrooke, Lord Petre of Ingatestone, and First Lord of the Admiralty Jervis, Earl St Vincent (then living at Brentwood, and himself a hard disciplinarian).[10]

That September, after the dreadful harvest, more trouble erupted. The housewives were up in arms. On 1st September they broke into the new Norwich flour mills and forced the millers to sell their product at half the market price until magistrates arrived and scared them off. On the 15th they argued with the stallholders at Harwich's Saturday market, not only about their bread prices but also those for meat, butter, eggs, potatoes and onions. Here too they began to grab the food and pay reduced prices. Then Mayor Rayner Cox (brother of the Harwich Naval Officer) showed up and parleyed with them. He offered a compromise ruling. But the visiting vendors from across the water in Holbrook and Walton (Suffolk) rejected this, reloaded their wares onto their boats, and left. Some young men chased them, took their food, and brought it back for sale in the town. Meanwhile a similar scene was being played out at Ipswich, as crowds gathered at the mill and grain store. Before they could get inside the Yeomanry mounted up and charged them into the River Orwell and nearby tar pits, though there were no casualties.[11]

John Jervis, Earl of St Vincent, in a portrait by Lemuel Abbott which can be seen at the National Portrait Gallery.

Interestingly most of the protesters had paid what they considered to be fair prices (i.e. 1799 ones) for the food and hadn't tried to steal it, which they could well have done. Even the Tory-inclined press reported this, suggesting that the authorities, while deploring riot, sympathised with the customers rather than the middlemen.

The part of north-west Essex most troubled five years earlier was again the scene of disorder. Persons unknown started a large fire near Halstead. Shops and mills in and around Saffron Walden were looted. The magistrates were shown an anonymous threatening letter which declared:

"Landowners and Yeomanry, You need not sharpen your Swords nor Pride yourselves with the Pleasure you will Receive by Killing a Starved multitude…we had rather be hanged then Starved in the midst of Plenty".[12]

"Midst of plenty" was not wrong, because as so often in economics, the situation was paradoxical. The volume of British trade, having fallen to 70% of its pre-war level by 1797, had almost recovered by 1800, and exceeded it in 1801. The increased grain imports were of course good for shipowners. Among other seaport projects the Chelmer Navigation (river canalisation), Lynn's first dry dock, and London's West India Dock was all under construction. Although Yarmouth's dried herring exports to Italy had ended because of Bonaparte's recent conquests, a 1798 parliamentary inquiry found that east coast catches were abundant, whether herring at Yarmouth and Lowestoft, cod at Harwich, or oysters on the Crouch, Colne and Blackwater.[13] Unlike in the 20th century world wars there were no minefields or enemy naval and air attacks to restrict them, and few privateers bothered to seize fish because it rotted by the time they got back.

Most importantly the high food prices had transferred wealth from consumers to producers, who sold less than hitherto, but at far higher prices. Much of their additional profit was invested in enclosures – that is, incorporating open land, whether traditional scattered arable strip fields or grassy heaths, into larger unified mixed farms surrounded by hedges and ditches. This process involved extra short-term legal and labour costs, but was accelerating because the landowners now had both additional funds and the promise of higher profits. In East Anglia it was mainly a matter of ploughing the chalky downlands of south-east Cambridgeshire, fens and marshes near Lynn and on the Essex coast, and sandy heaths of north-east Essex and south-east Suffolk. Enclosure had been going on in the region for 250 years, but proceeded during the French Revolutionary War at about double its pre-war rate, and this almost redoubled in the Napoleonic phase of the war. Whether the enclosures were of strip field, common pasture, or mere waste, they added not only to the income of landowners but also to national food production. On both grounds the Government, advised by Arthur Young and his boss Sinclair, was much in favour of them. However they were a protracted and piecemeal process and certainly did not boost grain supplies overnight.[14]

The shortages caused the government, along with shippers and dealers who saw the profit opportunity, to buy in twice as much foreign corn as they had five years before. It reached 10% of annual consumption – indeed probably higher, as there had been less importing in the earlier part of the year. At least 1,500 shiploads were involved. Many were unloaded on the east coast, at Lynn, Ipswich, Harwich, Mistley, and above all Yarmouth, apart, of course, from London. Such Yarmouth shipping firms as Hurry's, Preston's, Palmer's, Colby's and Palgrave's transported a good proportion. Some of the grain came from America, but the bulk from the countries round the Baltic.

However, Britain's own naval policy cut across this process. The Baltic countries were happy to sell Britain their corn (and also naval supplies), and to import other goods from Britain in return, but they also wanted to trade with France and her allies Holland and Spain. This we could not tolerate: otherwise the enemy would be as well fed, and as able to equip their navy, as ourselves. From the outset our men of war had therefore intercepted every suspect merchant vessel they came across in the North Sea (and elsewhere). If she was enemy they would seize her – if neutral they would do so if her cargo included contraband – that is, military supplies for the enemy. Britain classed as contraband not only weaponry, but timber for building warships, iron for guns, cloth for sails and army uniforms and innumerable other items. The confiscated ships and goods of neutrals, as well as of the enemy, were sold off in her ports, the government and captors taking their cuts. In other words, this was not just the legalised semi-private piracy of corsairs, but a strategy of systematic blockade, though, unlike in later wars, the distinction was still drawn between prohibited military and permitted civilian supplies.

Initially we did not have enough men of war in the North Sea to make many captures. Now our navy there was far larger, and encountered more Continental shipping as it went frequently back and forth to blockade the Texel and escort Baltic convoys. Occasionally the contraband fell into British laps. In 1799 a Hamburg ship, the *Peters*, came into Harwich after her anchors had been torn away in a storm. Appelbie, Master of the *Blazer* gun-boat, had been tipped off that she had been en route for France. On board he found incriminating papers and weapons and linen worth £45,000.[15]

No one objected to the seizure of "belligerent" merchantmen: the problem was the neutrals. All of those countries accepted that if their ships *were* taking contraband through a blockade towards a belligerent's port they would acquiesce in their capture and "condemnation" (as the confiscation of vessel and cargo was known). But none thought it legitimate for the British to interfere with those ships (arguably the majority) which were continuing their peacetime trade in civilian goods.

One of the most provocative Yarmouth squadron neutral seizures occurred in the New Year of 1799. When one of its frigates, the *Apollo*, was badly damaged by grounding near the Texel, her captain, Halkett, hailed a passing Prussian merchantman, the *Jonge Jacobus Baumann*, and persuaded her to take his men back to Yarmouth. On arrival the rescue ship and her cargo were confiscated as contraband and the crew were pressed. Wisely Marriott's Admiralty court ordered their release.[16]*

Unfortunately for us, though the controversy also concerned the Mediterranean and Atlantic, it came to a head in the Baltic. The governments there were either neutrals (Denmark, Sweden, Prussia) or, in the case of Russia, a disillusioned ally hoping to mend fences with Bonaparte. After several Scandinavian ships had been seized by the British, Tsar Pavel (Emperor Paul) suggested that the three other Baltic monarchs join him in an "Armed Neutrality". This was to be a defensive pact under which their navies would jointly escort their merchantmen against interception by either side, and then exclude from their waters both the merchant and naval vessels of whoever persisted with their boardings and seizures.

Paul's plan threatened either to stop Britain from fully blockading France and her allies (if Britain yielded to it), or cutting Britain off from her vital Baltic grain and naval supplies (if she defied it). By a grim coincidence the very August week he proposed it the English grain supply failed and therefore a 100-ship merchant convoy gathered off Yarmouth to shore it up from the Baltic. Just ahead of the convoy had sailed the Yarmouth naval fleet, under Admiral Dickson since Duncan's recent retirement. Its role was to force Denmark to let the convoy through the Sound (the narrow channel into the Baltic), should Lord Whitworth, Pitt's negotiator, be unable to persuade her to cooperate with us rather than the Tsar. On the 17th Dickson reached the Sound and came within sight of Copenhagen. Shots were fired by both sides, then the Yarmouth fleet was paralysed by a storm which nearly sank the *Ardent* and *Glatton* of Duncan-era fame. But, after another week's standoff, the Danes backed down and allowed Britain's merchant ships through. Dickson's convoy was able to load up with corn and other goods and get back to Yarmouth and then on to London and elsewhere.

But then the situation deteriorated. On hearing about the intimidation of the Danes Paul banned trade with Britain and seized all British property in Russia, including ships and their crews. By December Sweden and Prussia had signed up with him in his Armed Neutrality. Prussia occupied Cuxhaven, the port at the entrance to the River Elbe which not only gave us access to our crown domain in Hanover but was the packet station linking Britain (via Yarmouth) to Central Europe. In the New Year of 1801 Denmark started to pull away from her understanding with Britain and towards the other three Baltic countries. In March she excluded British ships from her ports, occupied Hamburg and Lubeck, and closed the Elbe. The Prussians occupied Bremen and Hanover, and, with Sweden, banned British ships from leaving and entering their ports. All of northern Europe was now closed to British trade. On top of this Napoleon made peace with Russia, declared himself a

---

* As well as being a judge, Marriott was Tory MP for Sudbury. His country house was the nearby Twinstead Hall.

champion of the "rights of neutrals", and supported Tsar Paul's quirky claim to be the rightful ruler of Malta – the key halfway house in the Mediterranean which Britain had seized from the French the previous year.

As a result corn imports into England shrank and bread remained scarce. Having slightly dipped, the average wheat price rose even higher than it had the previous summer. At King's Lynn rioters threw stones and mud through the windows of inns at wealthy diners. The Government was again very nervous, and exhorted patriots to help the war effort by giving up flour. The *Norwich Mercury* duly reported that the officers of the West Norfolk Militia had banned bread and pastry from their mess and substituted rice and potatoes.

Luckily Norfolk's greatest son, and loyal Britain's most beloved saviour, was now back home. On the rough afternoon of 6th November 1800 Admiral Horatio Nelson stepped off the *King George* packet from Cuxhaven and into a boat which landed him at Yarmouth. He had one arm and one eye less than when he had last visited, but two titles, a British baronetcy and, from the exiled King of Naples, the Dukedom of Bronte in Sicily. With him were Sir William Hamilton, elderly former British ambassador to that ruler, and his young, famously glamorous and low-born wife Lady Emma. The trio had travelled from the Mediterranean via Vienna. That Emma had become Nelson's mistress was already public knowledge: she was already six months pregnant. Their arrival was expected. A crowd pulled Nelson's carriage to the Church Plain, where Yarmouth's fish-merchant mayor, Samuel Barker, Admiral Dickson, and a line of aldermen and naval officers welcomed him. He was sworn in as a freeman of the borough and taken to dinner. Everyone processed into St Nicholas's church to thank God for his victories and safe return. He stayed the night at the nearby Wrestlers' Hotel, which was bedecked with flags and ceremonially guarded by Captain Lacon's local Volunteers. Bands played, shore and ship guns boomed in salute, and bonfires and fireworks lit the evening sky. Next day Nelson set off on the London road, escorted by Lacon's men. He stopped to visit Roundwood, but his wife and father had no wish to see the adulterer and were away. In nearby Ipswich he ate at Bamford's Hotel, and was greeted by the town worthies, army officers, and more crowds. On the 9th he was off again along the Colchester-Chelmsford-London road, between lines of flag-waving spectators.[17]

In early March 1801 he was back in the Roads as second-in-command of a fleet of 53 men of war, sent round from the Channel, and ranging from first-rate ships of the line to little gun brigs and "bomb vessels". His superior officer was the rather dilatory Admiral Sir Hyde Parker. Their mission was to attack Denmark, sink its navy, and force it out of the Armed Neutrality and the ports it had taken – though Nelson, with characteristic boldness, but perhaps also lack of political sense, hoped that instead it might sail straight through to Russia and take on Tsar Paul. The expedition lingered for a fortnight at Yarmouth, allegedly because Hyde Parker was distracted by his young bride, though more likely owing to adverse winds. On 2nd April, famously saying that he could not read Parker's cautious signal with his blind eye, Nelson closed in on the Danish battle fleet off Copenhagen, and bombarded it till its flagship blew up and the rest surrendered. A week later Denmark agreed to cease fire. Nelson did not land at Yarmouth again, but the Roads filled with a heart-warming array of returning British and captured Danish ships.

It is rarely the case in history that a triumph is all due to one man, and so it was on this occasion. By an extraordinary coincidence, while Nelson was en route to Copenhagen Paul was assassinated in a palace coup, and replaced by his more amenable son Alexander. An agreement was drafted with him whereby Britain agreed to be more selective in what she classed as contraband, promptly allow "innocent" ships on their way, and ban her privateers from boarding neutrals – but her basic blockade continued. Within a few more months Denmark, Sweden and Prussia had also accepted this, and released their grip on the British merchant ships and German grain-exporting ports they had been holding. Our Baltic trade resumed in full volume.

This portrait by Matthew Keymer was painted in 1801 whilst Nelson was back in Yarmouth, awaiting departure of the fleet for Copenhagen. The elaborate nature of the frame perhaps illustrates the glorification of his image after his death at the battle of Trafalgar.

Victories are also seldom unalloyed. It was during the Copenhagen expedition that East Anglian waters were the scene of a worse disaster even than that of the *Lutine*. On the afternoon of 16th March 1801 the old 74-gun *Invincible* was sailing north from Yarmouth Roads with guns and ammunition for Hyde Parker, when she ran aground on the Hammond Knoll, some 20 miles off Winterton on the curve of north-east Norfolk coast. Her pilot, from Harwich, had tried to take her on a supposed shortcut through an obscure channel. She was stuck there overnight, sliding off into deeper water at one point but then floating back on because she had torn off her rudder and jettisoned two of her masts. The fishing smack *Nancy* and her two boats, a passing collier, and a boat from Winterton rescued Admiral Totty and a number of others. Finally the wreck sank. At the last moment more of her crew crowded onto a launch and cleared her poop deck, using oars to push away other men trying to board. The captain, Rennie, was himself seen trying to swim to the launch, but was so exhausted that he lifted his hands up as if in prayer, put them over his face, and went under. For two days and nights five men clung onto the foremast, which still poked above water, till seen and saved by a Sunderland brig. The survivors were landed at Yarmouth. In all over 400 had died – more than at Camperdown and Copenhagen combined. They included the Harwich pilot. 119 corpses were buried in Happisburgh churchyard, others in a nearby drainage ditch.[18]

The 74-gun 3rd rate HMS *Invincible* of 1765 –1801 and the memorial to 119 of her crew who lie in Happisburgh churchyard.

There was nevertheless an even bigger story in the local newspapers that week. William Pitt, whose resignation had already been offered a few weeks earlier, finally stepped down. During the Irish rising of 1798 Suffolk's celebrated marquess, General Cornwallis, had gone over to Dublin as Lord Lieutenant. Despite ruthlessly putting down the rebels, he had, on Pitt's orders, tried to win over Ireland's Catholics with various concessions, in order to persuade them to accept more direct rule from England. At the end of 1800 Pitt put through the Act of Union, which closed the autonomous Dublin parliament and brought its members over to sit as a minority at Westminster. This was celebrated in England – not least by the Navy at Yarmouth – by the firing of guns and the hoisting of the new Union flag, with the diagonal red cross of St Patrick set between those of St George and St Andrew. Pitt and Cornwallis had already expressed their hope that Irish Catholics would be excused the tithes they paid to the Protestant Church, get state funding for the payment of their clergy, and above all have MPs at Westminster. Their insight was that the danger to contemporary Britain was not old religion but new radical politics. Pitt said that this "Catholic Relief" must go ahead. But the King, who had almost always backed him in the past, even in his most liberal measures, overruled him, arguing that by endorsing it he would be violating his coronation oath. "The most Jacobinical thing I ever head of!" George perversely declared, before relapsing into another bout of madness. Other ministers thought it wrong to allow members of a historically "disloyal" and "superstitious" church any legislative power over "sound" Protestants. Among the East Anglian establishment, apart from Cornwallis, Windham and Young supported Pitt, and Windham resigned with him. On the other hand many Anglican clergy and loyalists were horrified and thought he had gone as mad as the King. Coke, other New Whigs, and the radicals would not lend their support to the outgoing leader and instead vainly demanded that Addington, his successor, reverse all of his repressive laws.

Talking of law, authority was as concerned at this period about old-fashioned crime as illegal political conspiracy. Whether poverty was mainly to blame is questionable, since few offenders seem to have been dispossessed or unemployed. Poorly disciplined and under-officered troops and militiamen, far from the restraints of home, were responsible for much of it. Some were serial deserters: one defendant at Thetford admitted running away from 13 different regiments! Highway robbery was a problem on the vital main roads to Harwich and Yarmouth. Farmhouse burglaries were rife. So were forgery and fraud, encouraged by the widespread substitution of paper "bills" (cheques and notes) for coin. In 1800 a young lady drew a large sum in golden guineas from Gurney's Bank in Norwich. He later found that the signature on her cheque was forged, but by then she was on a ship for Hamburg.[19]

The criminal law was still a bizarre mixture of the chaotic, lenient and barbaric. There was, of course, no police force worth the name, though most places had their "constables" and serious offences usually caused local landowners and merchants to call together armed posses. At any one time the gaols in the assize-court towns – Thetford, Bury and Chelmsford – held an average of about 100 felons, most of them on capital charges. Prisoners (who included debtors and those held for minor misdemeanours) were given 1½ lbs of bread and a quart of weak beer per day, and 1 lb of cheese per week. Some got ¾ lb of meat for Sunday dinner. Courtrooms were busy, and much frequented by curious rich folk and reporters using shorthand. At Chelmsford, in 1800, the famous London barrister Garrow got his defendant acquitted after the judge had read him the death sentence when someone noticed that the supposedly unsigned cheque he had cashed had been signed after all – on the back. In the same court that day an 11 year old boy fainted when he was sentenced to hang for stealing from the post, but was told by the judge that he was likely to get a royal pardon on account of his age. Other trials had macabre outcomes. As late as 1794 one Bury St Edmunds murderer was exhibited in an iron gibbet after his execution. In 1800, at the same town, a young servant girl called Sarah Lloyd was hanged for helping her lover burgle her employer. Radical-Whig magistrate Capel Lofft (of nearby Troston Hall) had campaigned to get her spared, persuading his famous neighbour the Earl of Euston to sign his petition. After her death he climbed onto the scaffold and tried to revive her, then turned to the crowd and delivered a long denunciation of the injustice and cruelty of English law. As a result he was dismissed from the board of magistrates. In 1801 the hanging of another forger, militia sergeant Peter Donahue, went badly wrong when the noose broke an artery in his neck and showered him and those around him with blood: a watching journalist found it "most distressing".[20]

Meanwhile an infamous gang of Essex gypsy robbers were tracked down and hanged one by one. When the last of them, Stephen Lee, was sentenced to death at Chelmsford the judge took satisfaction in telling him that he could expect "no mercy on this side of the grave".[21]

The country again seemed to be under imminent threat for most of 1801. For the past year Bonaparte had been consolidating power in Paris, reconquering Italy and imposing another peace on Austria. But after Copenhagen he again proclaimed his intention to invade England and reassembled the army and flotillas of small warships and troop barges which had more or less disbanded in 1799. He boasted that given three days of easterly wind he could be on English soil. Brune, the victor of the Texel campaign, was put in charge of an army which at least in theory outnumbered Britain's entire home regular force. Rear-Admiral Latouche-Tréville was appointed to command the invasion flotilla, mainly based at Boulogne.

With the Baltic and food situations still partly unresolved, officialdom in the English eastern counties again grew anxious. General Balfour, the new Eastern District commander, surveyed the region's grain stores, bakeries and farm wagons so as to ensure that troops and civilians could be fed and invaders starved. The Earl of Euston, who lived near the village of that name in West Suffolk, helped him by touring the region that April. The authorities did have more precise statistical information at their disposal than in 1798, because the previous month the government had held the first national census. The plan for this had come from Charles Abbott, later Baron Colchester – though his only connection with that town was having been born there. Each Anglican clergyman in the country had had to send in a count of the people and houses in his parish, together with the numbers employed in agriculture and industry. As a matter of fact in 1796 Arthur Young had conducted and published his own census of Suffolk, and in exactly the same way. He had written to every one of the county's 400 rectors and vicars, of whom almost two-thirds replied. His estimate of 210,000 people for the whole county was probably just short of the true figure. After talking to Euston Young fell into an anxious mood, saying that the economic distress was such that if the invaders did appear half the county would join them.[22]

This opinion was widely shared by intelligent opinion – Tory as well as (and sometimes more so than) Whig. In its first (September 1801) issue the *Weekly Dispatch* alleged that…

"The cultivators of land, and the importers of corn have…ascertained that their profits increase with the public calamity … that a defective harvest is to them more lucrative than an abundant one."[23]

It claimed that land was being taken over by "upstarts without honour", who were forcing out the middling-rank yeomen, thereby opening up a gulf between landowners and labourers which threatened the Constitution. Though it did not name him, it may well have had Coke in mind when it deplored "monopolizers of land" who undermined "the monarchical edifice of England".

The Volunteers were called out several times that spring and summer in response to rumours of both enemy landings and food riots. Balfour's plans had allotted up to half of them to non-combat tasks such as guarding food stocks, evacuating civilians, escorting prisoners to Norman Cross and of course suppressing rioters.

At sea, the approach channels into "the River" (Thames) were now guarded by several floating batteries, mostly Dutch men of war captured at Camperdown or the Texel, and remanned by the British. The *Beschermer* (54 guns) was anchored in the King's Channel (today's East Swin, off Frinton), the *Batavier* (54) in the Queen's Channel (off North Kent), the *Vlieter* (44) in the Swin (off the Crouch), the *Alliance* (20) in the Wallet (close to Clacton), and the familiar *Glatton* (54), in Hollesley Bay.[24] *Beschermer* means "defender". The term "floating battery" suggests a ship without sails and incapable of movement, but in fact they were fully rigged and occasionally shifted position or called in at Harwich for repairs or supplies.

Meanwhile Nelson had been appointed to command the Royal Navy in the North Sea and Dover Strait. He did not relish this promotion. Unlike the site of his Nile battle, or Copenhagen, Boulogne was a narrow enclosed harbour which would be hard to raid. The French had gathered no great battle fleet he could engage – and accordingly his own ships, though numerous, were mostly small gun brigs and bomb vessels. And the Admiralty in any case told him (correctly) that probably Bonaparte was bluffing. However, that July he sent every man of war and Sea Fencible unit a letter which declared: "The moment the enemy touch our coast, be it where it may, they are to be attacked by every man afloat and ashore". He also stationed his old Mediterranean comrade, Captain Edward Berry, and the 64-gun *Ruby*, to defend Hollesley Bay, and promised to send him two new gun-brigs.

Between two frustratingly unsuccessful raids on Boulogne Nelson sailed up from Margate Roads on the *Medusa* frigate to muster the Suffolk and Essex Sea Fencibles. His visit to Harwich has been overplayed in Essex folklore. When he arrived off Bawdsey on the morning of 8th August the sea was rough and the Kent pilots he had on board said that they would not risk trying to enter the harbour. Feeling seasick, he went into port on the *King George*, one of three cutters which had accompanied him. He did not land, to the disappointment of "the Volunteers & C drawn up to receive us, and the people ready to draw the carriage". One of his officers, Edward Parker, did go ashore. Next day the four Sea Fencible Captains he had summoned were rowed out to him: Becher from Southwold, Edge from Woodbridge, Isaac Schomberg from Colchester, and Rudsdell from Maldon. He had told them that he "absolutely required" their volunteers to reinforce the crews of the

Captain Edward Berry, in a sketch made of some of Nelson's colleagues at the battle of the Nile.

guardships in the Thames Estuary. However, they were not very reassuring. Edge said that only about one in eight of his men had agreed to go to sea, and then only for three weeks. Schomberg (brother of the former *Glatton* officer Alexander Schomberg, and later a naval historian), said that his Colne and Blackwater men were worried about their fishing (the season was imminent), and would only do two. The local Sea Fencible training sessions had already been cut from four a month to two. Nelson told Emma Hamilton that the local fishermen were scared of naval officers, believing them to be "monsters" – perhaps understandably in view of the hangings and lashings they must have all heard about![25] Schomberg thought it was more that they did not want to work alongside the Revenue cutters who chased them for smuggling and illegal shipwreck-salvaging.

Nelson understood that the Sea Fencibles had civilian livelihoods which they might lose if they served full-time, but believed they were loyal and would "come forth when the whole country prepares for fighting and all other business stands still". He persuaded them to serve successively in two-week shifts – the Colne and Blackwater contingents on the *Alliance* anchored off Clacton and the Harwich contingent on one of their own smacks off the harbour. Their employers agreed to keep their jobs open for their return. Nelson sent Edward Berry to enlist more at Orford, but the men he encountered, obviously in the village pubs, drunkenly refused.

Next day Nelson left for the Nore. With the wind in the east-north-east he could not get down the harbour deep water approach. His pilots were no help, but an Admiralty surveyor named Spence came and offered to show him a navigable route southwards into the King's Channel, close to the Naze. The impatient admiral agreed, and so kept to schedule and got back to his fleet in order to mount another (unsuccessful) Boulogne raid. In honour of this the alternative channel was named after the *Medusa* on subsequent charts.

On the vice-admiral's orders six barges were armed with cannon and based in the Colne-Blackwater estuary, and two more in the Deben and Ore. As for the Sea Fencibles, between 16th August and 30th September 35 from Colchester, 27 from Brightlingsea, 42 from Mersea, 22 from Maldon and one from Bradwell joined the crew of the *Alliance*, together with 21 who volunteered (or were pressed) from merchant ships – mainly Scots and Scandinavians.

As it happened, reluctant Sea Fencibles, frustrated sailors, idle land forces, and anxious civilians had very little more time to wait before dramatic yet also anti-climatic news arrived from London. On 1st October Addington and Bonaparte had agreed to stop the war and start negotiations for a treaty of peace.

Amiens Interlude 10

The two chief negotiators of the peace treaty finally signed at Amiens, in northern France, were Bonaparte's brother Joseph and the Marquess of Cornwallis. Joseph Bonaparte spoke affably, but Napoleon had forbidden him from discussing British proposals for restoring independence to the Low Countries and northern Italy. When news of the treaty reached England at the end of March 1802 it was hailed almost everywhere with relief and glee. In East Anglia, hitherto economically depressed and threatened with invasion, it was celebrated as joyfully as anywhere. The Militiamen were allowed home. The Volunteers and Sea Fencibles were also disbanded, freeing them from the chore of weekend training. Trade with the Continent was re-opened. The enemy privateers, who had suspended their raids when negotiations started six months earlier, would no longer be a threat. Taxes, it was assumed, would be lower, and food cheaper. The Augustinian nuns even went back to Bruges from Hengrave.

One of the few Jeremiahs was William Windham. While Pitt and Fox accepted the treaty, he utterly rejected it. As soon as Addington had agreed to the preliminary ceasefire on 1st October 1801 Windham accused him of signing "the death warrant of this country".[1] Politicians had been realigning themselves. The anti-war New Whigs, including Coke, were in agreement with the government, crediting its claim that Bonaparte was not the menace his "Jacobin" predecessors had been, that he could be trusted, and that freeing England from the perils and costs of war was a solid achievement. They did say "Had you listened to us we could have had peace earlier", but they credited Addington for now "doing the right thing". The day the Amiens Treaty was signed the Irish-born traitor named Colonel Despard was hanged in London along with six co-conspirators. Coke and fellow Norfolk MP Astley sent congratulations to the King, whom the plotters had hoped to assassinate.[2]

The idea very briefly gained currency that, as he himself claimed, Bonaparte deserved credit for ending both the war and the revolution. Not only that: many a former and future enemy brought themselves to admire his energy, intellect and domestic reforms. Some were East Anglians. The Norfolk Whig Earl of Albemarle hailed the First Consul as a most enlightened reformer. Fanny Burney, who met him in 1802, judged him studious and sincere. The *Suffolk Chronicle* described him as abstemious, modest, unpretentious and working a 14-hour day. Amelia Opie *née* Alderson confessed that after seeing him on her visit to Paris "my frame still shook from the excitement".[3]

Capitalising on the euphoria, and probably aware that it would not last, Addington scheduled an election for July 1802.

This paid off. The result in no way loosened the Tory-Old Whig stranglehold. The government had their apparent treaty trump card. Luckily for them the wheat price had recently plummeted to the very reasonable 1798 level of 68/- (£3-8s) per quarter, suggesting that the economy was on the up and social unrest in decline. The usual loyalists were returned almost everywhere in Suffolk and Essex. Both candidates elected at Eye were Cornwallises, who utterly trounced their Whig opponents. The head of the family was of course, Addington's Amiens negotiator. One Bury MP was Lord Charles Fitzroy*, son of the Earl of Euston, whose mansion was ten miles north of town; the other was Lord Frederick William Hervey, son of the Earl of Bristol, who had been building the magnificent neo-classical Rotunda at Ickworth, four miles west, to house his art. Both were Whigs, but loyal. The Suffolk county, Aldeburgh, Bury, Dunwich, Ipswich, Orford and Sudbury constituencies were uncontested, so the re-election of the sitting members had been a formality.

At Harwich, in spite of its tiny electorate, all employed directly or indirectly by the government, one of Addington's loyalists, James Adams, was unexpectedly defeated by a "dark horse" named Myers, whose reliability was suspect even though he was married to the granddaughter of the other successful Tory candidate, the elderly minor office-holder John Robinson. Robinson, who had sat for Harwich for almost 30 years, and lived in the town in a fine seafront house which still stands, died a year later and was replaced by the prime minister's younger brother John Hiley Addington. Meanwhile Myers was conveniently unseated for "irregular" electoral conduct and Adams reinstated.

At Yarmouth a nephew of Admiral Earl St Vincent, and Troubridge, one of Nelson's Mediterranean captains, were elected. The town was flattered by its connection with the Navy which had saved England from disaster, had prospered from the war, and now hoped to enjoy the economic benefits of peace. There was otherwise still a respectable opposition Whig showing in Norfolk. Coke and his young friend Sir Thomas Astley were elected for the county. Bizarrely, the subsequently-famous diarist and radical Thomas Creevey was voted in at Thetford by a tiny Protestant electorate on the instructions of their absentee Catholic landlords, Lord Petre (of Ingatestone in Essex), and his brother-in-law the Duke of Norfolk. And, in the only sensational result of the region, Windham was narrowly defeated at Norwich by the radical barrister William Smith, formerly MP for Sudbury. In view of his 1796 vote Windham had expected his contest to be close, but his defeat shook him. He saw it as Jacobin revenge. It was probably more due to his denouncing Addington and his peace treaty, and thereby making himself seem an inflexible advocate of costly war. Indeed in view of his hardline position it is surprising that he did so well! He took up the offer of a rotten borough in Kent.[4]

Almost as soon as the peace celebrations, election and friendly visits to France were over criticism of the treaty and mistrust of Bonaparte came to the fore. They cut across the political and social spectrum. Disillusionment came so quickly that even before the treaty was signed some of its defenders resorted to saying that if it did not last it at least gave the country an essential breathing space before the war resumed. The French had just brought the Batavian Republic under tighter control. Though in theory British exports to France and her allies were permitted most were in reality prohibited bytariffs.

Thomas Creevey, lawyer, radical and diarist, elected Member of Parliament for Thetford in 1802 after nomination by the Duke of Norfolk.

---

* Charles Fitzroy would command troops at Ipswich. He was father of Robert Fitzroy, later captain of the *Beagle*, which would take Chales Darwin to the Pacific.

All but two of the enemy colonies taken during the war had been handed back. There was still the whole wartime national debt still to tackle. The economic situation in the eastern counties was particularly bad. One in six of the population of Norfolk was on poor relief – in spite of the reasonable price of wheat mentioned earlier.

Meanwhile Bonaparte had held another rigged vote which made him First Consul for Life and gave him more power than any French king. When Fox visited him in September 1802 (for which Coke rebuked him) he was repelled by his host's belief in militarism and censorship – even though the First Consul had praised him for opposing the war and hating Pitt and Windham! Tom Paine also concluded that Bonaparte had betrayed the Revolution, and left France for America at the invitation of the recently-elected President Jefferson.

By 1803 Anglo-French relations were again very strained. French "commercial agents" in Britain were spying. There were still French troops and warships in Dutch ports. There had been a French takeover in Switzerland. Britain was stalling over her treaty obligation to evacuate Malta. Bonaparte publicly denounced her for going against the letter and spirit of the treaty and trying to undermine the peace of Europe, and warned that if the war did restart he would invade. Addington, rather like Neville Chamberlain 137 years later, began to reactivate the nation's military and naval defences. Unlike in 1793, this time the government had almost universal support. This included both Pitt and Fox. When the Militia was re-embodied in March, Pitt not only approved, but spoke as if the war had already begun:

> "we must recollect…what it is we have at stake, what it is we have to contend for. It is for our property, it is for our liberty, it is for our independence, nay, for our very existence as a nation; it is for our character, it is for everything dear and valuable to man on this side of the grave".[5]

Waiting for Napoleon   **11**

"His Majesty's earnest endeavours for the preservation of peace having failed of success…The conduct of the First Consul to his Majesty's ambassador at his audience … furnishes another instance of provocation on the part of the French government".

In these solemn words, taken from the official *London Gazette*, the *Ipswich Journal* of 21st May 1803 began its explanation of why Great Britain had again just declared war on France. It listed Bonaparte's various aggressions, and related how he had insulted George III's ambassador Lord Whitworth, and threatened invasion. In the same small type it went on to promote a private lunatic asylum at Loddon, a toothpaste, a "spring physic", and a book on "modern gardening". The news was alarming but the paper needed its advertising revenue.

Fanny Burney was aghast at the situation, but Arthur Young wrote:

"War! To look into futurity is idle. The event is the Lord's hand, and will depend on the piety and fidelity of Christians amongst us, and not be governed by fleets and armies… France is so unprepared at sea, that no war opened with better prospects".[1]

(He had turned to religion after the death of a daughter a few years earlier).

Bonaparte had seized British ships and people, and invaded George III's domain in Hanover. Three Harwich Post Office packet boats, including Captain Flyn's, were taken at Helvoet. Their crews were held in Brill Prison by order of General Victor, French commander in Holland, and later marched far inland to Verdun, in France, where Captain Philip Deane jr of the *King George* died four years later, leaving a wife and children. On 20th June the Batavian ambassador was deported via Harwich on Hearn's packet *Prince of Wales*. The Duke of Cambridge, commander of the Hanoverian army, and Prince William of Gloucester, meanwhile fled from Cuxhaven to Harwich, missing the French by just a few hours. In August Dumouriez, the famous French émigré and one-time revolutionary general, also stepped ashore at the Essex port, having fled the German port of Husum, again on *Prince of Wales*. Soon afterwards the Harwich packets shifted their Continental termini to neutral Toningen (on the Holstein coast north of the Elbe) and Bremen.[2]

The events of 1793-1801 were repeating themselves, and sooner even than the pessimists had predicted. Within a month the French *Grande Armée* of

French general Étienne
Bruix, who was to be
responsible for the logistics
of shipping an army across
the Channel.

150,000 men was deployed along the coastline between the Somme and the Scheldt, principally in a camp just north of Boulogne, so large that it had streets, theatres and vegetable gardens. Already Bonaparte's Admiral Bruix had gathered more than 300 requisitioned barges and fishing boats. Within another two months he had over 1,400, and by August over 2,000.

The shortest crossing for the French invaders would be from Boulogne to Kent: if their landing craft were rowed or had a brisk easterly wind it could be done in 12 hours. However the longer approach from Flanders or Holland to East Anglia could not be ruled out by the defenders. The Dutch had agreed to provide some of the shipping, including five ships of the line (the French had none nearer than Brest) and five frigates. Bonaparte's love of surprise tactics was another consideration. In southern East Anglia the flat beaches and numerous river estuaries might invite invaders. And of course any direct seaborne threat to London would have to come from the east into the Thames Estuary.

On 17th May Admiral Keith became Commander-in-Chief North Sea and raised his flag on the captured Dutch frigate *Utrecht* at the Nore. His initial force was only about 15 ships, mainly small gun-brigs and bomb vessels. He was soon sent more, and within a month had 40 ships in three squadrons. By 1805 he had over 160, more than there were in the English Channel. Rear-Admiral Montagu, on the *Utrecht*, was based on the Downs, blockading the Maas, Scheldt and French Channel ports, and protecting British trade in the eastern English Channel. Commodore Sir Sidney Smith was on the *Antelope* sixth-rate in Hollesley Bay, and guarding the Harwich coastline with the gun brigs *Aggressor, Charger, Escort, Marmion* and *Vixen*. And Rear-Admiral Thornborough, on another captured Dutch frigate, the *Gelykheid*, was patrolling the coast and trade between Orfordness and the Humber with the gun brigs *Bold, Censor, Constant, Mallard* and *Snipe*. Each force was periodically to sally towards the enemy coast. Smith had been a household name since 1799, when he had landed sailors and marines at Acre, in Palestine, and thereby thwarted Bonaparte's march from Egypt into Syria.

The Thames Estuary "floating batteries" returned to their stations of 1801: *Beschermer* to the Wallet, *Leyden* and *Dictator* to the King's Channel. In the autumn the *Pegasus* anchored off Harwich, the *Defence, Romulus* and *St Albans* in Hollesley Bay. Several small, shallow-draught gunboats, mostly with sliding keels, were also posted: the *Adder* to the Wallet, *Borer* and *Nieuport* to the Colne off Brightlingsea Creek, *Aimwell* to the Blackwater off West Mersea, and *Boxer* to the Crouch entrance.[3] Captain Troubridge irritatedly wrote to Keith that "All the most remote estuaries want naval forces in their Creeks". But when the Barking fishing fleet asked Keith to provide them with an escort while they trawled off the Kent coast he refused to set such a precedent. Instead the plan was that all the guardships would help Smith repel an invasion wherever it came, rather than to tie them to merely local defence.[4]

The day after taking command Keith had all French and Dutch vessels in east coast ports seized. A month later he ordered the same move against enemy fishing craft found in the North Sea. The *Aggressor* seized five Dutch ones off Scheveningen just a week later, and within a month 35 had been taken into Yarmouth alone.

The Navy needed to re-man its ships in a hurry, and resorted to the usual methods. On 9th and 10th May, apparently in a simultaneous swoop so that ships could not slip away and escape the net, it sent press gangs into east coast ports, rounding up men and boys from merchant ships, fishing boats and quaysides. The operation was crude and heavy-handed. Of the 300 people seized at Yarmouth, 250 had to be released as exempt. Later the Mayor sent his constables round with officers from men of war in the Roads to press more, but when Captain Campbell, the Impress Officer, interviewed them he found that all but four had Protections or were of the wrong age. Rear Admiral Russell wrote to the Admiralty that Lt Borough, of the *Curlew*

George Elphinstone, Lord Keith, became Commander in Chief, North Sea, and sent out instructions for the revival of the defences of the east coast.

> "… was so violent in beating the Constable sent to support him, and violating the order and silence prescribed to him, that I have been obliged, in justice, to submit to his being left in the hands of the Civil Power."[5]

At Harwich, according to the seaman-diarist William Wetherell, the odious Captain Wilkinson of the *Hussar* frigate indiscriminately "plundered" the male population, including farmers and the parish priest.[6] The *Hussar*'s logbook and muster roll show that in fact she "pressed" 27, that she released them all within one week, and that Wetherell got the date wrong by a month. Meanwhile Captain George Wood, of the gun brig *Adder* in the Wallet, seized a similar number from passing ships and fishing boats, including one from Harwich, two from Brightlingsea, three from Yarmouth, and one from the neutral Prussian port of Emden. Harwich alderman, former packet captain and fishing-boat owner Philip Deane, senior, protested to him as follows:

> "I am afraid that you have taken an apprentice of mine, with an Act of Parliament Protection. I have to ask you will excuse him, or otherwise I shall be under the Disagreeable necessity of using the Act in force against you, which will be unpleasant and subject you to pay all Expenses occurring with a penalty of twenty pounds, for your detaining him."[7]

Wood replied that he was justified in pressing the boy (Ezekiel Gooding) because Deane's skipper, Roger Bates, had tried to bribe him. Deane angrily wrote back enclosing a denial from Bates – witnessed by Mayor Hopkins – and threatening to notify the Admiralty Board. Harwich was, of course, a borough linked to Addington himself. Deane must have kept his word, because two months later Gooding was discharged "by Admiralty order at Harwich". By then most of Wood's other recruits had also been freed.

Sea Fencible officers were not supposed to do impressment work for the regular Navy, but Captain Wollaston, former captain of the *Cruizer*, scourge of the French privateers, and now in charge of the Fencibles on the Colne, did so that October and also got himself into legal difficulty. He held a meeting at the *White Horse* inn, on Mersea Island, at which he told Lt Petit, of the gun brig *Aimwell*, to draft a local shipyard carpenter named Sopwith. Though he was middle-aged and had never been to sea before, this unfortunate man was held on the brig for seven weeks, until his brother obtained a writ of habeas corpus to free him. The Sopwiths then successfully sued Wollaston for £105 at Chelmsford Court.[8] Life on the *Aimwell* was obviously hated

A letter of objection to the seizing of an apprentice by the press gang.

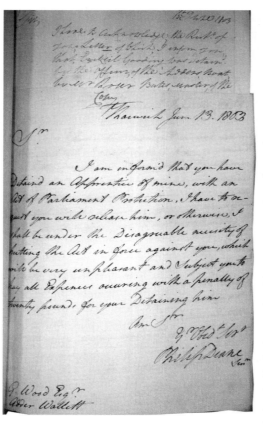

even by her volunteers: either that or the Mersea incident had undermined her officers' authority, because in the next two months 11 more of them deserted her – not difficult as she was permanently anchored just yards off Bradwell.[9]

A few miles away at Brightlingsea half the 50 crew of the gun brig *Borer* deserted within ten weeks, On 4 January, 1804, presumably to make up the lost numbers, she grabbed seven teenage boys at Wivenhoe. All but one had to be released because they were apprentices with official Protections.[10]

The Navy's hunger for pressed men was understandable. The captains of the Thames Estuary floating batteries were dismayed with the Greenwich pensioners sent them. In December 1803 the captain of the *Romulus*, in Hollesley Bay, wrote to the Admiralty entreating them to replace the 16 they had foisted on him, whom he described as so unfit as to be useless.

The recalled Sea Fencibles were again turning out four Saturdays a month to practice with muskets and cannon, on shore and on boats. Each district – for instance Blackwater-to-Stour or Southwold-to-Yarmouth – had two or three captains and four of five lieutenants instead of a single captain, meaning there could be an officer at each port. 900 Sea Fencibles were recruited in the Yarmouth-Cromer district (500 from the town of Yarmouth itself), 650 in Aldeburgh sub-district, 950 in Harwich (Stour-Blackwater), and 500 in Maldon (Blackwater-Thames). In the event of invasion they were to take their orders from the Army.[11]

The Admiralty had decreed that in the ports and estuaries south of Cromer they should man requisitioned fishing smacks and barges. Each was to have oars, a crew of between ten and 14 and mount one or two (mostly 24-pdr) carronades (short-barrelled cannon), loaded with solid, case or grape shot. The Army at Colchester lent a hand, and in October got the loan of six craft from the nearby River Colne. Over the winter the number of Colne Fencible smacks rose to 19, all equipped with 24-pdrs. The fitting out was done at Warren's Shipyard at Brightlingsea, with the aid of the gun-brig *Borer*. Meanwhile Captain Beaver of the Maldon Sea Fencibles oversaw the arming of no fewer than 33 for the Blackwater. He was fiery in his keenness to take on the enemy, and vainly offered to go over and attack Boulogne himself. 18 more gunboats were based around Cromer, the same number at Yarmouth, 19 in the Crouch and 27 in Harwich Harbour and the Stour. Willingness to man these craft varied. When he visited the River Crouch Keith found its fishermen keen to go to sea against invaders, but Harwich again protested about the disruption to its fishing.[12]

The will to fight also varied in the Army. One month's grace had been announced in the local press for those who had deserted or failed to report for the Militia. On 7th July the *Ipswich Journal* published the names of 21 such deserters and defaulters from Lord Euston's West Suffolk Militia – deplorably all were paid substitutes. A 40/- (£2) reward was offered for anyone notifying their whereabouts.

On 27th May 1803 General Sir James Craig arrived at Colchester to command the Army's Eastern District. The town had the largest barracks in the region, was close to the most vulnerable beaches and estuaries, and, in the usual phrase of the time, enjoyed a "centrical position". Craig was in indifferent health, prone to colds and chills. But he had a wealth of experience from the American War, which made him a believer in flexible modern methods in the style of Moore and Money. He was emphatic in claiming that, after Kent, north-east Essex and south-east Suffolk were the likeliest objectives for the would-be invader, and his troop deployment reflects this. No fewer than eight infantry and one cavalry brigades were to be based between the Crouch and the Alde, besides the artillery – a total of some 25,000 men. This was almost 90% of the full-time troops in the eastern counties.[13]

Craig was equipped with some of the first of the very accurate maps from the Ordnance staff's survey. From its printed six-inches-to-one-mile series coloured versions were hand-copied. Towards the end of June he wrote to the

General Sir James Craig, commander of the Eastern District from 1803.

In Colchester the *Artilleryman* public house stands on the site of the Napoleonic Wars artillery barracks. The street names themselves are reminders of those times.

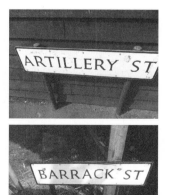

Duke of York saying that he had managed to visit the main danger areas in his command, in spite of cold weather and shortage of time, and drafted his defence scheme. Though he did not mention Sir John Moore in his letter, he had come to very similar conclusions.

He said that as the invaders would probably sail by night, and might be pushed off course by side winds, it would be necessary to spread the defence along a wider stretch of coast than they had planned to land on. "But it is utterly impossible to guard every spot", he warned. Instead he proposed to keep troops "in Central Positions so as to be able to march at the shortest notice … check him at the first instant, to afford time for the assembly of a more considerable Force … (and) profit of any Opportunity that his Ignorance of the Country may offer".[14]

Major-General Paget, later Earl of Uxbridge and Angelsey, who commanded the cavalry in east Suffolk and north-east Essex for several years. He famously had his leg shot off at Waterloo whilst mounted alongside Wellington.

He was least worried about Norfolk, owing to its lack of harbours and remoteness from enemy ports. He allotted only two regiments of Militia, backed by 6th Dragoons, to its defence. He also thought there was little risk to the Suffolk coast north of Southwold, but covered Hollesley Bay with a strong force made up of Lord Fitzroy's militia, Sir Eyre Coote's regular infantry, and half of Lord Paget's cavalry brigade, based mainly at Ipswich and Bromeswell Heath east of Woodbridge.

Like Moore, he was very anxious to secure Harwich, arguing that as an invader was likeliest to sail on a long autumn or winter night for the sake of concealment he would ipso facto risk rough weather and therefore need a sheltered anchorage. Though he had only one Militia regiment (the Royal Bucks) there, he put the whole of Lord Manners' regular infantry brigade on Bradfield Heath ready to move to its aid. Later he brought West Essex Militia down from Ipswich to reinforce the Royal Bucks at Beacon Hill. Like Reynolds six years earlier he was worried about Landguard Fort on the opposite shore, where the existing garrison was only one Militia and one small invalid company, and which he thought too small and feebly built – not to mention its "totally incapable" lieutenant-governor. He recommended its encirclement by a new ditch and palisaded rampart, the completion of two already-started outlying earth redoubts, and the digging of a well. While the fort held out, he thought, it would deny the invader the use of Harwich Harbour.[15]

Again like Moore Craig thought "Clackton Beach…by far the most accessible spot (to the invader) in the whole of Eastern District". It was to be the main concern of Hope's Highland Brigade which was then encamping at Weeley, ten miles east of Colchester. Hope was to hold most of his troops back at base so as to react to a landing anywhere round from the Colne to Harwich, but station one company at Little Holland and another at St Osyth so as to watch this beach from both ends.

Craig did not see the River Colne as a likely enemy objective, but thought that if the sea along Clacton Beach was too "boisterous" they might be diverted there. To cover this contingency he posted West Suffolk Militia at Thorrington Heath, from which it could reach the left bank of the river before Hope's Brigade at Weeley. The battalion was placed under Hope's command.

Craig wrote that "Next to Harwich Harbour the point that I am most anxious to secure is the entrance to the Blackwater River".[16] Though this had offshore sandbanks and marshy shores it was a potential anchorage as large and deep as Harwich, and even closer to London. He was bringing Lord Ludlow's militia brigade down to Colchester from Norfolk to guard its northern shore. He put one of Ludlow's battalions forward at Abberton, the spot found by Moore, so as to go onto Mersea Island should invaders come into the river. Two battalions from Lord Cavan's Brigade, on Purleigh Heights south of Maldon, were assigned to watch the southern shore.

The Duke of York was sufficiently convinced by Craig's concern about Clacton to reinforce him still further. Towards the end of July Lord Southampton's militia brigade – 1st and 3rd West York and East York – arrived at Elmstead Heath, two miles east of Colchester.[17]

Craig and Keith shared the view that the Suffolk coast was less threatened than the Essex. Not only was it one day's march further from London, but the easterly wind the enemy would rely on to bring him over while trapping the Royal Navy in port would cause a "wash" (surf) along the gravel beaches around Orfordness which spelt problems for landing barges and boats. Towards the end of the month Commodore Sidney Smith landed at Hollesley Bay to confer with Major-General Coote. They toured the local shore, then joined Major-General Paget to review all the troops on Bromeswell Heath, where, said the *Ipswich Journal*, "the Camp presents at once a busy and gay scene". The crowd of civilian spectators was "anxious to see the hero who taught the Corsican usurper that he was not invincible", it added. Smith disagreed with his superiors' view of the Suffolk coast. He claimed that almost the whole stretch from Landguard to Southwold could easily be landed upon. Bonaparte, he thought, must have been advised of this by Johnson, a smuggler who had deserted to the French*. He reported that if a ship was laid side-on to the beach it blocked the surf. He called for three cannon to be mounted on top of Orford Castle, and the flocks of sheep on the adjacent marshes to be removed.

A few days later Keith himself made a waterborne tour of the coast as far north as Suffolk. First he called in at Maldon and conferred with his old Mediterranean comrade Captain Beaver about his Sea Fencibles. Then he went on to Colchester and met Craig, renewing the professional partnership of nine years before when they had together taken Capetown from the Dutch. Sailing up to Hollesley Bay, he studied its potential landing beaches, then came back down the coast via Bawdsey, the *Beschermer* (anchored off the Naze), the Crouch, and Shoeburyness.[18]

Nearly all of Craig's army had arrived (from far inland) since May. Coote's brigade had already been on Martlesham Heath, east of Ipswich, but Craig shifted it to Bromswell Heath, on the other side of the River Deben, so as to be closer to Hollesley Bay. Coote, veteran of America, the West Indies, Ostend, Bergen and Egypt, was the nephew of the famous Sir Eyre Coote who had crushed Tipoo in India. Six Militia regiments all marched through Colchester within a few days late that month. The three regular "Scotch" Highland foot battalions landed at Harwich after a sea voyage from Leith. When one of their transports came into harbour an officer was amazed to hear them fervently singing a hymn of thanksgiving (presumably in Gaelic) down below. Essex folk called these kilted men "the petticoat soldiers".

Conditions in the new heathland camps were primitive. At first the Yorkshiremen at Elmstead had hardly any tents and most of them had to sleep

Orford castle was a fortification from much earlier times. Sidney Smith asked for three cannon to be mounted there as a part of the Napoleonic defences.

---

* On this he was misinformed. Johnson had been arrested by the French in Flushing and later claimed to have met Napoleon and been offered the job of guiding his invasion fleet. However he did not enter their service, and, legendary prison escaper that he was, got back to London in 1805 and signed up as a pilot with the British.

EASTERN DISTRICT ORDER OF BATTLE – July 1803
(less coast artillery, Volunteers & Sea Fencibles)

(King's) Lynn	Rutlandshire Militia Regt
Norwich-Thetford area	6th Dragoons (from Loftus's Brigade)
Norwich & Yarmouth	Shropshire Militia Regt, (Loftus's Brigade) 1 light artillery brigade.
Bury St Edmunds -Sudbury-Needham Mkt	
	7th Dragoon Guards (from Loftus's Brigade)
Bromswell Heath (east of Woodbridge)	
	Sir Eyre Coote's Brigade (53 & 69 Regts of Foot)
Woodbridge	1 dragoon sqdn of Paget's Brigade
Ipswich	Lord Chas. Fitzroy's Brigade (Royal North Lincs, West Essex, Herts Militia Regts)
	Lord Paget's Brigade (7th & 18th Light Dragoons – 5 sqdns)
	1 light artillery brigade
Foxall Heath	North Yorks Supplementary Militia
Harwich	Royal Buckinghamshire Militia
Landguard Fort	One company of the Herts Militia Regt & one Invalids Coy.
Bradfield Heath	Lord Manners' Brigade (24 & both btns of 30 Regt of Foot)
Colchester	Lord Ludlow's Brigade (West Norfolk, East Norfolk, Royal South Lincs Militia Regts).
	2nd Light Dragoons.
	2 light artillery troops
Abberton Green	Cheshire Regt, 1 dragoon sqdn of Paget's Bde
Elmstead Heath	Lord Southampton's Brigade (1st and 3rd West York and East York Militia Regts)
Weeley	Hope's Brigade (2 btns of 42nd & 1 of 92 Highland Regts), 1 dragoon squadron of Paget's Bde
Thorrington Heath	West Suffolk Militia Regt
Chelmsford	Finch's Brigade of Guards (1st & 3rd Coldstream Btns)
	Lord Cavan's Brigade (83rd and 85th Regts of Foot)
Purleigh Heights	Other 2 regts of Lord Cavan's Bde

in the grass, where 200 snakes were killed in one hour. At Weeley the Scots stumbled shin-deep in mud for months. Moore's 1797 report on Thorrington Heath had described it as "spongy and rotten". Not that the regulars, at least, were unused to hardships. Most had fought at the Texel and in Egypt. Meanwhile work was proceeding on wooden-hut barracks at Colchester, Ipswich, Woodbridge, Harwich and Weeley, respectively for 6600, 5800, 2000, 2500 and 1700 men. 1200 workmen came, mainly from London, to build at Ipswich and Woodbridge alone.

Once the barracks were completed their occupants were allowed to bring wives and children. Lt Grant, of the 42nd Foot, was joined at Weeley by his wife Mary Ann. She wrote to a friend describing their excursion to Frederick Nassau's St Osyth Priory, "picturesque ruins" where he and his fellow officers dined "*à la rustique*", and "the soul-moving harmony from the sounds of various instruments, echoing in different directions through the woods, exhilarated our spirits, and gave zest to those feelings which a contemplation of the glorious works of nature must always awaken".[19] 42nd were to become the famous Black Watch. Thomas of Norwich, then a legal clerk at Colchester, described them as "the noble 42nd, who wore black ostrich plumes in their caps, and were generally respectable and well-conducted Scotch gentry".[20] This is a cue to comment on the changing appearance of the British troops in general. The 18th century pattern of uniform, with jacket open over waistcoat, and tricorn hat, had been replaced by a double-buttoned tunic and cylindrical hat – as on traditional tins of Quality Street chocolate. Jackets were still red, except for riflemen, who wore a dark green which gave them a degree of camouflage for fighting in open order as opposed to *en masse*. The same applied to the Volunteers. Cavalrymen and dragoons wore brass helmets with plumes folded down over the tops, like birds' crests.

It was also in the July of 1803 that Major-General John Money published his alarmist *Address to the People of Norfolk and Suffolk*, and got every local newspaper to quote it. He conceded that a landing on the east coast was likely to be a secondary one for the sake of diverting the British from the south, but warned that it was nevertheless a grave threat. "Do not flatter yourselves with the notion that we are perfectly safe while we are the masters of the sea", he declared. He warned that the French were familiar with the coastline and sandbanks of Suffolk and Norfolk because Semonville, their ambassador in the Batavian Republic, was a former émigré and resident of Yarmouth. The Navy, he claimed, would be powerless if an east wind held it back in port but brought over the enemy. The Militia was, he said, quite unequal to the French veterans. It was therefore essential for local civilians to rejoin the Volunteers, turn up for training, and have their weapons ready. He urged them not to "wait till the roofs of your houses are on fire". Windham was equally jittery about the coastline north of Aldeburgh, believing that it could be seized before the Ipswich and Bromswell garrisons could react. And the *Ipswich Journal* thought it its duty to add:

> "All persons arriving from France and Holland and witnessed the immense preparations which they are now making for the invasion of this country express astonishment at the apathy and indifference which prevail here".

Largely as a consequence of such propaganda the part-time Volunteer corps rapidly reassembled under their socially notable former commanders, and agreed to sign up for one-month periods of permanent duty rather than just for weekend training. Some 15,000 enlisted throughout Essex and East Anglia. 1,000 joined at Norwich, 600 at Yarmouth, 700 at Ipswich, and almost 800 at Colchester – among them the magistrate and subsequent mayor Thomas Hedge.

Meanwhile Addington had taken a radical step himself. He put through a new Defence of the Realm Act whereby in the event of invasion the Volunteers would be multiplied fivefold with conscripts, without selection by gentleman officers. This would have brought their total strength in East Anglia to some 75,000, nearly all of its young men less those already in the permanent forces and Sea Fencibles. In the prime minister's support Pitt declared in the Commons: "There was a time when it would have been dangerous... But that time is now past".[21] The masses no longer had any sympathy with revolutionaries, he said. At Norwich the leftist writer William Taylor jr. almost frothed at the mouth in patriotic agreement:

> "Let us therefore with exemplary docility acquiesce in the governmental arrangements ... let us rise with method, with unanimity, like a great and powerful people determined to live free or die ... The invader must be attacked from every direction by night and by day ... War must now be our business, our amusement: it must occupy every hand and mind".[22]

As it turned out this enrolment was never needed – to Tory relief and Taylor's disappointment..

It was obviously desirable to prevent invaders landing in the first place. In the autumn work began on the installation of coast artillery (mostly 32, 24 or 18-pdr), and at more locations than in the previous war. In addition to the Yarmouth-Lowestoft coastline, by the spring of 1804 batteries had been emplaced behind moats and earthworks at, among other places Holt, Cromer, Southwold, Aldeburgh, the entrance to the River Ore, Landguard, Harwich, Frinton, Little Holland, Clacton Wash, St Osyth Point, Brightlingsea Westmarsh Point, Fingringhoe, Mersea Island, Bradwell Point and the entrance to the Crouch. Since there were not enough soldiers to man all these, some (e.g. on the north Norfolk coast and at Clacton and Walton) were handed over to the Sea Fencibles. Each infantry brigade was also given a few light 6-pdr guns.

Craig then turned his attention inland. Should invaders get onto the road to London he proposed to halt them with fortifications around Chelmsford. A four-mile semi-circle of trenches and gun pits was dug between the town and Springfield, across the Colchester road, and a shorter section at Moulsham to the south. Two 30-acre star-shaped earth and timber forts were built at Widford and Galleywood nearby. In between the River Chelmer and various streams were flooded. These positions would force the enemy westwards, buying time for the reinforcement of the capital and enabling the Chelmsford garrisons to cut his communications back to the coast and attack him from behind. Craig thought the invaders were unlikely to try to storm these defences since he had "always assumed as a datum that the Enemy cannot bring any heavy artillery with him". However his own (rather Napoleonic!) instinct was to manoeuvre and fight in the open, and not to "shelter behind works", and he resisted suggestions to fortify Colchester.[23] The Chelmsford work was held up during the 1803/4 winter by repeated rain which made earth slip back out of place and flooded diggings. It was not completed till 1806, by which time any immediate peril had passed. It annoyed some. The Chelmsford brigade HQ had been installed in the Moulsham mansion belonging to the tetchy Whig Sir Henry Mildmay, and a rampart was dug across his garden. He protested about the "great inconvenience" and thieving soldiery, and demanded generous compensation, on the grounds that although he did have another house a clause in a will obliged him to live for part of the year at Moulsham. Eventually he got £4,000.[24]

Craig and Keith were more concerned and systematic about signalling than

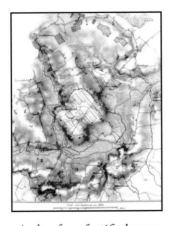

A plan for a fortified camp at Springfield, between Chelmsford and Boreham, drafted by the Eastern Distirct Engineers in 1804.

Moore. The Nore-Yarmouth chain had been dismantled, so that in May Keith had it reinstated. The East Anglian press printed a list of its posts that June – very odd by modern security standards. In addition he installed a post on Prittlewell church tower, enabling him to signal from the Nore to the army near Chelmsford. Chains of army posts were also set up, equipped with a white and red flags and lamps. The single white signal showed that a post was ready to receive or send, a red was the invasion warning. The first two of these stations were on the towers of Brightlingsea church and St Mary's church in Colchester, which were within line of sight. Thereby Craig himself could be immediately told of invaders showing up off Clacton or the Blackwater. It took a full year, however, before the rest of his chain was complete right across the county. In June 1803 another link was provided between Yarmouth and Norwich, via Strumpshaw Mill and Filby Church, and also later extended west right across to Cambridgeshire. In 1804 the Colchester post was moved to the Barracks – since it cost £1000 it must have been on a purpose-built tower. The naval chain – still only ball and flag – was extended westwards along the north Norfolk shore from Yarmouth to Lynn in 1805, with a post on such high ground at Trimingham that it became a lookout far inland as well as seawards.[25]

Craig ordered that once his troops had hoisted the red warning flag at a signal post, civilians on standby were to raise similar flags on every church tower from which it could be seen. T W Coke had one to hoist over Holkham Hall. At night this general alarm warning was to consist of brushwood beacons. Concerned that these could be accidentally ignited in dry weather, Craig ruled that they should be double – only if two fires were seen at the same point should others be lit.

In the event of an enemy landing the British artillery which could not be moved was to be spiked, and bridges and roads were to be blown up. All the 1797-1801 plans for moving livestock and food stocks inland were revived, and local meetings held at which civilians were chosen as drivers. So as not to clutter the main roads needed by the defending army the herds and wagons were to move on the minor roads, where necessary crossing the highways only at certain designated places. What could not be shifted would be set fire to. Compensation would be offered to those suffering financial losses from invasion, but only if they had already signed up to help with the evacuation scheme.[26] The Government was most anxious to prevent law and order breaking down in the event of invasion, and, above all, the looting of the property of the wealthy. Each Lord Lieutenant drafted a plan appointing reliable gentry to take emergency legal authority in the various towns and hundreds of his county, together with "superintendents" and special constables in each parish – in effect, a wartime police force. Women and children were to be evacuated inland: those from Tendring Hundred to Samford Hundred near Ipswich, those from Dengie Hundred to the Bishops Stortford-Dunmow area, those from Rochford Hundred to Ongar.[27]

Meanwhile another defence survey of the area was drafted for the Duke of York by none other than the celebrated émigré General Dumouriez. He too anticipated a landing at Harwich and/or in the Blackwater, but thought the enemy would avoid the exposed Clacton shore. Like Moore he recommended that the Colchester and Ipswich cavalry should concentrate on the left of the British line and push east so as to retake or relieve Harwich. He wanted artillery and mortars installed at Bradwell, Mersea and St Osyth to fire from all directions on ships entering the Blackwater. It may be that his plan was based only on maps, and not inspection of the actual terrain. On the other hand he was familiar with French military methods and had studied the issue from the invaders' point of view ever since the American War.[28]

In mid-August the Duke of York, accompanied by his brother the Duke of Cambridge, visited Ipswich. They inspected Fitzroy's militia regiments on Westerfield Green, local Volunteers on Parker's Fields, and Coote's regulars on Rushmere Heath. In the evening they dined with cavalry commander Paget at Christchurch Mansion. Next day they did a similar tour with Craig, Ludlow and Hope at Colchester.[29] Craig was keen not to be caught napping and to keep his men on their toes. Each day he had them march to the positions towards the coast where they were to fight their first delaying actions.

In September one of Coote's foot regiments moved to Chelmsford, and two of Manners' left for the South Coast. Militia replaced them. The following month Coote was succeeded by a Major-General Smith. Later Major-General John Baird took over the militia infantry brigade at Colchester from Ludlow. Baird had served three times in India, been four years a prisoner of Hyder Ali, found the dead body of his successor Tipoo at Seringapatam, and taken part in the conquest of the Cape of Good Hope and Egypt.

Major-General John Baird, commander of the militia brigade at Colchester during the 1803-4 invasion alert, and later prominent alongside Moore and Wellington in Spain.

The Yarmouth fleet had been enlarged so as to contain the ships the Dutch were fitting out at the Texel. For the next several years it consisted of about 16 ships of various types. They still included the *Director*, once captained by the infamous William Bligh, and *Monmouth*, another of the mutinous ships of 1797. Vice-Admiral Dickson, previously in command at Yarmouth, had died at his Hardingham Hall home in the spring, so Rear-Admiral Russell took over and raised his flag on the *Gelykheid* (soon afterwards shifted to the larger 3rd Rate *Repulse,* and later mostly on the *Roebuck* frigate). Later Rear-Admiral William Douglas (usually called "Billy", even officially) arrived as Yarmouth Port Admiral, in charge when Russell was away blockading the Dutch.

That October alarm on the East Anglian coast reached fever pitch. Colchester was most affected. Dissenting minister Isaac Taylor sent Jane* and his other children inland to their former home town of Lavenham. The lawyer Daniell buried his valuables in the garden and the Classical scholar Rev. Twining fled St Mary's rectory. At St James's Church on East Hill the Mayor, Volunteers and leading citizens listened to the Rev. Round preach from the Book of Maccabees, and compare Bonaparte to Goliath and England to David. Mrs Taylor wrote to her daughter Jane at Lavenham with this prayer:

> "Thou comest to me with a sword and with a spear, and with a shield, but I come to thee in the name of the Lord of Hosts, the God of the armies of Israel…"[30]

Lt-Col Bawtree's "Loyal Colchester Volunteers" met and drilled every morning at seven. Earl Fitzwilliam, Old Whig statesman, Pitt's one-time viceroy in Ireland, and Colonel of the West Yorks Militia, was told and travelled down to join his regiment,[31] though I visualise him staying with Craig at Colchester rather than in the snake-infested Elmstead field.

Visiting his native Aldeburgh, the poet George Crabbe was briefly caught up in the panic, as warship and shore guns fired, alarm drums beat, and men rode off to alert the army. His father told him not to worry.[32]

---

* Jane Taylor was author of "Twinkle, twinkle, little star."

The excitement seems to have had several causes. The orders had just been issued about civilian evacuation and special constables. On 20th October an American ship coming out of the Zuider Zee reported to Captain Hope, of the *Defence* frigate, that they had seen 50 "large stout boats", each with four gun ports, moored at Amsterdam, plus 12 more under construction nearby. Hope had also been told that there were two new ships of the line in the port, and two more at the Texel. Next day Smith's *Antelope* and the *Ruby* found a flotilla of Dutch schuyts off the Texel, capturing 13 and sinking one.[33] On the 24th the predominant westerly winds shifted to the east and, unusually, held there for 11 days.[34] Nor can the alarmist writings of Money and speeches of Windham have helped, or a poem in the *Ipswich Journal* entitled "The hour of battle now draws nigh".

With the wind back in the west and no further sightings of the enemy a steady tension replaced the wild alarm. The King himself decided to take the field should the blow fall, and base himself in Chelmsford with the Guards, while the rest of the royal household evacuated to Worcester. Some of his staff and baggage were moved to Essex in readiness. The Norwich Volunteers were sent to Yarmouth for permanent duty. The Lord Lieutenants of the maritime eastern counties – especially Essex – were told by the Government to order a watch for Dutch spies, posing as neutral Prussians, landing on the coast.

Three days before Christmas the concern flared up again. It came to light that on 4th December Bonaparte, after visiting Boulogne, had decreed that 50 more troopships be requisitioned and "emphatically evinced a determination to hasten the embarkation and departure of the Armament by all possible means". He was said to be about to return to the coast, along with his reserve troops, and to have scheduled the sailing of his flotilla for Christmas Day. "Have you heard this new alarm? It is said the French are actually embarking", Jane Taylor wrote to her mother at Colchester.[35] Next evening, a rainy Friday, a report reached the town the French were right off the coast. A theatre play broke up in confusion. Women ran round the streets screaming. The party of Scottish officers from Weeley in the audience commandeered coaches, horses and even donkey carts and rushed off down East Hill heading back to camp.[36] It was another false alarm, apparently caused by neutral ships passing Clacton which had failed to answer signals from shore.

Consequently on Christmas Eve, as scheduled, most of the troops in the open-air camps near the coast went into winter quarters at the newly completed barracks at Colchester, Ipswich and Woodbridge. (Lt Grant's regiment were an exception, as he complained to Mary Ann). 24th Foot went up from Bromswell to Norfolk to fill a longstanding gap there. Throughout the Christmas and New Year period there was no further news of invasion. Numerous reports and letters testify to local opinion being divided between officials and officers who were professionally obliged to take the situation with deadly seriousness and civilians who had "heard it all before" and become complacent. Mrs Taylor replied to her daughter: "all here is perfectly quiet: and still no thinking people at all doubt our being invaded". She worried that the more short-sighted were now complacently mocking Craig and his previous alarms, but soon afterwards did allow her children back from Lavenham.[37]

The Crisis Passes: 12
Pitt, Trafalgar & All the Talents

The defenders of Great Britain enjoyed one great coincidental benefit at this period: wheat prices were at their lowest since 1797, ranging from just 51/2- (£2.11s 2d) per quarter in Essex down to 47/- (£2.7s) in Cambridgeshire. The cost of living had fallen by around one third since the grim 1801. Apart from cutting the expense of feeding the army and navy, this kept the urban population quiet and largely banished talk of internal disorder or a pro-French fifth column. The plentiful corn supply was partly due to excellent growing weather in 1803, partly to cheap imports from the Baltic now that the Armed Neutrality was a thing of the past. Indeed corn prices were so low that protests were lodged by landowners and farmers, who warned that they were producing at a loss, and that the foreign imports needed excluding lest the country became so reliant on them that its security was undermined.

The army continued its preparations. In order to accommodate a full-scale army for battle in Essex or Suffolk, in April 1804 Craig had his staff list all the churches, inns and warehouses in Chelmsford, Colchester and Ipswich. He estimated that around 21,000 men could be crammed into the first and second, and over 38,000 into the third – apart from the barrack accommodation in each case. Somehow 600 were to billet in Ipswich Town Hall and 450 in St Peter's church, Colchester![1]

We know from Thomas Brightwell that at least one full scale battle rehearsal was held all along the proposed main defence line, because he wrote that he and his Colchester Volunteers had marched to the ridge at Ardleigh to take part in an exercise involving between 80,000 and 100,000 men – a number equal to twice the total strength of Eastern District.

Meanwhile the Navy were also very much on the alert. The Yarmouth-based men of war were the reconnaissance force and advanced guard against the supposed right wing of the enemy "armament". On 7 January 1804 reports reached the port, originally from an American merchantman bound from Rotterdam to South America, that there were flat-bottomed invasion barges at Flushing. Next day Captain Manby, on the *Africaine* frigate off Goree island, reported that there were now 52 gunboats ready for sea at Rotterdam and 38 others building. On the 26th Captain Weir's *Ferriter* sloop captured the smuggling vessel *Friends of Yarmouth*, which had been carrying Dutch gin from Emden to Lisbon. Her captain, Merells, imparted some most useful news. He said that when he had called in at Flushing he had counted 110 new schuyts there, each armed with one long gun and "adapted for transporting troops", as well as 19 schooners, each with three 24-pdrs and six 6-pdrs, and also the French frigate *Le Farie*, some of whose crew were stationed on the other craft. He had also seen several gun-schooners on the stocks, only three weeks from completion. Moreover he had spoken to a local man, at one time imprisoned by the French, who told him that 150 more schuyts were en route from other Dutch ports, each for transporting 60 to 80 soldiers and armed with one long 10 or 12-pdr astern. There were already 6,000 French troops on Walcheren island, who each day practised boarding and disembarking from the invasion craft.[2]

Intelligence received by Captain Weir on the invasion barges being prepared in Dutch ports and (above) an enlargement of the bottom left, showing a gun mounted on a barge.

On 22 March several Dutch gunboats emerged from Flushing and were intercepted by Sir Sidney Smith's squadron. Two were captured, and their crews landed and imprisoned at Yarmouth.

It was at first unclear whether the invasion craft in Dutch and Flemish ports were meant for a descent on the east coast, or whether they were to sidle along to the Dover Strait for the short passage to Kent. But the second possibility began to gain ground. Keith set up a standing sloop patrol within sight of each port– the *Africaine* and *Rattler* off Helvoetsluys, the *Antelope*, *Penelope* and *Aimable* off Flushing, and the *Cruizer* and various gunboats off Ostend.

On 7th May Sir Sidney Smith reported to Keith from the *Antelope*, anchored off the Maas, that the number of enemy ships at Helvoetsluys, Flushing and Ostend suggested "the probability of a great movement from those ports".[3]

On the 15th the Flushing flotilla left harbour and headed west along the Flanders coast. The *Antelope*, *Cruizer* and *Rattler* intercepted and exchanged fire with it off Ostend. After *Rattler* had duelled with an armed praam (sea barge) and taken several hits (with three men dead and ten wounded), the enemy flotilla doubled back into the Scheldt.

Six days later Manby's *Africaine* boarded and took 11 Dutch schuyts (shallow-draught coasters) coming out of the Maas, and sent them back to Yarmouth. While he was rounding them up he was fired on by shore guns, and in retaliation he seized no fewer than 40 Dutch fishing boats off Scheveningen. While one of his crew was rowing back a "jolly boat" he got lost in mist and was captured and imprisoned on shore. The Scheveningen town commandant sent him back out to Manby under a flag of truce, with apologies and a claim that he had been forced to fire by the French. Manby sent back a bottle of beer for the Dutchman and a ring for his wife. Evidently at least some Dutchmen had little desire to help their French masters.[4]

On the 30th Smith told Keith that "the number of armed vessels at present in the port of Flushing ready to sail, which as well from intelligence as from

Sir Sidney Smith, active in many aspects of the war. Of him Napoleon Bonaparte, later in his life, is reputed to have said: "That man made me miss my destiny".

our own information, we reckon to be above 350 vessels of all descriptions". He estimated that there were 28,000 French troops encamped round Ostend, of whom half were ready to sail on barges some of which already had horses and field cannon on board. "They appear to perform their evolutions and firings with order and precision", he had gathered. On 23rd June there was another action in which the *Rattler, Galgo* and *Inspector* waged a gun battle with Ostend schuyts, which they drove onshore, and batteries round the harbour. "The enemy have been in motion all along the Dutch coast … to get the different flotillas to Boulogne … it is possible the threatened invasion may soon be brought to a trial", recorded the Admiralty.[5]

Over in America Tom Paine was following the news. His departure from France did not mean that he wished her to stop its war with England, whose ruling class he saw as the arch-enemies of liberty in Europe. He published more of his views on the strategy Bonaparte should adopt, and with particular mention of the East Anglian coast, whose shores he called "as level as a bowling green", "clean firm sand where a flat-bottomed boat may row dry aground" and "the weak and defenceless part of England".[6]

The invasion scare, and naval skirmishes off the enemy coast, had been going on for the better part of a year when politics again took centre-stage.

Local Tory opinion, except where tied to him at Harwich, had long been disenchanted with Addington, and whatever they thought of Catholics, awaited a comeback by Pitt. On 28th May 1803 the fallen hero's birthday had been celebrated at the Nelson Hotel, Yarmouth, by a company of the faithful led by Norfolk MP Colonel Wodehouse. He had toasted (apart from Pitt himself), the royal family, Nelson, General Cornwallis, Windham, Whitworth, and the Bishop and Mayor of Norwich, but not the prime minister.[7]

The following week Windham accused Addington of inadequate preparations. He argued that the 50,000 militia he planned to transfer to the Regular Army would dilute it, since the quality of the militia had been degraded by randomly conscripting the reluctant along with the keen, allowing substitutes, and exempting men in the Volunteers. Better just to pay more men to volunteer straight for the regulars. The Volunteers, he claimed, were unsuitable for coastal defence, and pitched battles, but instead should be trained as guerrillas. He thought it complacent to discount the possibility of invasion on the Norfolk and north-east Suffolk coasts.[8]

On 15th March 1804 Pitt told Parliament that, in relation to the threat now facing it, the country had a weaker navy than in the previous war. A redoubled, not merely an equal, effort was needed. Addington and Earl St Vincent (now First Lord of the Admiralty) were wrong to concentrate most naval shipbuilding in the royal dockyards: it needed to be farmed out to the merchant yards. Putting guns onto barges and lighters was to invest in "trash". Instead purpose-built gun brigs were needed, but few had been built. More coastal fortifications were also required, in view of the doubtful superiority of the Navy.[9] Windham and Pitt shared the view that troops, cannon and gunboats needed to be packed along the coastline of south-east England, rather than relying on the large men of war at Portsmouth, the Downs and Yarmouth to contain the enemy by blockade.

On 25th April, the majority vote for Addington's Additional Force Bill was so slim that he had clearly lost the confidence of most of that part of the House which was not in his pay, and he resigned. On 10th May Pitt returned to Downing Street, having, for the sake of the King, agreed not to revisit the Catholic issue or include Fox in his cabinet. At first sight surprisingly, Windham was not included either. In fact he and Pitt had never got on, in spite of being political allies and for seven years in the same government. Pitt was essentially a calculating rationalist, averse to ideological passion and manic enthusiasm, who had shared Windham's (and Burke's) fear of the Jacobins but rejected their idea that Britain could force France back under her old regime. When Windham accused Addington of "signing Britain's death warrant" by talking to Bonaparte, Pitt thought he was as fanatically misguided as when he had applauded the fall of the Bastille.

One month later newspaper readers learned that First Consul Bonaparte had been declared "Emperor" by his tame elected assembly. There were now very few indeed, even at Norwich, who saw him as anything other than an aggressor and enemy of liberty, whatever they thought of their own government. Foxite New as well as Old Whigs accepted that invasion must be resisted – including by them. Nevertheless Pitt still believed colourful propaganda was necessary. With Treasury money the *Anti-Gallican* compendium was published – in its own words "the Standard of British Loyalty, Religion and Liberty" and a "Collection of Papers, Tracts, Declarations, Speeches, Poems and Songs on the Threatened Invasion". Issued in the spring of 1804, it announced:

> "GRAND EXHIBITION. Mr Veritas begs to inform the Inhabitants of Norwich that he is about to Exhibit in their City a superb and valuable Collection of Pictures, illustrating the Character of the FIRST CONSUL of France ..."

The display depicted such Bonaparte atrocities as his looting and burning of towns, his massacres of civilians and prisoners of war and his "renouncing his redeemer". In the 20th century it would have been a film.

More fun was the patriotic performance at the city's Theatre Royal by the comic singer Holliday, who contrived to work the name of every one of its 100 pubs into his marathon song "The Loyal Norwich Landlord's Defence Against Invasion".[10]

Pitt took back with him into government his old right-hand man Dundas, now raised to the peerage as Lord Melville, and appointed him First Lord of the Admiralty in place of St Vincent. But St Vincent claimed that Dundas was a corrupt hireling of the private contractors and in 1805 led an attempt to impeach him in the House of Lords. This failed, but caused his resignation and tarnished the reputation of his patron Pitt. True to form Thomas Coke took a Commons petition to the King in agreement with St Vincent. One of Dundas's defenders was Commodore Sir Sidney Smith, who doubled as MP for Rochester.

Since it was in the distant Atlantic that the French fleet manoeuvred, and the Dutch and Belgian ports were so closely watched, the impression grew that the danger to the east coast was fading. In August 1804 the floating batteries were removed from the Thames Estuary. The same month the brigades commanded by Finch and Beckwith at Chelmsford, Southampton at Elmstead, and Baird at Colchester all crossed the Thames and encamped in Kent, in case Bonaparte might at last be ready to invade, but not in Essex. In 1805 Baird led an expedition to retake the Cape of Good Hope from the Dutch,

Craig and Sir Sidney Smith went to the Mediterranean, and Thornborough left for the Atlantic. Eastern District at Colchester was taken over by none other than the Earl of Chatham – though as this elder Pitt brother was still Master of the Ordnance he was rather an "absentee landlord" and his work was mostly done by Lord Charles Fitzroy at Ipswich.

Though Emperor Napoleon had just paid his third visit to Boulogne, and issued another menacing and optimistic public declaration, he too had become increasingly doubtful about his grand plan. To synchronise the movement of thousands of craft from a dozen bases, in the face of tides, unpredictable weather, and the growing British fleet, was not comparable to the great land campaigns he was used to. Whenever he visited and watched an exercise, he saw his vessels struggling to get out of harbour against contrary winds, grounding on sandbanks, and capsizing in rough seas. He concluded that a single surprise blow was out of the question, and that instead there would have to be a series of ferrying operations over several days. For these to succeed he would have to command the Channel, and this was not possible unless he could rid it of the main British battle fleet.

The late 19th century American historian William Sloane argued that Napoleon assembled his huge "armament" as a bluff, to force Britain into negotiation and mislead his Continental enemies into assuming that he would not attack them. An exactly similar argument has been advanced about Hitler's "Operation Sealion" in 1940. This is a tricky problem, but I would say that in both cases the invasion preparations were not so much a bluff as a scheme to be activated if, in the meantime, the British will or ability to resist crumbled. In 1940 that will and ability were demonstrated by Churchill's truculence and the RAF in the Battle of Britain. In 1804-5 they were exhibited by Pitt's truculence and the Royal Navy in the Channel, Atlantic and North Sea.

In 1940 Hitler hoped that the British fleet could be kept away from the invasion area by his bombs, mines and torpedoes. 135 years earlier Napoleon, not possessed of such weaponry, thought his only strategy was to decoy it to distant waters long enough for his scattered fleets to rendezvous in the Channel and escort his armada across. For a year and a half he and his admirals attempted this geographically vast plan for uniting their fleets while dividing Britain's – frustrated by endless changes in wind and weather and successful responses by the Royal Navy. This inconclusive phase of the war – really a long game of manoeuvre – created a situation on the east (and south) coast of England which, again, resembled that of 1940. The invader was just over the horizon but never appeared. When bloody or dramatic events occurred it was almost always somewhere else. The war was more invisible threat than reality. People were unsure whether to be anxious, optimistic, or merely bored. Their government and commanders – not least Craig – worried about the possible demoralisation and lack of fighting spirit this uncertainty implied, and constantly cajoled them to be ready – psychologically as well as tactically.

In the autumn of 1804 Britain's isolation was brought to a (temporary) end by the alliance with Russia. The negotiators of this, Lord Leveson Gower and Sir John Warren, had been ferried between Harwich and St Petersburg by the *Amethyst* frigate. When Warren and his wife came back to Harwich on 4th December they were greeted by booming cannon and pealing church bells.[11]

The waiting game was finally brought to an end by the Battle of Trafalgar, the news of which reached eastern England on 7th November 1805. The bells of Norwich Cathedral and every other Norfolk church pealed in celebration of the sinking of half the combined Franco-Spanish fleet off Cadiz, then tolled to mourn the victorious Nelson's death. There was self-congratulation at Graham's shipyard, Harwich, when it was learned that the French admiral, Villeneuve, had been captured by HMS *Conqueror*, built there four years earlier. Also at Chigwell in Essex, home of Captain Eliab Harvey of the *Téméraire*, and at Catton near Norwich, home of Captain Berry of Nelson's old ship the *Agamemnon*. Both had distinguished themselves in the fight. A cutter rushed from Yarmouth to the Elbe with 3,000 copies of a special Government gazette quoting the victory despatches of Nelson's successor Collingwood. On the 17th the elite of Norwich attended a victory celebration at the Assembly Rooms, where brilliant lights shone through painted glass sheets to project images of the hero and his battle onto the walls. On 9th January 1806, the day of his funeral in London, the Norwich bells tolled for two hours, punctuated by gun salutes. Contingents from 79th and 92nd Highland Regiments at Weeley, the Scots Greys at Colchester, and 21st Light Dragoons from Woodbridge had gone up to London and joined the guard of honour. "No procession that has ever taken place in this country will equal the grandeur and pomp … displayed at the funeral of Lord Nelson" declared the *Ipswich Journal*. The publisher Boydell ran an art competition with a £500 prize for a painting to commemorate the late admiral, and through the *Journal* invited participants to submit their work to the region's bookshops. The winner was Arthur William Devis.[12]

There were victory celebrations at public buildings across the region, including the Assembly Rooms at Norwich.

Nelson's titles passed to his elder brother, a clergyman like his father. His widow Fanny was given £2000 a year from the Civil List. Emma and her little daughter Horatia got nothing. The wasteful Emma even spent some time in a debtor's prison. Some have judged this unjust, especially as the Admiral's last words included a request that they be looked after. Cold-shouldered by English society, ironically they went to live in France after Napoleon's first abdication. Emma died just before Waterloo. The teenage Horatia was adopted by her paternal aunts back in Norfolk, and later married the curate of Burnham Westgate – within two miles of her father's original home. The Nelson wheel had turned full circle.

A return to Norfolk – this stone in the chancel of Trunch church in Norfolk marks the resting place of Horatia, Nelson's daughter by Emma Hamilton.

Since he fought and died far from his native Norfolk, it would not be appropriate to say much more about that county's greatest son here. Few have ever doubted that his great and decisive victories were due to his willingness to attack, his calculated skill in doing so, and his imparting these to his subordinates. I will only venture the following.

First, Trafalgar was not in itself the event which saved England from invasion. Napoleon had already taken his army from Boulogne and was leading it eastwards against Austria and Russia. The enemy fleet wrecked by Nelson was not en route to England but the Mediterranean. Arguably another East Anglian, Admiral Sir William Cornwallis (brother of General Cornwallis) should have equal credit for having blockaded the largest French fleet, and the one best placed to support an invasion, in Brest harbour for the last two and half years. However once he had defeated his Continental enemies and turned his strategy back on Britain, Napoleon's naval losses at Trafalgar meant that, short of building a new fleet (which would take years) he could no longer even consider invasion.

Admiral Sir William Cornwallis, brother of General Charles Cornwallis.

Second, Nelson was not merely an apolitical naval officer, but one who saw himself as the sword of monarchy, aristocracy, established church, and class system. It was ironic that the Mayor of Norwich who half-heartedly led the city's Trafalgar celebrations was Dr Edward Rigby, the old radical of the French Revolution.[13] Certainly Nelson was not some sub-Burkean fanatic who feared and despised the masses, and Rigby had come round to believing in patriotically defending England against invasion, but their views cannot be equated. Although Nelson described himself as an "Old Whig", not a Tory, that faction had become just as fervently opposed to reform and keen on the war. We can appreciate that, as a serving officer, he could hardly have accepted the invitation Coke had sent him to come and celebrate the centenary of the 1688 Revolution at Holkham Hall, because he knew his host would be criticising the King.[14] But Nelson was more obsequious to all royalty (not just George III) than he needed to be, even when they were notorious fools and tyrants. Again, when he considered becoming government parliamentary candidate for Ipswich in 1796 there was nothing untoward. It was quite standard for army and naval officers to be MPs at this period – usually on the Government side – contrary to the modern expectation. (In the event Snape-Hammond, a member of the Navy Board, stood instead). But two years later Nelson went out of his way to aid the hated Bourbon king of Naples in his savage repression of liberals and democrats, for which some fellow officers as well as the New Whigs and radicals attacked him. The title "Duke of Bronte" was a reward for helping a brutal autocrat, not for a naval victory.

I cannot agree with the Nelson admirers who depict him as somehow transcending the political and social assumptions of the circles in which he moved – for instance, as an opponent of aristocratic privilege or a "champion of the lower deck".

Third, he hogged the limelight at the expense of fellow officers, both superiors and inferiors, in a way which can only be called small-minded and even sly. Some have attributed this to an immature craving for attention, or the social insecurity of a country parson's son surrounded by haughty aristocrats. When Sir John Moore saw him in the Mediterranean he thought him a shameless poseur. At their only meeting Wellington was appalled at his boastful monologue. St Vincent was one of several admirals to absent himself from his funeral.[15]

Of course neither Nelson's politics nor his character detract from his greatness and achievements as a warrior. He would most certainly not have been a better admiral had he agreed with Coke and Rigby, or been less personally ambitious – quite the contrary, since he believed in ruthless attack and glory, not cautious defence and modesty.

Finally, how justified is Norfolk in claiming him as one of its own? Obviously anyone who leaves home in pursuit of a career in distant places, and rarely returns, becomes at least partly an outsider. He spent only a few days in his native county after the outbreak of war in 1793, and his fleeting visits to East Anglia arose from his duties, not personal choice. His naval career owed little to his having been brought up within a stone's throw of the North Sea. He was steered into it by an uncle (Captain Maurice Suckling), whose own son also joined the Navy, initially on Nelson's *Agamemnon*, but showed little aptitude for it and ended up as a neglectful local Sea Fencible lieutenant. Nelson's abandonment of Fanny to live with Emma in Surrey was in itself a renunciation of Norfolk.

On the other hand, it cannot be claimed that Nelson was alien to that county because he and his known forbears had never tilled its soil or fished its sea. By origin he was as much a local man as any local farmer or fisherman. He was educated at Norwich and then at Sir William Paston's school at North Walsham, as was one of his protégées, William Hoste. He retained a Norfolk accent. His mother had been a Walpole – one of Norfolk's old gentry families. They, like much of the East Anglian upper crust (including Windham, Coke, the Cornwallises) had lived in the region longer than many of its middle-class intellectuals, such as the Rigbys and Martineaus. And the title he attached to

N.Spilman was quick off the mark in Yarmouth to produce an engraving, albeit it in a naïve style, of the victory off Cape Trafalgar. It is dated 17th November 1805. Doubtless he hoped to cash in on Nelson being a native of Norfolk.

his Nile baronetcy was "of Burnham Thorpe". So "Norfolk man" is largely apt.

Pitt recognised Trafalgar as a great victory and Nelson as a great commander, but, in his characteristic cool and rational fashion, refused to share in the popular belief that one man had eternally saved the country. In his last days he was preoccupied with Napoleon's second defeat of Austria and Russia. Bonaparte might not be crossing the North Sea or Channel but beyond them his military and political power was so great that he would not be defeatable for unknown years to come. And, with this dominance over the Continent, he would still be a danger to England.

On 25th January 1806, just a fortnight after the admiral's funeral, the *Ipswich Journal* announced (as usual in the middle of one of its long small-print columns):

"It is with the deepest regret that we have to pronounce the death of the Rt. Hon William Pitt, First Lord of the Treasury and Chancellor of the Exchequer … (he had) abilities of the most transcendent description…the purity of his principles was admitted by all. It is therefore impossible that such a man could have any personal enemies among those possessing genuine British hearts."

It explained that the late prime minister had been ill for some weeks, that his sufferings had "terminated in violent fever and water on the chest". He had, in all probability, died of liver failure brought on by drinking and stress. But the *Journal* had always admired him, and so admitted to feeling a "regret bordering on despondency". Not everyone agreed. The Welsh-born King's

Lynn radical dissenter William Richards thought that Pitt's reputation was bogus, that he had shown a "vindictive disposition", and that his "reign of terror was long and grievous".[16]

At this crossroads moment the British political scene again shifted. Windham joined the New Whigs Fox, Grey and Sheridan, and the Tory Addington (now called Lord Sidmouth), in the "Ministry of All The Talents" formed by Pitt's reform-minded cousin Lord Grenville. He became Secretary for War and the Colonies. For several years the opposition New Whigs had been voting with the Tory-Old Whig coalition on many bills, and Pitt himself had hoped to widen the government to include them. Nonetheless the atmosphere around the Cabinet table, between Fox, Addington and Windham in particular, must have been tense! One other East Anglian Whig MP, Thomas Creevey of Thetford, took the minor post of Secretary to the Board of Control. The majority of ministers were long-term advocates of parliamentary reform and "Catholic Relief", but the King was reassured that these policies were not on the agenda.

Thomas Coke sought no involvement, and soon had the sad duty of paying heartfelt personal tribute to Fox, who died after only six months in office. He declared that his old friend had been his reason for being in politics and was the great national leader who should have been. Nevertheless in the general election held that autumn he invited Windham, in the spirit of the new coalition, to stand with him for the two Norfolk county seats against the son of Coke's old Tory rival Sir John Wodehouse, who opposed Tories sharing power with "Foxites". Both were elected. Two Tory women from Norwich got up a petition to say this was through bribes, and early in 1807 the victors stepped down in favour of Coke's former election partner Astley and Coke's brother Edward. When the contest was then re-run Thomas Coke stood again with Astley, defeated Wodehouse, and sat till long after the war. Their supporters dressed up two dummies as prostitutes and paraded them through Norwich in reference to the two Tory petitioners. Windham again took a rotten borough outside the region. At Yarmouth another radical Whig, Dr Stephen Lushington, was also elected in 1806. Whiggism, with its dislike of the Crown, and belief in electoral reform and civil liberties, refused to lie down in Norfolk, for all the adulation many of its inhabitants had lavished on Pitt and Nelson. There was even a mild outbreak of it in Tory Ipswich: two Whigs were brought up from London (after an appeal in the newspapers there), and were only narrowly defeated by the sitting members.[17]

Although the new ministry was united in the defence of the country it did hold "talks about talks" with Napoleon, in the hope of another non-aggression pact like the one at Amiens. The Emperor freed Lord Yarmouth, former MP for Orford, from his long detention in France, and the Suffolk peer acted as intermediary between him and Fox. There was considerable publicity and hope for this mission, reflecting not so much a revulsion against bloodshed as a dislike of taxes and economic disruption. But by 1807 Yarmouth was back without success.[18]

Grenville and the 1806-7 parliament made one great reform, the abolition of the slave trade. This was not very controversial in eastern England, largely because, unlike the west, it was not commercially dependent on the Caribbean plantations. Thomas Clarkson, the second most famous anti-slavery campaigner after Wilberforce, was an East Anglian – born and brought up at

Wisbech, and later married and resided at Bury St Edmunds. It was his *Essay on the Slavery and Commerce of the Human Species* that had launched the issue into the public sphere back in 1785. Dissenter (especially Quaker) and radical opinion at Norwich and Yarmouth was wholly behind him, though he and Wilberforce were Anglicans and Tories. Like his mentor Fox so was T W Coke. Another ally was the Bury humanitarian magistrate Capel Lofft. The Colchester MP Thornton, though all over the place politically, was a devoted follower of Wilberforce. Captain F P Irby, whose father lived at Blofield Hall in the Norfolk Broads, and who had fought at Camperdown and then led the River Colne Sea Fencibles between 1805 and 1807, became a local hero when, as an Atlantic frigate captain, he captured Spanish and Portuguese slave ships and freed their "passengers". In May 1813 the Norwich newspapers reported that he had sent three of his liberated "African youths" to the city for their education, and that they had been baptised at St Peter Mancroft.[19]

The slave trade's one vocal defender in the region was Admiral Earl St Vincent, who went from Brentwood to the House of Lords to argue that Britain's economy and therefore ability to fight the war were fundamentally dependent on the supply of cheap and captive labour in our colonies.

I should add that the Government did not share Clarkson and Wilberforce's intention of abolishing colonial slavery itself – only the traffic in slaves. This went some way to answering the St Vincent objection.

The "Talents" had but a brief spell in power, because when Grenville pressed the King to allow Catholics to be army officers he rejected the idea, which led to the cabinet's resignation and the general election of May 1807. The King then entrusted the government to the solidly Protestant and illiberal "Old Whig" Portland. No East Anglians held office in his administration, though, as usual, many old faces remained on the back benches, such as General Fitzroy at Bury, Sir John Hippesley at Sudbury, and Sir Thomas Bunbury in Suffolk. Absentee members, who lived elsewhere and hardly ever visited their constituencies, abounded. This was most evident at Eye, whose two so-called representatives were the Marquess of Huntly (from north-eastern Scotland) and Lt-Gen Sir Arthur Wellesley's brother Henry, who had been elected for a seat in his native Ireland at the same time! Rear-Admiral Sir Home Popham, previously one of the Yarmouth MPs, now shared Ipswich with one of the Crickitt banking family, who had long represented it. Popham, still only 44, had had a chequered naval career, among other achievements inventing the Sea Fencibles and the Navy's signal code, but also commanding an expedition to South America in 1806 which had ended in defeat. He had gone back and forth between Harwich and St Petersburg arranging the movement of the Russian ships involved in the Texel Expedition. The Liverpool Pittite-Tory merchant William Huskisson was elected at Harwich and became a Treasury Lord. He was befriended by the port's resident naval officer and sometime mayor, John Hopkins, but disliked by other local worthies because of his disdain for the sort of state-monopoly and uncompetitive economic interests by which they lived.[20]

Dockyards & Shipyards   13

Contrary to Pitt and Dundas's claims, in 1804 Addington and St Vincent had already ordered additional sloops, gun brigs and schooners from private East Anglian firms, some of which had not worked for the Admiralty before. And more contracts followed. The main local yards to benefit were Thomas & Josiah Brindleys' (Lynn), Nathaniel Palmer's, John Preston's, and Parsons Custance & Isaac Stone (Yarmouth), Jabez Bailey's (Ipswich), James Betts (Mistleythorn), Joseph Graham's (Harwich) and Matthew Warren's (Brightlingsea). In 1812 Edward Larking & William Spong, and from 1814 William Bottomley also built at Lynn.[1]

These builders generally had two slips each and therefore worked on two ships at a time. Fitting out was done at Chatham. Their workforces were surprisingly small by 20th century standards: around 50 for two-slip firms. They were "protected" against the press gangs.

Their small warships were fast, shallow-draft and manoeuvrable, better able to get at invaders coming inshore than larger vessels. It turned out that they were not needed to repel invasion, but in the coming years they hunted privateers, raided the enemy's coast and helped ensure an ever-tighter blockade of his naval and merchant shipping.

Of their various productions the schooners were the smallest and least effective. They had, by definition, fore-and-aft sails on two masts, with one small square sail mounted crossways on the upper foremast. Only 56-foot, 75-ton, four-gun, and 20-man, they were very manoeuvrable, but thought too small for ocean voyaging. Six were built at Yarmouth in 1806 – four by Custance & Stone and one each by Crane & Holmes and James Lovewell.

Most of the gun brigs were *Archer* class, 80 feet long, 177 tons, 12 guns, 50 crew. Their shallow draft made them roll sickeningly in even moderate seas. By 1806 the *Cruizer* class sloops were more prominent – 96 feet, 382 tons, 18 guns, 121 crew. Both were existing standard designs from the Surveyor of the Navy, Sir William Rule. The original *Cruizer* has already often cropped up in this narrative as a very successful anti-privateering vessel. She had been built by Teague's yard at Ipswich in 1797. Another class of Rule sloops, the *Cherokees*, was introduced in 1808. Smaller than the *Cruizers*, they were to be so vulnerable to bad weather that they earned the nickname "coffin ships". The guns on both types were short-barrelled (short-range) 18-pdr carronades.

In civilian usage a brig was a small ship with square sails on two masts, and a sloop a faster, more manoeuvrable, craft with fore and aft triangular sails on a single mast (resembling a yacht). However the gun brig and sloop of war differed only in size and number of guns. Each had one gun deck, all her square sails on two masts, two triangular sails forward secured to the bowsprit, and a triangular aft steering sail on a boom. The *Cruizers* are sometimes termed "brig-sloops", but were usually called "sloops of war" in their logs and other contemporary documents. The next size of warship up, the frigate, differed from both in having three masts. Above that the ship of the line (1st to 4th rates) also had three masts, but guns on two or three decks. The gun brigs differed from the more lightly-armed gun vessels, some of which had hitherto defended the Essex rivers. These were small captured French craft of miscellaneous sorts.

The gun brigs standardly cost £6,800, and the sloops £7,200. Just under half the money went to the builders, the rest was spent directly by the Navy on guns, stores and fittings.

Most of the sloops and gun brigs had the standard elm bottoms (plated with copper against worms and barnacles), oak beams, decks and sides, and fir masts, but some were all-fir, scorned as "pasteboard" by fussier captains. Most of the oak and fir came from the Baltic, though Arthur Young supplied some of the former from his Suffolk property.

Small though these ships were, their adventures spanned the globe.

Matthew Warren at Brightlingsea launched his first Admiralty contract, the Archers *Sparkler* and *Tickler*, within two days in August 1804. *Tickler* was captured by Danish gunboats in the Baltic after a heroic four-hour resistance in 1807. *Sparkler* was wrecked off the Dutch Frisian island of Terschelling in 1808, with most of her crew taken prisoner. His *Kite* and *Raven* were 282-ton, 16-gun sloops, from a rare class intermediate between the Archers and Cruizers, and not designed by Rule. *Kite* captured one of the notorious Fourmentin privateer brothers in the Dover Strait in 1807. Six years later half her crew were killed or injured when they landed on the Macedonian coast and were pelted with rocks from the cliffs above. *Raven*, serving at the Downs, daringly reconnoitred the enemy fleet in the Scheldt in 1812, notwithstanding her having a First Lieutenant who was so "deranged" (to quote his captain) the purser protested to the Admiralty on behalf of the crew.

Warren was a London trader, and ship and insurance broker, who had a country house at Ingatestone called Furze Hall. Till 1806 he was still in partnership in London with one Fielder Jenkins. He started building ships for the merchant service at Brightlingsea in 1797, having bought out the bankrupt Philip Sainty, who after the war built yachts for the Earl of Uxbridge and Anglesey (the former General Paget), and settled at Wivenhoe. His Brightlingsea yard was on the site of the subsequent Aldous's. He also took over Sainty's "New House" (nowadays the *Brewer's Arms* pub) in the main street. His shipwrights seem mostly to have come with him from Rotherhithe and Deptford on the Thames, and may have lived in three cottages which he owned in the town. After his bankruptcy in 1811 he had no more local connection.[2]

Betts at Mistley can be traced back to at least 1778, when he is recorded ordering iron bolts from a foundry in Scotland, probably for his frigate *Terpsichore*. His most celebrated man of war was the 32-gun frigate *Amphion*, launched in 1798 to replace one of the same name which had recently blown up at Plymouth. She took Nelson out to the Mediterranean when he took command there in 1803. Later, as flagship of his one-time protégé

William Hoste, she sank and captured ship after ship off Portugal and later in the Adriatic. Betts' sloop *Clio*, based mainly on Leith, captured an almost unrivalled number of Danish ships and raided the Danish Faroe Islands. During the 1812-15 war with America his *Raccoon* sloop ventured all the way to the Canadian Pacific coast to capture the famous fur-trading post set up there by Astor of New York. Betts went bankrupt in 1809, and his assets were sold off at the *Thorn Inn*.

Betts was also the name of Warren's foreman, but he came from Rotherhithe, and not Mistley.

The *Thorn* inn at Mistley continues to serve the town.

The largest East Anglian building yard was Joseph Graham's, which shared a site with the Admiralty repair yard at Harwich. He had built for the Navy before the war, and been visited by Arthur Young and his French guest de Liancourt during one of their tours of local businesses. His first ship in this new conflict was the 32-gun frigate *Alcmene* (1794), followed by the gun brigs *Beaver* and *Busy* (1795 and 1797), and the frigate *Ethalion* (also 1797). He then spent a controversial four years on the 74-gun ship of the line *Conqueror*, launched in 1801 and prominent at Trafalgar. His *Fearless* sloop (1804) took part in the second Copenhagen raid and was wrecked on the coast of West Africa five years later.

By 1805 Graham was £5,000 in the red and, pleading more delays, tried unsuccessfully to renegotiate his contract for the *Undaunted* frigate, which lay incomplete on the stocks. The Admiralty took the work away from him and she was towed to Chatham and finished there. He had no more naval work till given the 3rd rate *Vengeur* in 1810. The ups and downs of his business did not disturb his position in the town's tiny ruling group: he was a local magistrate and many times mayor right up to his death, which took place at his yard in 1814.[3]

Jabez Bailey built at the "Upper Yard, Stoke", on the opposite bank of the Orwell from Ipswich proper just below the bridge. He was highly regarded by the Admiralty, who continued to order from him after most of the other local yards ceased to be given contracts. He was proud to make maximum use of Suffolk oak, which he claimed to be immune from dry rot.

His ships were often in the news. He built the region's only four Cherokees. His *Sappho* sloop won considerable fame for taking a Danish privateer off the Yorkshire coast in 1808, and was later in action against American shipping off Florida. His *Imogen* sloop captured many enemy merchantmen in the North Sea and Mediterranean. His *Hearty* gun brig took a Danish gunboat in the Baltic in 1812. Early in 1813 two more of his sloops pursued the American *Hornet*, a ship equivalent to their own, off the Demerara River, Guiana. While his *Espiegle* stood idly by his *Peacock* was sunk in a fierce action. The former's crew included a young Lt Maryatt, the future author. Bailey's *Favourite* sloop, after serving in the western English Channel and liaising with the Galician junta in Spain, carried the British ratification of the 1814 Anglo-American peace treaty to the USA. Towards the end of the war, after a long run of sloops, Bailey launched two of the small 6th-rate frigates sometimes known as "post-ships". Rather ironically he was bankrupted after peace returned.[4]

There had been no warship building at Yarmouth in the Revolutionary, as opposed to Napoleonic, War, but it then took off in a major way.

The original Yarmouth yards all seem to have been on the South Quay, immediately below the town and on the same bank of the River Yare, but by the end of the war others had appeared opposite at Southtown. John Preston lived on the corner of the Quay and Friar's Lane. His father Jacob had run the business, built some large merchant ships before him, and was still an alderman and sometimes mayor. Other brothers were local ship owners. They were from an old-established Norfolk (and before that Suffolk) family with some titled forbears. It was Preston who launched the first men of war built at Yarmouth for at least a century – the *Helena* sloop in May 1804 and the gun brig *Mosquito* in September.[5] *Mosquito* was most active capturing enemy privateers and merchantmen in the North Sea. His *Exertion* gun brig, disguised under a Danish flag, hunted down the third of the North Sea *Jena* privateers in 1808. His sloops, most of which were initially based at Yarmouth, were also notable. *Pandora* was wrecked off Gothenburg in 1811, with all her crew either dead or taken by the Danes. *Hyacinth* took numerous enemy vessels off Holland and later southern Spain.

Nathaniel Palmer, who lived in Middlegate Street, was a brother of the major ship owner John D Palmer. The Palmers were equal in local prestige and influence to the Prestons, in spite of being Congregationalist Whigs in two minds about the war. Nathaniel was only a naval shipbuilder for a short time, however. He launched the *Cygnet* and *Aerial* sloops in 1804 and 1806 – the first was lost in the Caribbean, the second survived the war.

Custance & Stone, a longer-lasting Yarmouth firm, are something of a mystery. Parsons Custance was a surgeon who had lived next to the Market Place, and died there in the 1780s. His presumed son was a mariner according to the 1796 and 1807 voting lists. Isaac Stone was a shipwright. Between 1805 and 1807 their Southtown yard was successively called Stone & Cox, Stone & Custance, and Custance & Stone. In spite of the subsequent bankruptcy of these last two, Stone seems to have continued in (civilian) shipbuilding. He was a guest at the 1814 victory celebration dinner, but not Custance, possibly because he had just enlisted as a master (mate) in the Navy. A year later Stone was living at Aldeburgh and married a woman from Gorleston. Shortly after that he may have been one of those charged for attacking HMS *Cadmus's* press gang in the Yare – along with several other men with the same surname. After the war he still voted at Yarmouth, but lived in London.

This firm's small frigate *Boreas*, which had recently been rearmed with heavier guns, was sunk on the Guernsey rocks with most of her crew in 1807. The following year their *Comus* sloop boldly seized several Spanish merchantmen from inside Gran Canaria harbour. On the south-west coast of Italy their *Cephalus* sloop captured or destroyed a great number of small vessels from the navy of Napoleon's brother-in-law, Joachim Murat, King of Naples. In 1813 several of her crew were tried, and one hanged, for planning to desert her in a French ship they had taken.

Of the little Yarmouth schooners built by Custance's, and by Lovewell's, two, the *Woodcock* and the *Wagtail*, were wrecked by the same storm in the Azores in 1807. No more were built after 1806, at least at Yarmouth.

Brindleys', at King's Lynn, was a relatively large and old-established concern with a second yard on the Medway, where they had built the *Shannon* frigate which later became famous for her capture of the American *Chesapeake*. Their first Lynn man of war, the gun brig *Tigress*, had been launched in 1797. They were not related to the famous canal builder of the same name, nor (contrary to local belief) to Admiral Nelson. Like Bailey at Ipswich their yard went bankrupt in the 1820s, and Thomas later emigrated to America.

Their *Minorca* sloop was active combating Spanish privateers off Southern Spain between 1805 and 1808, and thereafter French ones off Italy. Their *Zenobia* sloop captured numerous American ships off Portugal during the 1812-15 war with the USA. Their *Kangaroo* took part in the Walcheren campaign, where she briefly flew Admiral Strachan's flag. After the war she was for many years an Essex customs vessel, and survived so long that Victorian photographs exist of her mastless hull laid up on the mud.

Some of the builders were also merchant ship owners, operating vessels they themselves had constructed. This was true of Preston's at Yarmouth, who owned ten or eleven such ships. Graham's, Bailey's and Brindley's each owned one – Brindley's switched theirs from the London run to Lynn-Chatham, probably to ferry materials and workers up from their other yard on the Medway. Warren owned four, which he had built at Brightlingsea before his naval contract: three of them plied between London and the Iberian Peninsula.[6]

In addition to the shipyards employed by the Admiralty, there were many others building merchant ships to replace those lost to privateers, storms, and age. Big and enthusiastic crowds attended their launchings. Such was the excitement at Cattermoule's Yard, Thorpe, Norwich, in 1803 that a hundred spectators climbed onto a new brig and capsized her: all were pulled out of the water but one young girl had drowned.[7] Other East Anglian firms building wartime merchantmen included Stuttle's at Colchester, Prentice's at Ipswich, various Preston brothers, Douglas and Chamberlain at Yarmouth, and Mark Watson and Joseph Wales at Lynn.

Meanwhile a little on the shore activity of the Navy.

Harwich already had a 150-year history as a subsidiary naval "base", or "outport", not in the sense that it had a Port Admiral or naval barracks, but because its great harbour offered a safe anchorage for warships operating off the Naze-Orfordness coast and because of its naval repair and fitting-out dockyard, located at the north-easternmost tip of Essex. The wooden treadwheel crane which today stands on Harwich Green was still inside the yard and in use in the early 1800s, in spite of dating from 1667. There was only one shore-based Admiralty official at Harwich – for the whole Napoleonic phase of the war John Hopkins, a local civilian who was in charge of work on the ships, finance, supplies, and medical matters! His office staff consisted of a single civilian clerk. Hopkins was also repeatedly mayor of Harwich and captained its Volunteer company. His naval store yard, separate from the shipyard, fronted the harbour between Church and Kings Head Streets, next to today's Trinity House offices.[8]

At Yarmouth, the other East Anglian naval base, John Day was the "Naval Officer" in charge of the dockyards, and Robert Warmington, the packet boats agent in the Revolutionary War, and twice mayor, managed the pay and stores. Thomas Alldridge, a local shipping agent, acted as clerk – and effectively civilian liaison officer – for the Port Admiral, who, though he had a flagship, mainly lived onshore[9].

There were also officials based inland, with such titles as "Vice-Admiral of Essex[*]". These were not in fact serving naval officers, but administered the Admiralty's legal affairs in the counties concerned.

---

[*] The word "vice" here means "instead of", not "second-in-rank to".

Privateering & Blockading   14

Given France's inability to invade Great Britain, her strategy was still more economic than anything else. The *lettres de marque* now issued from Paris were no longer headed with the idealistic ideological slogans of 1793, but gave their purchasers the same authority to pirate British commerce. Napoleon's privateers – ships and crews – were the same as the Republic's, and used the same tactics.

On 1st July 1803 Lloyd's Insurers announced : "It is reported that several colliers have been taken by privateers between Lynn and the Humber and carried into Ostend". On 7th October the *Constance* gun brig made the first capture of a French east coast privateer, the little 16-man *Caroline*, and took her into Yarmouth.[1]

On 4th November the coal brig *Economy* was bringing a cargo from South Shields to her home port at Woodbridge in Suffolk when another small cutter privateer seized her off Cromer. The same day she was retaken by two pilot boats from Lowestoft, which had been guiding ships through the local shoals, and next day sailed into Yarmouth with five French prisoners.[2] On the 16th the 6th-rate *Circe* chased a French privateer across the sandbanks off Cromer, but grounded and tore off her rudder. She became a wreck, though local fishing boats rescued her crew and took them back to her Yarmouth station. Then the *Censor* gun brig brought a London collier into Yarmouth Roads, together with the news that she and four other merchantmen had just been captured by the famous Dunkirk privateer captain Blanckeman, back in action since the Amiens Treaty and his repatriation. A few days later two more French privateers were seen from the Suffolk coast and two warships left Lowestoft Roads in pursuit. That night the *Monkey* gun brig recaptured the merchantman *Orford* off Orfordness and took her into Yarmouth.[3]

On 11th and 12th December 1803 two small ships were seen hovering off Lowestoft. Lt Thomas Bean declined to take the *Censor* out to them, but off Southwold Matthew Gunthorpe boarded one from his revenue cutter *Badger*. She turned out to be the Dunkirk privateer *Vigilant*, crewed by Capitaine Vanderwall and 32 men. Bean was reprimanded by Russell for his inactivity, after Gunthorpe had reported him. He protested: "My character is very much abused and the account being entirely false I beg you would be pleased to request their Lordships to order an inquiry".[4] Meanwhile, further south, about 20 miles off Orfordness, another gun brig, the *Vixen*, found and captured the second intruder, the Dunkirk privateer *La Lyonnaie*, with Capitaine Jean Foley and 20 crew. The same day a captured British merchantman, the *Dutton*, came close to shore at Happisburgh. The nearby Winterton Sea Fencibles manned their boats and retook her and her six-man prize crew. Most of the prisoners from the three vessels were detained at Yarmouth (the first such prisoners of the Napoleonic half of the war), and later sent to Norman Cross, but Vanderwall and the *Dutton* prize master somehow escaped. Once again it was evident that the enemy privateering was as much an international mercenary activity as a French naval strategy. On the 23rd 21 of the Yarmouth prisoners volunteered to join the Royal Navy – 12 Swedes, six Russians, one Pole, one Dane and one Portuguese.[5]

The year ended with letters of protest reaching the Admiralty from east coast merchants and ship owners about the privateering "depradations" between the Wash and Yarmouth. In March 1804 Russell stepped up the protection patrol from two to four gun brigs: *Ferriter* for the Suffolk coast, *Snipe* for the Norfolk coast inshore route, *Vixen* from Burnham Flat to the Haisborough Sands, and *Censor* from there back to Yarmouth.[6] They were, however, having to keep an eye on scores of ships at the same time, scattered along a 100 mile stretch, including in darkness and fog, when visibility might be down to a few yards. On 5th May a Hull-bound ship was hailed by a French privateer in Yarmouth Roads itself – the base for all four of the aforementioned gun brigs and for Russell's own main force! But occasionally the privateers came unstuck. On 16th November the Newcastle coal brig *Eve* sailed into Yarmouth. Her five occupants told an unusual story. They had been put on board as a prize crew by a French privateer, but two of them (Americans) had overpowered the other three (Frenchmen), and decided they would steer for England.[7] Whether their motive was political, mercenary, or just dislike of their French crewmates, was not recorded.

Two days later 2,000 people lined the jetty and beach at Yarmouth. The word had spread that the Navy had pulled off an important capture and was about to land a famous prisoner. Recently raiders had been off the Tyne, and merchantmen had gone missing at a rapid rate. Ashore – for the second time during the war – stepped the legendary Dunkirk corsair Étienne Jean Blanckeman, guarded by men from the familiar and almost equally famous *Cruizer* sloop.

At 9pm on 17th November, while on her usual anti-invasion patrol off the Flanders coast, *Cruizer* had sighted an enemy armed lugger headed south. The wind was east-north-easterly, so both ships sailed parallel with the shore. *Cruizer* was already the most accomplished privateer hunter, and refused to be shaken off. She chased all night and for nearly 100 miles. The wind became a gale, and tore away several of the lugger's yards and sails. At 4am she suddenly furled her remaining sails and anchored, apparently in the hope that her pursuer would overshoot and be unable to turn back into the contrary wind. However the British ship got close enough to hail, whereupon a voice unconvincingly replied in poor English that he was from Philadelphia. At 7am Hancock, *Cruizer*'s captain, readied his guns, fired three shots over the lugger, and hailed again. This time her flags were seen to fall, and French shouts of surrender and cheering from British prisoners in her hold could be heard. Hancock had already guessed his enemy's identity, and when he boarded and rounded up her crew he was not disappointed. The ship was the privateer *Contre-Amiral Magon*, sailing from Ostend, and her captain the celebrated Blanckeman. The *Cruizer* towed her to Yarmouth Roads.

The seizure of *Le Contre-Amiral Magon* by the *Cruizer* off East Anglia was of sufficient popularity for it to be engraved on this tobacco box alongside an image of the action betweeen HMS *Victory* and the *Santissima Trindad* at the battle of Trafalgar.

Her prisoners numbered 67. Two-thirds had Dutch or Flemish names. They included an army officer and civilian clerk who had been along for the ride. As usual each name was neatly recorded in the Tolhouse prison book, but the scribe allowed himself the luxury of writing Blanckeman's name in red ink. The captain was then rowed to the *Monmouth*, officially because his name was Dutch, and Dutch prisoners were held separately – though many Dunkirkers had such names and he was a native of the town. Later he was moved to Chatham. Some of his captors protested that this had been a trivial act of spite. His second-in-command, Nicholas Brandt, went to Wales on parole. The other prisoners were marched by Fifeshire Militia via Norwich to Norman Cross.

The captured ship had been built at Dunkirk two months earlier at the yard owned by Blanckeman's brother, and had been funded jointly by him, the captain, and local merchants. Étienne had insisted that only the best oak be used in her construction, and had sent 200 miles to buy it. He had intended to carry a huge crew of 200, including experienced sailors from Holland, but decided to set sail with only 84 (some allegedly recruited from gaol) so as to catch a convoy due to leave north-east England for the Thames. He had taken three ships close to the Tyne, and put 19 of his men onto them, but two had been recaptured: the third, the *Belisarius*, was to reach Dunkirk.

The captors and captives spoke kindly of each other. The privateers said they despised Napoleon and normally spoke in English instead of French. Their captain was described by the British press as courteous and chivalrous, and as a masterly sailor who "took every vessel by trick and finesse" rather than force. His tactics were already famous among the seafarers of both France and England. He knew every mile of the English east coast from pre-war fishing, but it was said that his instinct for deception had originated from his other one-time career as an actor at the Dunkirk theatre. He disguised his ships as British colliers by staining their sails black and following them down the coast as if en route for London. However he avoided taking coal-carriers, because they were slow and took too many men to sail, concentrating instead on smaller, faster, craft that were likely to hold more valuable and portable goods. He used to boast that with a fishing boat costing £600 he could capture merchant ships worth £6,000. He had been, in the words of a French writer, "the terror of London's commerce". He had taken 34 ships in the previous war (till captured on the *Anachreon*), and 40 in the present one. Napoleon had awarded him the Légion d'Honneur, while Lloyd's of London had put a prize of £1,000 on his head.[8]

The *Contre-Amiral Magon* was named after the French admiral who, as Villeneuve's second-in-command, was himself captured at Trafalgar a year later. A week after reaching Yarmouth she was driven onto the beach and swamped by another gale, but was eventually brought into Palmer's Yard.

The capture of Blanckeman did not stop commerce-raiding off the east coast. On 29th January 1805 the Dutch small privateer *Vlieg* and her collier prize were brought into Yarmouth. On 2nd March, as she sailed along the Norfolk coast, the coal brig *Sea Dog* was attacked by a lugger privateer. Rather than face a French prison, her crew scrambled into their boat and rowed to shore at Winterton. Three weeks later the *Charger* gun-brig brought the small Flushing-based raiding cutter *De Zenno* into Hollesley Bay. On 12th May the Yarmouth-based *Mosquito* brought back the French privateers *Orestes* and

Pylades, which she had boarded off Yorkshire, along with 54 prisoners.

The Yarmouth Navy also came across some regular enemy warships. On 27th April 1805 Captain Cartaret's sloop *Scorpion* brought in the Dutch "armed ship" *L'Honneur* from off Scheveningen. One of the prisoners turned out to be Jean de Saint Faust, a French naval captain who had been given the Légion d'Honneur for beating off an attack by a British frigate, and was en route to Curacoa in the Caribbean to command the Dutch naval force there. Since he had sailed from Delfzyl, in north-eastern Holland, his intended route must have been the risky one via the Dover Strait.

The privateers still came audaciously near the coast on occasion. On 24th October 1805 a Yarmouth fishing boat was taken near Orfordness. The *Forward* gun brig left Yarmouth Roads in pursuit after the news had reached her via the coastal signal chain, but Admiral Douglas stopped her because Keith had told him to gather up all spare ships to escort the expedition about to sail from the Downs to north-west Germany. At the very same moment Lt King reported from the Gunton signal station that the same, or another, privateer had just seized a merchant brig coming in to Lowestoft. "I am not able to send anything in chase of her", Douglas signalled back. On 7th February 1806 the merchantman *Silva* came into Harwich and reported that an enemy privateer had just taken no fewer than ten ships near the Kentish Knock, 30 miles from that harbour but only ten from the Kent coast. A week later this raider appears to have come closer, because four more merchantman were seized while passing the Essex port. Within a few days Yarmouth port had three of its own trading ships taken, two in the same area.[9] And on the 18th the London-based cargo brig *Polly* was found empty and drifting down the Swin, 20 miles to the south and within sight of the River Crouch: her crew had been taken off by a privateer who may have abandoned her because a British man-of-war approached.

However the most celebrated Yarmouth Roads event of this period involved a regular French man of war, not a privateer. 26th July 1806 marked the arrival of the British frigate *Blanche* and the fast and powerful 50-gun French frigate *Le Guerrière*, which she had captured one week before as far away as the Faroe Islands. The Frenchman had sailed into the Atlantic on a raiding cruise, and gone that far north in order to capture British whaling ships bound for Greenland. 20 Frenchmen had been killed and 30 wounded, compared to only five wounded on the *Blanche*, in their 45 minute gun duel. An unprecedented 297 prisoners were sent up to Chatham, since Norman Cross had been full for some time.[10] Incidentally it was from Chatham that five captives had made a daring escape the previous January. After three months confinement Captains de Tarie and Vautier and three other Dunkirk privateer men had trekked along the coast, stolen an oyster smack near Harwich, and got across to Blankenberg. But there a gale had capsized their craft and drowned the two captains. How exactly they had crossed the Medway and Thames to Essex, and exactly where they found their escape boat, are unknown.[11]

1807 was another year of successes against privateers for the Yarmouth Roads men-of-war. Just eight days into the New Year the famous *Cruizer*, now captained by P. Stoddart, captured another "remarkably fast" raider, the *Jena*, which had been operating off Flamborough Head and had taken three stragglers from a Baltic convoy, one of them the Yarmouth ship *Felicity*. Within a fortnight she confronted another privateer, *Le Brave*, drove her ashore on

Blankenberg beach east of Ostend, and liberated her two prizes. Among naval gentlemen the *Cruizer*'s fine reputation was somewhat marred when it came to light that men she had put aboard one of these recaptures had beaten up a Frenchman. One of her crew was held responsible and whipped round the fleet back at Yarmouth – a grim punishment.[12] As ever, there was repetition and room for confusion with privateer names: two more *Jenas* were brought into Yarmouth that year, one just three weeks after the first. They were named after Napoleon's great victory over Prussia the previous autumn.

In August 1807 three ships, two of them bound from Riga in Russia to English Channel ports, were captured by an 11-gun privateer near Longsand Head, off Harwich.

What made the encounter between French privateer and English ship on 19th September a bloody one when 100 others had involved only a few token shots is unclear. The privateer was *L'Étoile* ("the Star"), captained by the most famous of the Boulogne Fourmentin brothers, Jacques-Oudard, the so-called "Baron de Bucaille". The Englishman was the veteran Harwich revenue cutter *Argus*, commanded by John Turner. *L'Étoile* had left Ostend on the 9th, captured the merchantman *Endeavour of Arundel* near the Galloper light (off Orfordness) on the evening of the 18th, and then had her prize snatched back by the *Argus* on the morning of the 19th. That evening Fourmentin caught up with the revenue cutter. For half an hour the two vessels battered each other with cannon. Then, since he had less firepower but more men, the famous corsair rammed and boarded his opponent. The first officer to jump across was pushed off, and for a while the French were held off by Englishmen firing muskets from their higher deck, but then the attackers swarmed on board shouting "Vive l'Émpereur!" (at least according to Napoleon's official newspaper *Le Moniteur*), brandishing cutlasses and pistols. For another quarter of an hour there was a savage hand-to-hand battle. Seven of the *Argus*'s crew were killed, and six wounded – one of them the captain, who took a pistol ball in the arm. Two Frenchmen died and four were injured. Both ships had been badly battered and before she could be taken in hand the revenue cutter sank, taking four more privateers and one more Englishman to their deaths. The captives ended up in a prison at Arras. They included Ipswich man Edward Catchpole, brother of the celebrated criminal and prison-escaper Margaret Catchpole.[13]

Fourmentin, another recipient of the Légion d'Honneur, as well as his "Chevalier de l'Émpire" title of "Baron", was the most successful privateer of all, claiming a total of 99 prizes. Just seven weeks later he was himself captured off the North Foreland on another vessel. He told his captors that *Argus*'s captain was alive but had had the arm amputated.. In fact Turner had died, as his widow at Harwich is on record as receiving a pension from the Revenue.

Three days after this celebrated event, far to the north in the heart of the North Sea, another privateer called *La Décidé* fell victim to the Yarmouth-based (and one-time French) frigate *L'Aimable*. A "beautiful large lugger" (according to Captain Lord George Stuart's report), she had been notorious at east coast ports for three years, and had taken 30 ships – the last being the *Mary*, which had been transporting artillerymen and their horses for the British campaign then being waged in Denmark. It was also *L'Aimable* which captured the French naval corvette *Joste* in February 1809, along with

Jacques-Oudard Fourmentin of the privateer *L'Étoile* in old age. He ranks as the most successful North Sea corsair of the war.

her 200 crew, cargo of flour for the French garrison on the West Indian island of Martinique, and chest of silver coin.

Yet for every capture of a privateer or recapture of one of their prizes many got back safely to port. In all waters enemy privateers were still taking between 400 and 600 ships a year throughout the years 1804-1812 – much less than the peak number of 949 taken in 1797 (during the previous war), but still costly for owners and insurers. In 1807 Vice-Admiral Russell assured the Admiralty that he was doing his utmost, but the following year Lloyd's Coffee House (as the famous London insurers still called themselves) publicly protested that:

> "The successful predatory excursions of the French privateers are not restricted by the vigilance and activity which might be expected from the Admiralty".[14]

But the merchant shipping war was far from one-sided, because meanwhile the Yarmouth and Thames Estuary men-of-war had been continuously intercepting enemy and suspect cargo craft. Some were Dutch, usually bound for Amsterdam from Norwegian or Baltic ports, occasionally from Holland's far-distant tropical colonies. They and their cargoes could be seized and "condemned" outright. Complete ships, with contents, were auctioned at Yarmouth. This was welcome to the townsfolk. In one auction, on 30th September 1803, they were offered the following, seized by Rear-Admiral Thornborough's squadron:

> "70 casks of genoa oil, 177 barrels of American rice, 10 Parmesan cheeses, 1600 Edam cheeses, 30 Gouda cheeses, 35 barrels of raisins, 50 logs of pearl barley …"[15]

At first, hoping to enlist major neutrals to their cause, the British were restrained in intercepting their trade with the enemy. In November 1803 the Admiralty told Rear-Admiral Russell to allow a convoy of 30 Russian and Prussian merchantmen to pass through the North Sea to France, even though they were carrying contraband for Napoleon's fleet. But Prussia could not be won over. By 1805 her trade with the enemy was becoming intolerable. The Yarmouth squadron was ordered to take a tougher line with merchantmen flying her "colours". The problem was "the prostitution of neutral flags", wrote Yarmouth author John Brown in 1805, continuing:

> "Both hemispheres resound with reiterated and aggravated charges against England, for being the tyrant of the seas, and the oppressor of neutral commerce; and half the world credits the accusation, little thinking that England, formidable everywhere, and on the ocean irresistible, is passively suffering the main pillars of her might to be undermined, and her arm rendered nerveless, for the wont of a vigorous exertion of her naval preponderance in curbing the unlawful traffic of neutrals … Every (enemy) creek is choked with armaments insolently menacing the extinction of the British Empire … Whence came the materials and stores (for) these enormous fleets and flotillas but from the boundless violation of maritime neutrality?"[16]

In addition to her main territories on the Baltic, Prussia ruled the North Sea district of Ostfriesland (East Frisia), or Papenburg, lying between the estuaries of the Ems and Weser on the North Sea and next to French-controlled Holland. Papenburg – especially Emden – ships were bringing contraband under their neutral flag back to their home waters, then taking it along the Wadden See (between the Frisian Islands and the Dutch mainland) to enemy Amsterdam.

Brown also claimed that "neutralization" of enemy merchantmen was an industry between Emden and Hamburg, employing, it was said, over 100 companies which hired ships to carry contraband and supplied them with Prussian papers. At Leer they were financed by a prominent Berlin banker, with whom they split their profits. They bribed the local magistrates to turn a blind eye. Brown avoided alleging that the Prussian government colluded in this, but implied it.

His main source of information was the veteran captain of the Yarmouth-based revenue cutter *Hunter*, Thomas Riches, who had a personal grudge against the Papenburg-Prussia neutralisers. In October 1805 Riches seized the Dutch merchantman *Sara Cornelia*, and put three of his men on board to bring her into his home port. En route the Dutchmen he had left on the prize overpowered the Revenue men and took them back to Holland. Riches had taken one Jan Kalle and three more Dutchmen with him on the *Hunter*. Kalle swore that he was a Prussian national, and that his ship was registered at Emden. In any case she carried no contraband. So an English Admiralty court ruled that he had to send her back along with his prisoners. Riches complied, but wrote an angry protest to the Dutch authorities claiming that Kalle was really one of their compatriots, and would be detained until his missing crewmen were brought to Yarmouth. After stopping two more "Prussian fishing vessels", with "the papers to prove it", he claimed to have found that both their owner and crews were really Dutchmen.

Relations between the two countries finally broke down when Napoleon persuaded King Frederick William to take over Hanover from him in return for closing his ports to British trade. In April 1806 the "All the Talents" government fiercely responded. All Prussian merchant ships in British waters were detained. Fifteen, mostly carrying coffee or sugar, were seized at Harwich on 15th April. More were boarded in Hollesley Bay by the gun brigs *Aggressor* and *Boxer*. Seventeen were brought into Yarmouth from the open sea in June – and eventually a total of eighty were laid up at that port. Their captains were held on board, but the seamen went to Norman Cross. Some had returned to European waters from ports on the other side of the Atlantic quite unaware of why they were being detained! The Yarmouth navy blockaded the Prussian-controlled north-west German coast. Jackson, British ambassador in Berlin, was brought back home (also via Yarmouth), on the *Ariadne* frigate. And Britain declared war. The days of the Armed Neutrality crisis were back. Neutral ships were allowed through the German blockade provided they had not come from, or were not carrying the usual contraband to, a French, Dutch or Spanish port. But by the time the navy at Yarmouth had got used to the situation changed again. France and Prussia had fallen out over Napoleon's carve-up of the rest of Germany, and the Emperor was marching on Berlin. Britain and Prussia became allies, the blockade was lifted, and British troops were shipped to Hanover to help fight the French on the Rhine.

If the Royal Navy in the North Sea were not perplexed they certainly must have become cynical. Between 1795 and 1813 they were told successively that Prussia was an ally, a hostile neutral, a peacetime trading partner, a hostile neutral, an enemy, an ally, a hostile neutral, and an ally! So when they boarded and searched her ships they had to know their business, especially as the vessels carried papers written in German, prefaced by King Frederick William's 70 official titles, and strewn with diplomatic and legal verbiage! And soon their task became more complicated still.

In January 1807 the Royal Navy was ordered to put the whole Continental coast – neutral as well as enemy – under blockade. This applied to all of Scandinavia, the small states of north-west Germany, and Russia, as well as Prussia. It was done under the Order in Council declared by Canning, now Foreign Secretary, in response to Napoleon's "Continental System", under which all mainland Europe was forbidden from trading or communicating with Britain. Neither blockade was ever in reality total. Almost from the outset Napoleon, by means of pre-issued licences, let in neutral ships from British ports, if these carried goods he personally needed. In the winter of 1807 he imported cloaks for his troops in east Prussia through Hamburg. The British government's permission to export them was perhaps connected to Lord Yarmouth's attempt to obtain peace with the Emperor.

From November, under a second Canning order, the Yarmouth Navy stopped ships sailing between neutral countries complying with the Continental System as well as between those countries and enemy ones – for instance ones bound from north-west Germany to Sweden or Russia. *Yet at the same time* they were to allow these ships to land their cargoes in England, either selling them there or re-exporting them after paying British duties and provided it was to neutrals. For this purpose licences, or "certificates of origin" – one per voyage – were sold to neutral captains. By 1809 15,000 were being granted annually. The historian Holland Rose claimed British policy was less to choke the Continent's overseas trade than to divert it to this country. Nevertheless Napoleon still saw this as a threat and immediately retaliated to Canning's second order by telling his navy and privateers to seize any neutral ship (and cargo) coming from British waters – unless she carried a French licence.[17]

Another complication was the Dutch. Napoleon's brother Louis, whom he had imposed on Holland as king in 1806, was happy to allow, even patronise, trade between his adopted country and Britain in order to prop up the crumbling Dutch economy and make himself popular. Napoleon reckoned Louis was letting 25 ships a week leave for banned destinations. A packet boat to carry licences, orders for goods, and merchants, was even run between Katwijk and Harwich. From Yarmouth three ships were still regularly sailing to Amsterdam and one to Rotterdam. This was no secret. In 1807 the newspapers remarked on it. The ships involved were listed by Lloyd's. The Dutch admiral at the Texel, Kikkert, was distinctly pro-British and often released captured English vessels and their crews against the wishes of the French – for instance the Harwich fishing smack *John and Mary* in April 1809.[17]

Nevertheless, the east coast Navy and Customs went on seizing *unlicensed* vessels, not least Dutch ones. For example, on 19th September 1807 five captured Dutch merchantmen were moored on Yarmouth Quay: the *Jonge*

Anna Margharetha, Vrow Margaretha, Jonge de Wert, Jonge Tobias and little *Vrow Rebecca*, along with the Danish ketch *Christian Frederick*. Their cargoes – and in the case of the Dane the whole ship – were publicly auctioned at the *Star* tavern. The cornucopia of goods on offer included cheese, butter, pickled herrings, pork, bacon, barley, oats, flour, carrots, turnips, pumpkins, bay leaves, sugar, treacle, coffee, geneva (gin), wine, spa water, tobacco, timber, steel, oil, clothing irons, brushes and even an anvil. [18]

Forged licences and ships' papers abounded. Many neutral ships were buying papers from both sides and only showing British ones to the British and enemy to the enemy. Though the British war effort benefited overall from Dutch and Scandinavian collaboration, and therefore continued access to such vital imports as wheat and naval supplies, the transfer of so much trade to neutral flags angered the East Anglian shipowners and merchant seamen.

En route to their Copenhagen raid in 1807 the British seized the small Danish island of Heligoland, 60 miles off the Elbe. In 1809 they also took Anholt, right inside the Kattegat within 90 miles of Copenhagen. From rapidly-erected wooden warehouses there German and Scandinavian cargo and fishing boats smuggled British-originated sugar, coffee, cloth, china and cutlery back to the nearby Continent – especially the Danish Elbe port of Altona – in defiance of Napoleon. By 1811 at least 20 Yarmouth-owned merchant ships ran to Heligoland, mostly from London but in two cases from the Norfolk port itself. The Harwich packet ships also operated a regular service between their home port and the two islands. [19]

According to an American guide significantly entitled *European Commerce, Shewing New & Secure Channels of Trade with the Continent of Europe*, in 1807 Yarmouth was exporting carriages, coal, cotton, oysters, sugar and woollen goods to Continental System countries, and importing beer. Beer was going in the other direction from Colchester, and more oysters from Brightlingsea. As late as 1810 Thomas Mortimer's *General Dictionary of Commerce, Trade & Manufactures* said that Yarmouth still imported the full range of naval stores from Norway and the Baltic, Harwich traded with Germany, and Lynn exported to the Baltic and French-ruled Spain.

Throughout the war the licensed trade with the enemy ran alongside that longstanding east coast black economy, smuggling. Every week pairs of cutters, one Excise and one Revenue, left on one-week round trips to combat this. The *Fox* and *Repulse* patrolled from Bradwell and Wivenhoe over to the Dover Strait and back, the *Argus* and *Viper* from Harwich along the Suffolk coast, and the *Hunter* and *Badger* along the Norfolk. Onshore or in small boats there were "Tide Waiters" and other customs men watching the many estuaries and creeks. [20] However, the smugglers were undeterred. If anything the war encouraged them, since such Continental products as "geneva" (Dutch gin) were so scarce they commanded record prices. Under cover of mist or darkness hundreds of "ankers" (nine-gallon barrels) of this beloved tipple were often landed from a single ship, via small boats conveniently left nearby. The troops guarding the coast tended to be more interested in getting their share than helping the Customs. When a smugglers' boat ran ashore near Landguard Fort in October 1811 four of its garrison drank themselves to death on the spirits on board. [21]

The Navy was also troubled by the smugglers, especially as some were neutrals – or claimed to be. On 15th July 1804 the Yarmouth patrol sloop

Vixen boarded a ship off Norfolk, not far from Nelson's birthplace at Burnham Thorpe. She flew "Papenburg (i.e, Prussian) colours" and appeared to be a merchantman called *Good Intent* with a crew of five. However a search revealed two more men hiding below decks (one in the woodwork!), undeclared casks of spirits, false windows, and that paint was hiding at least four other names which she had used. One concealed man had American papers, the other claimed to be Prussian but had none.[22]

An extract from a French chart of the coast from the Humber to Lowestoft, published in the 'VIth year of the Republique', thus 1795. The chart indicates that it is based on Hamilton Moore's chart of 1789, published in London.

The interchange of information and straightforward copying of maps was well-established, with rare legal challenges on copyright. In the American War of Independence, British engineers would survey whilst based in the United States and feed their findings back to London publishers like Faden and Moore. Copies soon found their way to France - and in that period, were supplied back to the American forces. Doubtless in 1795 the French privateers welcomed the seamarks provided by this chart.

Continental Expeditions 15

When Fox had met Bonaparte in 1802 the First Consul accused Pitt and Windham of plotting his assassination. In spite of his own dislike of the Englishmen concerned, Fox had denied this. However, two years later the British government was almost certainly involved in the loose conspiracy, involving royalists and various French generals (including Pichegru, the conqueror of Holland in 1795), which did indeed involve such a plan. Early in 1805 the exiled Frenchmen Bonard and Lesimple travelled from London to Hamburg with the intention of reaching France and killing Napoleon. They stayed at the *Three Cups* at Harwich to wait for the Cuxhaven packet, but fell out, took knives from the table, and fought in the nearby churchyard. Nevertheless they both embarked next day. When Bonard reached Hamburg he went to see its French governor, de Bourriene, and denounced his accomplice and the British government. He shocked Bourriene by suddenly opening his shirt and revealing a dreadful gash in his side.[1]

The barracks at Colchester and Weeley, the anchorages of Yarmouth and Harwich, the quick and direct road access from London to the coast of East Anglia, made the region a staging point for the naval and military attacks on the fringes of Napoleon's Empire which Pitt's successors repeatedly carried out between 1806 and 1814. Germany, Sweden, Denmark, Holland, and Spain – to or from all these countries went these expeditions.

Finch's Guards and Paget's brigades, stationed in Essex and Suffolk a year or two earlier, embarked from Ramsgate and Deal for Cuxhaven in November 1805 in the hope of driving the French from Hanover while Austria engaged their main armies in southern Germany. But since Napoleon's victory at Austerlitz and the peace treaty of Pressburg almost immediately followed they were back in England in the New Year. Paget's cavalry landed at Yarmouth and then rode back to its Ipswich base.

After Nelson's funeral in January 1806 79th Regiment (the Cameron Highlanders) were successively based at Colchester, Weeley and Harwich, for a total of a year and a half. On the afternoon of 18th April 1807 two of their companies, with their families and some local civilians, were returning to Harwich from detached duty at Landguard Fort, crossing the harbour in a small cargo ferry they had hired. A sudden sideways gust capsized the boat, and drowned 98 people – 73 soldiers, 13 women, eight children and three sailors.[2]

That same month the *Ipswich Journal* announced:

"A glorious opportunity for youths of true courage … Young men who find themselves glowing with military ardour and are anxious of becoming defenders of their native Country against the common enemy are invited to step forward in this most important crisis, and lose no time like true Britons in joining his majesty's Suffolk Regiment of Infantry, or others that will be submitted to their choice".

But the East Suffolk (12th) Foot were then in India. There is no evidence that any Suffolk men were shipped out to them that year. And when their second battalion was raised five years later this was in Ireland from Irish militiamen. In the late 1790s most of the regular regiments named after East Anglian counties had spent time in the region and recruited there. But since then the connection had in most cases been broken. The regiments had been repeatedly moved around the country and remanned wherever they happened to be, either with local civilians or militiamen – themselves often serving outside their own counties. Irishmen (Protestant officers and Catholic other ranks) abounded. On the other hand east of England men had joined regiments from outside their area, both those stationed locally and in other parts of the country or abroad. Both battalions of 4th ("King's Own") Foot spent long periods at Colchester between 1806 and 1813, recruiting many hundreds of locally-based (and locally-born) militiamen. Officers from a hundred miles away came to Norwich and Ipswich to recruit, just as Nore or Portsmouth-based warships sent press gangs into Yarmouth, Lynn and Harwich.

Meanwhile, at the War Office, following Pitt's death, Windham and his successor Lord Castlereagh had drafted more army reforms. Windham's plans included shorter periods of enlistment in the regulars, the abolition of flogging and doubling the size of the Militia. They fell through, arguably because he lacked the patience to explain them in practical detail. But in 1808 Castlereagh ordered that militiamen transferring to the regulars for seven years' service would start on a 50% pay rise, and that new local Militia regiments, confined to four years' service near home and so without the higher pay, would be raised by ballot and without the right to hire substitutes or claim exemption through membership of the part-time Volunteers, who would be phased out. Thereby home defence would be performed only by full-time conscripts, and 40,000 home-based regulars could be formed into a "disposable force" which could be immediately embarked for whatever foreign opportunity cropped up. When Lt-Col Beckwith and Quartermaster Surtees came (incognito!) to Ipswich in the spring of 1809 they recruited no fewer than 1100 militiamen for their Rifle Brigade, then down in Kent earmarked for Portugal.[3]

The "crisis" in the Ipswich recruiting appeal was Napoleon's virtually complete conquest of Central Europe and impending imposition of peace on Prussia and Russia. In these worrying circumstances Portland's government and the Earl of Chatham were alarmed when hundreds of their best soldiers (including the Highlanders) at Colchester, Weeley and Maldon reported sick with an eye infection. Men unable to see are of course unable to fight, and therefore would have to be sent home. The regimental surgeons said it was an epidemic of ophthalmia, and suggested that it had originated from their mens' campaign in Egypt six years earlier. But the Government was suspicious, and sent down its own doctors to investigate. In July 1807 28 men from 28th Foot, at Maldon, were arrested under the Mutiny Act and sent to Chelmsford Gaol on a charge of self-inflicting the illness. A London newspaper, *The Courier*, accused them of "a most wicked and diabolical conspiracy" to undermine the defence of the county. Apparently the men knew that their blindness would only last three weeks, and was caused by an eye ointment rather than the disease itself.[4] The famous radical William Cobbett wrote in his newspaper, the *Political Register*, that it was unlikely that such brave campaign veterans would be so disloyal, that few would tamper with their own eyesight for the sake of discharge and that even if some had, the authorities ought to be asking themselves why troop morale was so low – not whether there was a plot. 28th Foot, incidentally, later fought just as courageously with Wellington in Spain and at Waterloo as they had in Egypt.

However, the Government had good reason for keeping its Essex-based regiments intact and under discipline. They were urgently needed for another expedition. Napoleon's final triumph on the Continent was imminent. He was already leaning on Denmark. This might mean French control of the Baltic and then a revival of their plan to invade England, this time involving the Danish navy and merchant fleet. On 24th July these fears were confirmed: a packet returned to Harwich with the first news of the Treaty of Tilsit, the pact of mutual recognition and non-aggression with which Napoleon and the Russian Tsar Alexander had ended their war.

Just two days later a new expedition assembled off Yarmouth. Its naval fleet was commanded by Admiral Lord Gambier, and consisted of 69 vessels, over one third of them ships of the line. The army, under General Lord Cathcart, was carried in a further 84 ships, each also bearing three or four flat-bottomed landing craft. On board various ships were Sir Sidney Smith, Popham, "Bounty" Bligh and Major-General Arthur Wellesley (the future Duke of Wellington). His reserve division included 28th, 79th and 92nd Regiments, which, less ophthalmia cases, had come from Maldon and Weeley via Harwich. The objective was again Copenhagen. The expedition caused havoc in the Danish capital, sinking dozens of ships at their moorings, blowing up forts, burning the dockyards (along with a sizeable part of the city), and seizing over 60 prizes. Yarmouth, Ipswich and Harwich merchant seamen volunteered to help bring these home.

Some of the British troops returned to England via Yarmouth. Among them were the 43rd, who marched from there down to Maldon and later moved to Colchester. At the former some of their young officers got into a fracas. When they disrupted a public lecture the speaker sprinkled them with water. They came back later dressed in silly costumes and masks, whereupon 20 civilians beat them with sticks. Constables were called and locked up the officers for three days until they had paid fines. One of them was Captain William Napier, later to fight and suffer under Moore and Wellington, and write a superb history of their Peninsular campaigns. What the brawl was about seems to be unrecorded. Napier was a radical, even in 1807 critical of the government, but his own correspondence makes it seem that from his side the incident was a prank and not a protest. He had made many friends in the town with his wit, charm and artistic talent.[5]

That December King Louis XVIII landed at Yarmouth from the Swedish frigate *Freya*. One of the late French king's younger brothers, in recent years he had committed himself to constitutional monarchy and acceptance of the moderate early stage of the Revolution. So as not to cause too much controversy he styled himself "Comte de Lille". He had been in exile at Mitau, on Russia's Baltic coast, but after the Tsar's Tilsit Treaty with Napoleon had been given

Admiral Gambier's fleet forces the Sound en route to attack Copenhagen, 1807. On the left is the castle of Elsinore. Gambier's ships had assembled off Yarmouth, as had Hyde Parker's and Nelson's a decade earlier.

notice to leave. England was just about the only country to recognise his kingship at that time. The 16 British sailors who rowed the famous refugee ashore with Admiral Douglas in his barge later returned the 15 guineas Louis had given them, writing to Douglas:

> "PLEASE YOUR HONOUR – We holded a talk about that there £15 that was sent us, – and hope no offence, your honour. We don't like to take it, because as we knows, fast enuff, that it was the true King of France that went with your honour in the boat: and that he and our own noble King (God bless them both! and give every one his right,) is good friends now; and besides that, you honour gave an order, long ago, not to take money from nobody, – and we never did take none; and Mr Leneve, that steered your honour and that there King. Says he won't have no hand in it; and so does Andrew Young, the proper coxes: and we hopes no offence: so we, one and all, begs not to take it…From your Honour's dutiful servants …"[6]

Louis XVIII returned after agreeing to a constitutional monarchy and initially styling himself as Comte de Lille to minimise controversy.

Gratifying for authority, though it does seem slightly curious that the sailors should remark on the British and French kings having become allies when this had been the case for the last 14 years.

Louis landed with the Ducs de Berri and Angoulême. They were met on shore by his younger brother Charles, Comte d'Artois – later king of France himself, and at this period referred to simply as "Monsieur", who had come up from London. In the town the royal party breakfasted with Admirals Douglas, Russell and Hood, and several captains. "The scene was truly interesting and effecting", recorded the *Ipswich Journal*. It noted that Louis had complemented Douglas's daughter Rose with "a happy simile" of that flower and her character. Then the Frenchmen got on the road in two coach and fours. They stopped for afternoon refreshments at the *Great White Horse* inn, Ipswich (later described by Dickens in his *Pickwick Papers*). Halting again for dinner at "an elegant new room" in the *Three Cups* at Colchester, they were greeted by a "huge concourse of all ranks". Late that night they reached Gosfield Park, near Halstead, which had been loaned to Louis by its owner, the Marquess of Buckingham.

On 29th August 1808 the rest of the exiled French court arrived at Harwich from Mitau via Sweden and then travelled on to Gosfield. No fewer than 70 in number, it included Marie Josephe, Comtesse de Lille (wife of Louis XVIII), the Duchess of Angoulême, a duke, a marquis, and the uncle of Talleyrand, the Napoleonic minister who had recently fallen out with his master and was intriguing with the royalists. True to form, the *Ipswich Journal* and other newspapers revelled in the chivalry and kindness of the local crowd. "We live as a nomad people, carrying everything with us for when we change countries", the Duc d'Angoulême replied to a British naval officer who had remarked on the huge amount of baggage his men had just unloaded on the quay. At Gosfield Louis and his queen received English and French visitors, including Louis Philippe of the rival Orleans family. The would-be king often walked the grounds, being too overweight to ride. The press seems to have most admired "Madame Royale", as the Duchess of Angoulême was known, whom they described as "amiable", "virtuous" and "benevolent".[7] The following year the exiles moved from Essex to Oxfordshire.

Uniforms of many regiments were in evidence across the region; here the the 95th Rifles, the 71st Foot and the 79th Foot.

Meanwhile 79th and 92nd Regiments of Foot had spent the 1807-8 winter back at Weeley, with part of 95th, a new formation armed with the short-barrelled, accurate, though slow-firing Baker rifle. On 29th April 1808 they again sailed from Harwich for Yarmouth Roads to join a third expedition to Scandinavia led by Sir John Moore. It was known as the Baltic Expedition, though in fact its destination was the Swedish port of Gothenburg on the Kattegat. An eight-ship squadron, commanded by Admiral Saumarez from the celebrated 100-gun Trafalgar flagship *Victory*, escorted it.

In the wake of Tilsit the Swedish king Gustavus IV had enlisted British support against France's ally Denmark, to his west, and Russia, to his east. One of the riflemen, Captain Grant, got no further than Harwich, because he was killed in a pistol duel with a lieutenant of the same battalion outside the barracks.

Gustavus wanted Moore's army to help him fight the Tsar's invasion of Finland. But, though technically now at war with Russia, the British would not commit themselves to this. So he confined them to Gothenburg and, having mended fences with Napoleon and agreed to join his Continental System, asked them to leave. However from the Swedish coast the Royal Navy did successfully raid Danish ports and shipping bound between Jutland and Norway, thereby consolidating the work done at Copenhagen. In October the British evacuated back to Yarmouth, and Thornton, Britain's ambassador in Stockholm, was also landed there (from the *Daphne* sloop).

By contrast the army effectively commanded by Wellesley had successfully landed in Portugal that summer and cleared it of its French invaders. On the eve of his victory over General Junot at Vimeiro, north of Lisbon, he had been reinforced by Major-General Acland's brigade, with 2nd, 20th and part of 95th Foot (Rifles), which had embarked at Harwich. Soon afterwards 43rd (Napier's regiment), 59th, 76th and the rest of 95th followed them via the same port.

By the end of the year many of the troops formerly based in east Essex and east Suffolk were back together under Moore, contesting Napoleon's occupation of Spain. They included the 42nd and 79th Highlanders from Weeley, the 1st Bn, 4th Foot from Colchester, Paget's 7th Light Dragoons from Ipswich and Napier's 1/43rd Foot from Maldon. Very soon they were all retreating across snow-swept mountains to the north-western port of Corunna. In the battle fought there, to buy time for the British evacuation, Hope commanded the left, Baird the right, and Paget the reserve. Baird was badly wounded, while Moore himself was killed and buried in the town. By February Napier had returned to Maldon, and 79th were back at Weeley for the fourth time.

At the same time the light dragoon cavalry of the King's German Legion, commanded by Major-General Count von Linsingen, arrived at Ipswich from Corunna. Most of them stayed for the next five years. The KGL had been formed from members of King George III's Hanoverian army when they were driven out of Germany by the French in 1803. Before going to Spain its cavalry had been based at Weymouth in Dorset, near the King's summer residence. Naturally Linsingen was a favourite of the royal family, who were often seen in the KGL uniform.   The people of the Ipswich area – at any rate its Tory gentry, merchants and clergy – much admired the Germans for their discipline, law-abiding behaviour and attachment to their royal patrons. Linsingen's son and little grandchildren settled at Birkfield Hall, Belstead, after the war, and only moved away in 1824. Both son and daughter married east Suffolk people.[8] Predictably the radicals saw Linsingen and his men as brutal royal hirelings. In July 1809 some KGL rode to Ely to round up Cambridgeshire Militia who had mutinied when told they would have to pay for their knapsacks. The Germans surrounded the prisoners and gave them hundreds of lashes, an incident which led to the condemnatory article by William Cobbett which earned him two years in Newgate Prison.[9]

Soon after Corunna Wardle, a radical Devon MP, attacked the Duke of York over his affair with Mrs Mary Anne Clarke and their alleged corrupt sale of army commissions. Though Parliament rejected his demand that the Duke be dismissed from command of the Army, he resigned. The affair stirred up the liveliest party-political controversy since the 1790s. The remaining East Anglian radical Whigs, like Thetford MP Thomas Creevey and Montagu Burgoyne of Harlow, claimed that the alleged crookedness of the Duke was endemic among royalty and Torydom. T W Coke made a strong speech to this effect in Parliament. After the Ipswich, Bury and Colchester borough corporations had voted against doing so Cobbett got his East Anglian readers to send in pro-Wardle petitions. The one-time Cambridge "heretic" William Frend also re-emerged in his support.

The affair had some Essex connections. Mary Ann Clarke lived at Loughton, where the Duke visited her en route to his inspections of Eastern District. Colchester lawyer Daniel Sutton jr, son of a famous inoculating doctor, was summoned to the Parliamentary inquiry because he had been clerk at the recent Weeley court martial of her army officer brother Captain Thompson, who had been charged with forging his mother's handwriting on cheques. When she testified on his behalf she had falsely called herself a widow. Thompson's solicitor at the trial had been Francis Smithies, son of the Colchester town clerk of that name.[10]

Then came an echo of the revolutionary past. News arrived from New York of the death of Norfolk's exiled Thomas Paine. He had been buried under a tree on his farm, with only six people including a Quaker and two black former slaves in attendance. In its predictable smug fashion the *Ipswich Journal* described him as a historical curiosity rather than an ongoing ideological force. Paine's reputation would survive this sort of dismissal, but at the time it was not totally wide of the mark, because he had done himself no favours by supporting France's war against Britain, advising Napoleon on invasion, and even attacking the American hero George Washington.

Though Wellesley was more than holding his own against the French in Portugal and Spain, and in Foreign and War Secretaries Canning and Castlereagh the government had its two most determined war leaders since Pitt, another British military disaster soon rekindled controversy.

In late July 1809 the largest expedition so far mounted from Great Britain set off for the mouth of the River Scheldt, ninety miles east of Harwich. Austria had recently come back into the war against Napoleon, who was also facing unexpected resistance in Spain. Between them the Allies hoped to expel the French from their conquests and bring down the Emperor. The British plan was to seize the island of Walcheren and peninsula of South Beveland, on the north side of the Scheldt, Cadzand on the south, and eventually Antwerp 50 miles up-river. Over 39,000 British troops were to be carried over by 600 transport ships and men of war. The Earl of Chatham led the army, and Admiral Sir Richard Strachan the fleet. Many of the officers and men who

William Napier, the hero and historian of the Peninsula War became well-known at Maldon while his regiment was there, before sailing for Portugal.

Soldiers of the Rifles
leaving Walcheren after the
doomed expedition.

had defended Essex and Suffolk five or six years earlier took part, including Paget, Hope and Coote. Most of the troops from Colchester, Weeley and Ipswich shipped off for the expedition from Harwich, some directly, others via Kent. They included the Scottish Highlanders, most of 95th Rifles, and two regiments of the KGL Light Dragoons.

The Walcheren campaign, as the whole effort was soon called, was doomed to fail from the outset because Napoleon had already decisively defeated the Austrians at Wagram (near Vienna). But initially hopes were raised in England. Most of Walcheren and South Beveland, though not Cadzand, were secured. After a two-week siege Flushing fell. Nearly 500 French and collaborationist captives were landed at Yarmouth by HMS *Agincourt* and HMS *Monmouth*, held in the town gaol, and then marched to Norwich by the Yorkshire Militia. Their attitudes and ultimate destinations varied. From one batch ten volunteered for the Royal Navy. The 200 who reached Norwich cavalry barracks on 4th September included several wives and children, who received food and blankets from the city's civilians. Their officers were moved to write the mayor a letter of thanks before leaving on the 6th for parole at Northampton.[11] Most of the other ranks were of course shut up at Norman Cross.

Meanwhile the Earl of Chatham had been waiting to march on Antwerp until Strachan sent his ships up the river in support, while Strachan waited for Chatham to take the enemy gun batteries before doing so. Though Napoleon himself was still away in Austria his ministers took the initiative and sent the out-of-favour General Bernadotte to Antwerp. With a smaller force he held the British invaders away from the city. Then they fell ill by the thousand, till whole regiments, brigades and divisions were incapable of marching and carrying equipment, let alone fighting. So just behind the enemy prisoners came a stream of invalids. The barracks at Harwich, Ipswich, Woodbridge, Weeley and Colchester had to be extended or cleared to accommodate them. The first large batch, comprising 11th, 59th and 79th Foot, came into Harwich harbour on 13th September. A military eye-witness later recalled

> "the emaciated figures, and long pale visages of the poor sufferers as they lay stretched in the boats and on the wagons … the piercing shrieks and agonising groans …"[12]

The Secretary at War, Lord Leveson Gower, sent Sir Lucas Pepys, Physician-General of the Forces, to investigate. Asked to proceed to Walcheren, he declined, claiming that he had no experience in inspecting camps and billets. 13 transport vessels were gathered at Harwich as an evacuation flotilla for future sick.

Whereas fewer than 40 soldiers had died in Eastern District between May and August, between September and December the figure was 681.[13] Of the 400 invalids from 1/92nd shut up in Woodbridge Barracks, three or four died each day. Among the1,000 at Colchester it was eight to nine. Over the next three months 150 died at Ipswich. Almost every churchyard in these towns, and also at Harwich and Dovercourt, was used for the burials, which for morale reasons took place after sunset. Many of the victims had shown no symptoms at Walcheren or while travelling back. Having marched back to Weeley from Harwich, many of the 79th immediately collapsed on the ground,

44 of them unable to rejoin their comrades when they marched out weeks later. Some men only reported sick many months after returning, and deaths occurred as late as 1814.

42 of the Harwich and Ipswich dead were given post-mortems. Pepys defined the infection as "bilious remitting fever", and said that he was already perfectly familiar with it. All agreed that the disease was not contagious, and with some victims flared up again after they had apparently recovered. Many called it the "ague" or "marsh fever", and the doctors themselves blamed it on "marsh effluvia". It was in fact malaria, common not only in the marshy polders of the Netherlands at that period, but equivalent areas of the Essex coast and Cambridgeshire Fens – as Davis, one of the Ipswich army doctors, observed. The standard treatment was chewing quinine bark, tons of which were stored at Harwich and the nearby camps. Davis and another army surgeon, Dawson, argued as to whether mercury should also be a treatment.[14]

Meanwhile Canning and Castlereagh had blamed each other for the military failure, duelled, and resigned. The prime minister, Portland, who had coincidentally suffered a stroke, left office a fortnight later, and was replaced by Spencer Perceval. The Earl of Chatham, attacked from all sides, also quit. For some months what was left of his expedition remained on Walcheren in order to hold a beachhead for a future offensive, but in December they too returned. The whole campaign went down in history as one of the most mismanaged and futile ever waged by Great Britain.

Early in 1810 the remaining sick were removed from the Essex and Suffolk barracks. At Woodbridge the officers celebrated with a sumptuous dinner, which ended with a disgraceful brawl among the junior diners.

Chatham, Strachan, Coote, Hope and Pepys were among the host of officers to testify to the parliamentary inquiry which convened in the New Year.[15] Because it sat in secret radical Whigs alleged a cover-up. Tory MPs counter-claimed "breach of parliamentary privilege", and when Perceval's government proceeded to detain Sir William Burdett and others on this charge angry crowds gathered in London. 2/11th Foot, back from Walcheren, was sent from Chelmsford to help keep order. Arthur Young wanted "the rascally authors, printers and publishers of those inflammatory papers which have done so much mischief seized and imprisoned", and said "It is a question of whether we are to be governed by Parliament or the mob".[16]

In June 1810 William Windham died in London from complications caused by a hip operation the previous year. He was privately buried at his native Felbrigg. The one-time libertarian Whig, counter-revolutionary, anti-appeaser, and uneasy ally of Pitt had been out of government since giving up his Norwich seat in 1807. In later years he had lapsed into reactionary social attitudes which even many Tories deplored, such as defending the slave trade (which he used to attack), cruel sports, hanging petty criminals and the unreformed voting system. He was still convinced, Burke-style, that even if criticism of authority had a factual basis it would be used by malignant schemers to undermine the war effort and cause bloody revolution – though he had supported the Walcheren Inquiry.

On 25th October 1810 George III completed his fiftieth year as king. In the wake of the Duke of York controversy, Walcheren, and another poor harvest and rising bread prices, loyalists all over the country staged lavish celebrations. At Ipswich General Burgoyne's infantry and von Linsingen's cavalry joined the town's Loyal Volunteers for an outdoor religious service on the New Barracks parade ground, then marched past General Loftus, now Eastern District commander-in-chief. Every soldier was given 1/- with which to drink the King's health. The officers dined at the *Bear and Crown*, and next day at the coffee house. 100 poor people ate three sheep at the Stoke Hill farm of Messrs Bleadon and Steward. The prisoners in the town gaol and the paupers in Melton "House of Industry" (workhouse) had roast beef, plum pudding, and porter, and the inmates of the debtors' prison received a generous one guinea each. The Marquess of Salisbury held impressive festivities at his Aldeburgh seaside retreat: cannons were fired from his terrace and fireworks from his garden. At Colchester, after the Mayor and Corporation had held their thanksgiving in St Mary's Church, the army's cannon and muskets made a deafening cacophony. The garrison's officers dined at the *Three Cups* and drank toasts proposed by John Round jr, while 6,000 poor ate, among other things, an ox roasted at Hawkins' timber yard. In the evening there was a supper ball at the *White Hart*. At St Osyth Priory Frederick Nassau's sons danced with the servants till 3 a.m. The most stylish celebration was held by the aged Admiral Lord St Vincent at Rotchetts, his mansion near Brentwood. The place was festooned with 10,000 lights, some making up a huge royal coat of arms. "The ornamental decorations have every mark of loyalty and judiciously-blended taste", reported one magazine. The Prince of Wales had been invited, but had been kept away by "a sudden attack of the gout", it sadly admitted. Elsewhere the parties were more modest: at Harwich, though there were the usual flags, bells and cannon, the Volunteers had to content themselves with cold food in a tent.[17]

At Lynn William Richards scoffed: "It was a political manoeuvre; and not the first to which the British public have been the dupes".[18]

It was common knowledge that the King was far from being in the healthy state his celebrants wished, either mentally or physically. Within a few weeks he lapsed into his final madness, and in 1811 the Prince of Wales was proclaimed Regent. The Whigs had hoped that he would dismiss Perceval and bring them into the cabinet, but he failed to oblige.

Denied sight of their own royals, the eastern counties had to be content with another visit by an exiled foreign one. On 10th November 1810 the sloop *Tartar* landed ex-King Gustavus IV of Sweden at Yarmouth. He had been ejected by Napoleon's marshal Bernadotte. Gustavus was now to be styled Count Guttorp. His awkward attitude two years earlier was diplomatically forgotten. Lord Gardner, now Yarmouth Fleet Admiral, met him at the jetty with his carriage, flags, a band, and an escort from the Yorkshire Militia. After lunching at the *Angel Inn* the ex-king took the road for London. At Colchester he was met by King George III's messenger. The town's annual fair happened to be taking place. Local landowners Du Cane and John Round junior, who had been presiding over this, "waited on" the exiled king (as bowing and scraping was called), and Du Cane persuaded him to stop off and dine with him at Braxted, near Witham. From there Gustavus went on to Burgoyne's house at Mark Hall, near Harlow, and finally to London.[19] Unlike Louis XVIII, he never retook his throne, since Bernadotte, once a Jacobin (!) had installed himself as Crown Prince and after the war became king. (His heirs have been Swedish monarchs ever since).

Meanwhile most of the regiments which had populated east of England barracks, and gone off on the various brief Dutch, Scandinavian, and/or

Peninsular campaigns, had joined Wellington in Portugal. They included the Weeley Highlanders (42nd, 79th and 92nd Foot) and 95th Riflemen, Sir Stapleton Cotton's cavalry brigade, with 14th and 16th Light Dragoons, at Woodbridge prior to the KGL, and 1/4th and Napier's 1/43rd, formerly at Colchester. Most were to fight in the Peninsula for the next five years, at Talavera, Torres Vedras, Busaco, Fuentes d'Onoro, Cuidad Rodrigo, Badajoz, Salamanca, San Sebastian, Toulouse. By 1810 Wellington was also sent two foot regiments named after East Norfolk (the 9th) and East Essex (the 44th). The last-named were famously to capture a French eagle (regimental standard) at Salamanca in 1812.

The desperate courage displayed in the storming of Badajoz in particular was phenomenal. However, it is sadly true that the brave and the brutal are – at least in war – often the same people. After they had stormed the city many of the British troops ran amok robbing, raping and murdering the civilians they were supposedly liberating from the cruel and godless French. They included men from 1/4th, 1/43rd, and 95th Rifles, all based in north-east Essex two or three years earlier. Such behaviour confirmed the view among Tory statesmen and British generals that the noose, the lash and the refusal of political rights were the only way of controlling the "lower orders".

The soldiers' lawlessness was not entirely a product of the bloody Spanish war. With some it had begun long before. In 1803, before the renewal of war, Skerrett, the colonel of the 83rd, was dismissed and put on half pay for tolerating the rape of numerous women in the Chelmsford area by some of his men. A searching inquiry had been mounted by Calvert, Eastern District Adjutant-General, and a very strongly worded condemnation of the situation was issued by the King and the Duke of York, who were genuinely shocked.[20] On Christmas Eve 1808 four privates of the 4th beat up Lincolnshire militiamen in the Woolpack Inn at Colchester. One was sentenced to hang at Chelmsford for killing his victim with a poker.[21] Not long afterwards an ensign of the 11th shot and killed a surgeon of the same regiment in a duel near Maldon – over accusations of cheating in a game of cricket.[22] No doubt authority saw the one case as mere thuggery, the other as an honourable tragedy, but in both a life was needlessly lost.

While these battalions were away many of them were reinforced from their home depots or former bases in East Anglia. For instance, almost throughout Wellington's campaign 2/4th at Colchester made up the losses of his 1/4th. In 1811 three foot regiments kept depot staffs at Maldon, and in 1812 three others did so at Danbury – although none had originated in the region or been stationed there for many years. So, while we are sure many local men went to fight abroad, it would be very hard to discover how many or who they were. 54th (West Norfolks) were unusual in being based, and mainly recruiting, in the eastern counties after 1810.

The last, and probably most dubious regiment to train for the Continent at Colchester were the two battalions of the Piedmontese Legion, at the end of the war in 1814. These Italians, who had originally been captured by the British in Spain, were so reluctant to go back and fight Napoleon that they set fire to their barracks and many deserted.[23]

The various campaigns swelled the prison population of Norman Cross to more than 6,000 by 1810. Trouble had been brewing there. Several guards had been attacked. Escapes had become frequent. In September 1808 one fugitive, Charles Bourchier, killed a civilian, and, after recapture and trial at Huntington, was hanged at the camp in front of all its prisoners and guards. A search through every hut then found 700 home-made or smuggled daggers. A year later two officers got out concealed in the cart removing the night soil, but were eventually recaptured. More dramatically, soon afterwards 500 prisoners rushed the inner wooden fence, broke it down, and began to attack the outer one. They were beaten back by the militia, who bayonet-wounded 40 of them. A 14-foot brick wall was then built all round the site. However the following year one man got out by simply walking behind the night watch as they filed out of the camp!

The blockhouse and fencing at Norman Cross prison camp as drawn by Captain George Lloyd of the 2nd West Militia in 1809.

The inmates' craft production also became problematic. Two men were caught forging banknotes, in English law a capital offence. They were lucky to suffer no worse than removal to Huntingdon Gaol. Others were making and selling blasphemous and obscene pictures and toys, occasioning a protest from the Society of the Suppression of Vice in 1810.

It had probably been to pacify the prisoners, as well as to divert them from crime and depravity, that the Government had appointed the French émigré de Gales de Tours, former Bishop of Mélun, as Catholic camp chaplain in 1807. He stayed in the nearby village of Stilton.[24]

Between 1811 and 1813 the guards included Lt Thomas Borrow, of East Dereham and the West Norfolk Militia. The camp made a deep impression on his young son, George, who decades later described it as a place of hunger, degradation and misery, and a "sad cross for many a Norman", in his book *Lavengro*. He thought it a national disgrace. Though the place was undoubtedly grim, his account was perhaps overly tragic-romantic, and not uninfluenced by his postwar literary mentor William Taylor, one of the Norwich radicals of 1789.

Forts, Signal Posts & Lifesavers 16

While Napoleon was busy in Central Europe and Spain, the fear of invasion was in abeyance. The ruthless raid on Copenhagen staved off trouble from that quarter. The guardships in the Essex rivers were removed, and Volunteer and Sea Fencible training fell back to only once or twice a month. The warning beacons were abandoned. When locally-based regular regiments went abroad they were only partially replaced. By 1809 there were only half as many troops in Eastern District as during the invasion scare of 1803-4.

However in the longer term the threat could not be discounted. No one knew then that Napoleon would eventually overreach himself, and suffer disaster in Spain, Russia and Germany. In 1804 he had controlled the west European ports, shipyards, shipping and coastline only from south-western France to north-eastern Holland. But in 1809 he controlled them from Spain to Norway. He had crushed Austria and Prussia, forced peace on Russia, made Denmark an ally, overrun most of Spain, and occupied the small states of north-west Germany.

By then the British had discovered that there were a dozen French ships of the line building or fitting out at Antwerp and Flushing. The Dutch had an equal force at the Texel. The Emperor was making up for the losses inflicted by Duncan and Nelson. One of the objectives of the Walcheren expedition was the elimination of the new enemy fleet in the Scheldt. It only accounted for one major French ship, so the Royal Navy had to stay in the Downs, and in the case of Admiral Ferrier's three ships of the line, Hollesley Bay. In the autumn of 1811 Napoleon spent two months touring the ports, dockyards and shipping of northern France, Belgium and Holland. When Downs vessels reconnoitred the Scheldt in 1812 they saw 16 completed French ships of the line, six frigates, and numerous sloops and gun brigs, a far stronger force than the one during the 1803-1805 scare. Only towards the end of that year, with his Russian disaster, was Napoleon's invasion ambition finally scuppered.[1]

If France was to be a permanent danger, the English coast would need permanent defences.

In the 1808 Commons militia debate Cambridgeshire MP Sir Charles Yorke warned what a successful French invasion would still mean. It would, he asserted, resemble the Norman Conquest:

> "Nobody should flatter himself that it would be possible, after an unsuccessful (British) campaign in this country, to patch up any kind of peace with France that would preserve property in its present channel. The victorious armies would be distributed over the country to colonise the soil they had conquered."[2]

He demanded to know why the Essex and Suffolk coasts had not been

The west side of the Circular Battery, or Redoubt as it is generally known today, at Harwich It was not armed and manned as a fort in the 20th century world wars, but was a military prison and stores. Today it is a museum..

fortified like the Kent and Sussex. He was not entirely up-to-date, as the Government had been making appropriate plans.

The vulnerability of Harwich Harbour had worried the Army for many years, and steps were taken to strengthen its defence. Across the water at Landguard Fort the parapets were heightened, stronger gun platforms were installed, the moat was deepened, and the Ordnance Depot on the north-east side was dismantled and rebuilt at Harwich. A more ambitious plan was also drafted for a large Harwich "Circular Battery", and approved in May 1806. It was built of brick and stone on the open land halfway between the town and Beacon Hill Battery, and south of the new Ordnance Depot, after the road had been diverted westwards to make way for it. About 35 feet high and 150

The right of the two towers is Tower A, at St Osyth Point. On the left is Tower E, at Clacton. The former is now an aviation museum, the latter now overlooks the beach – and served for a while to support the system for Butlin's holiday camp. The term "Martello" is a corruption of Martella, a place on the coast of Corsica where the Royal Navy was beaten off by a similar round fort manned by the French.

Built of brick, some were given an outer coating of stucco.

Seen from the air the ovoid shape of the Martello towers becomes apparent. They were built with the point towards the sea in the hope that cannon balls fired from ships lying off the coast might glance off without doing much damage so long as they did not strike the actual point.

feet in diameter, it was surrounded by a moat, and beyond that an earth glacis which sloped down for well over one hundred yards all round, right to the road and the shore. Work was completed on it in 1810. Mounting ten 24-pdrs, it looked out unobstructed in every direction over the harbour, town and sea (and still does). The total cost was around £52,000, of which the civilian contractor, Frost, received about four fifths.[3] To the left of this "Redoubt", as it later came to be known, a new five-gun battery was placed at Angel Gate, south of the Harwich dockyard.

Colonel Money, the artillery major Reynolds, and Windham had influenced the building of Martello towers along the Kent and Sussex coasts in the 1790s, and called for the chain to be extended north of the Thames. In

The most northerly of the chain of Martello towers on the east coast, Tower CC at Slaughden, just south of Aldeburgh. This was the only tower to be quatrefoil in shape, and is said to have been built to the design of one that was to have been erected on the south coast but was not proceeded with. There was a battery in front of this tower, but both the battery and a large part of the moat have been taken by the sea.

his 1798 report on coastal defences Reynolds had argued that open batteries were too easily knocked out by shipborne cannon, and that the best place for army defensive guns was "a simple Tower of Brick defended by a Handfull of Resolute Men".[4] He had proposed a total of 61 of these towers for the coastline between Purfleet and Yarmouth Jetty, 24 of them to be built immediately, 18 more in the medium term, and the remaining 17 eventually. During the alarm late in 1803 Windham had again called for their construction along the Suffolk coast, in the visibility gap between the warships in Yarmouth Roads and those in the Thames Estuary. The following year General Craig had suggested such towers at Harwich, Hollesley Bay, Bradwell, Mersea, and the River Crouch, varying in size according to the degree of threat. In an open letter to Windham in 1805 Money renewed his call for the towers, claiming that, although the Navy would very probably halt any invasion at sea, if the enemy ever *did* get through they would be able to land and march on London. He suggested that some towers be built inland to command key roads. "They cannot be carried by a *coup de main*", he argued, and by forcing the enemy off into the fields would give the defenders time to deploy for the counter-attack.

In the summer of 1805 the Ordnance Board sent the Eastern District engineer Major Bryce, architect of the Chelmsford fortifications, to survey sites for possible North Sea coast Martello towers. On his six-foot-long map he marked almost as many proposed sites as Reynolds eight years earlier. They ran from No.1 at Foulness to No.58 at Aldeburgh. Two of his towers were to guard the Crouch, seven the Blackwater, three the Colne, 14 the Clacton-Walton beach, 11 the Felixstowe shore, and ten Hollesley Bay and the mouth of the Ore.[5] The cost in money and labour would certainly have been too high, and two years elapsed while Napoleon was busy fighting on the Continent. Then Bryce's map was brought out again and a scaled-down chain decided upon.

Early in 1808 the relevant plans were drawn up by Colonel Twiss and Captain Ford at the War Office, and entrusted to Captain Whitmore, chief engineer of Eastern District. That spring purchase orders went to the owners of the proposed sites (total purchase costs were estimated as £8,000) and surveys were done. In early August the region's press reported that 500 men were at work at Grays making the necessary bricks – some 700,000 for each tower. That September the *Ipswich Journal* said that materials for the Felixstowe and Bawdsey towers had been landed, and that their foundations were being dug, adding some inaccurate details about their heights and armaments. The towers were not cheap: each cost some £20,000, about three times as much as one gun brig.

29 east coast Martello towers had actually been scheduled, and were built, covering the possible invasion beaches between the Rivers Colne and Alde only. Where there was an existing open gun battery, which was so in most cases, the tower was located just behind or alongside it. The chain began with Tower A at St Osyth Point, continued with B-K along the coast of north-east Essex as far as Walton Creek, resumed with L and M at Shotley, and continued along the Suffolk coast via Z at Alderton and AA at Shingle Street to CC at Aldeburgh – and was built in that order, probably on the grounds that the closer a site was to London the higher its priority had to be. The towers clustered along the stretches of flat, dry and open coast which the Army had been most concerned about. There were no fewer than four on the two-mile

stretch between Lion Point and Clacton Wash, seven at Felixstowe, and five between Bawdsey and Shingle Street. The first six were all on sites bought from Nassau of St Osyth Priory.[6]

The work was shared between private contractors, Royal Engineers from Colchester and Ipswich, and militia – 200 Hertfordshires were employed at Shotley and 500 Dumfrieshires between the Deben and Alde. Tower A was completed in 1809 and Z only in 1812, while the Aldeburgh castle was left still unarmed when the tide of war finally turned in 1813. It had a different design from the rest, quatrefoil instead of round.

The towers were built almost entirely of small brownish-grey brick, with stone for door lintels and gun mounts. In a period before the ferro-concrete of 20th century forts, and in a region devoid of natural stone, numerous thicknesses of brick made sense, and were widely used in the forts built by many nations in the 19th century. The bricks were fused together with hot mortar. High-explosive shells each weighing hundreds of pounds would have demolished such walls, but the standard small shot of the era would merely have dislodged a few bricks – and very protracted multi-ship bombardments would have been needed to cause fatal damage, during which the towers would have given more punishment than they received. Some evidence of the strength of the brickwork cropped up in 1811, when Tower C, at St Osyth Beach, began to lean. The engineers dug round under the opposite side and the whole structure settled back on the horizontal without a crack.

Most of the towers were 33 feet high and 55 in diameter at the base, tapering to 50, with walls eight feet thick. Unlike their somewhat smaller equivalents on the Kent and Sussex coasts, they were not absolutely circular, but slightly flattened on three sides, like very rounded triangles. The curvature was of course to avoid vulnerable corners and to deflect fire coming from acute angles. Each tower was two-storey, with the upper floor and roof held up by a stout central column. Stores were on the ground floor, men upstairs. The single door was on the upper floor, and reached by a drawbridge if the tower was sunk within a moat, otherwise a ladder. Each floor had two small windows, and also a fireplace, so there were two chimneys in the roof. There, shielded by a five-foot parapet, were three cannon mounted on wheels running on semicircular rails – standardly either one long 24-pdr and two short, or one long 24-pdr and two 5.5-inch high-angle howitzers.

Each tower was to be stocked with 160 cannon shot (round, grape and case), 80 hand grenades, and 380 small arms cartridges, and to be defended by one officer and a dozen men.[7] Though evidence on this is inconclusive, it seems that, if ever actually manned at all, this was only by the odd caretaker or two. An Ordnance Board report of 1812, the year the east coast chain was finished, says that the defenders were being held inland, at Weeley and Woodbridge, and were only to occupy the towers if the alarm was signalled back from the coast, in each case the march being possible in two hours. For this it gives the unhealthy coastal environment as a reason, perhaps with the Walcheren experience in mind.[8]

Their late construction date led some to dismiss the east coast Martello towers as little more than follies, even at the time. But they tended to be Whig-radicals who had never seen much need for military spending.

In anticipation of heavier naval action in the North Sea now that Napoleon dominated Germany as far north as the Baltic, the Admiralty kept up its

The maps of the positions of the Martello towers used throughout the book are all taken from one large map in the National Archives. The maps show both numbered towers and letters, indicating the inital towers proposed and then the ones that were actually built. This extract shows the area around Walton. Initially the towers were numbered; when the plan was revised, they were lettered, with the letters being doubled when the alphabet ran out – hence AA, BB and CC..

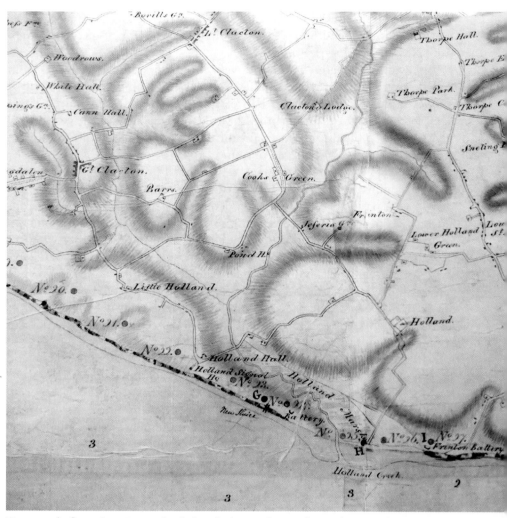

Yarmouth fleet. In 1806 it had decided on a barracks and arsenal across the River Yare at Southtown and a new naval hospital on the South Denes, to replace the smaller improvised ones in the town. The Southtown buildings, which cost £15,000, were to hold up to 10,000 troops and the stores for ten warships. Work proceeded slowly. Admiral "Billy" Douglas laid the first stone of the hospital only in 1809, and building did not finish till 1811. It consisted of four blocks round a courtyard, with patients in three and staff, stores and administration in the fourth. A chapel and clock tower were included. Great pride was taken in its modern and healthy design. Its capacity was 200 patients and the cost was £100,000, in addition to £20,000 for an adjacent officer's house, which drew a protest in Parliament from the Norwich radical MP William Smith.[9]

In 1807 Yarmouth was also provided with a "receiving ship", for signing on and holding naval recruits, in the form of the captured French sloop *Utile*. She was moored in the river near the Tollgate. She was sometimes used for local naval court-martials. Two were held in March 1810. One was of a teenage midshipman from HM gun brig *Orion* who had beaten a seaman and caused him to fall overboard and drown. *Orion*'s captain, who happened to be the brother of the late Admiral Dickson, and the *Standard*'s captain, acting as court president, did their duty and got the boy discharged from the Navy. By

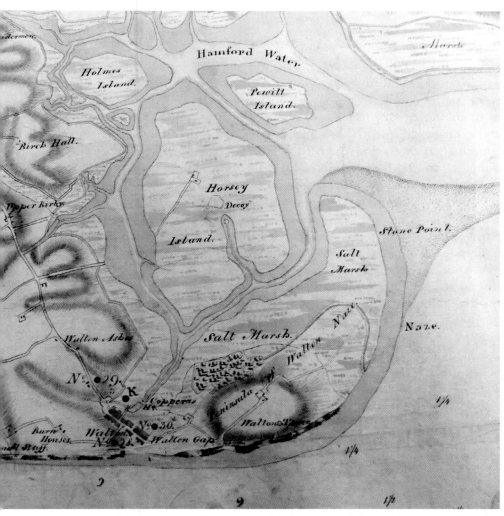

contrast, when a seaman from the *Désirée* was tried for striking an officer he was sentenced to death.[10]

Vice-Admiral Murray took over from Douglas at Yarmouth at the end of 1811. In view of today's Scottish separatism, it seems remarkable that they and their predecessors Dickson, Duncan and MacBride, not to mention the Army's Moore, Craig, Baird and Hope, were all Scots.

The coastal signal posts are described as "signal towers" in contemporary documents. This, together with their locations, suggests that they were raised structures – probably wooden latticeworks high enough to be clear of trees and house roofs. A few, such as the one at Beacon Hill, St Osyth, went onto Martello towers. Some of their lieutenants had been in charge since the Revolutionary War, such as Leckie at Bradwell and Shirley at Little Holland.[11] One of their duties was to report smugglers. A very unusual incident occurred at the "South-end" (presumably Prittlewell Church) signal tower in 1804. Lt Norman got into a fight with a former Admiralty bureaucrat named Ibbotson, who died of his injuries two days later.[12]

To link Yarmouth directly to the Admiralty in Whitehall, as the Channel naval bases were already linked, in the summer of 1808 a shutter telegraph was erected on the overland route Strumpshaw–Norwich–Ickingham–Newmarket–Royston–St Albans–London. Even though each shutter was the size of a door, and the whole frame the height of a tree, at anything between six and 12 miles apart each station was only just within sight of the next. When George Roebuck, the Admiralty surveyor, first travelled the proposed route he thought it impractical, and instead suggested upgrading the flag and ball chain which already ran up the coast to the Thames. However the inland posts, many on quite high ground, were less troubled by London fog and sea mist, and fewer were needed. At night, of course, combinations of hidden and exposed lights, corresponding to open and closed shutters, were used. Amazingly each word in a signal could be sent along the whole chain in 17 minutes.[13] In 1811 the existing coastal chain (Yarmouth-Nore) was converted to shutters. The same year the army's inland chains of flag stations were scrapped.

Popham's numerical signal codes, sent with flags and balls from ships' masts as well as land poles, had many hundreds of permutations, and could not only spell out such messages as Nelson's famous "England expects every man to do his duty", but even "anxious" and "envious". However the English east coast signal posts and men of war normally used a simpler code. Their most common signals were the challenge "275" and friendly response "125".[14]

Though the naval code numbers were secret, "telegraph" technology was not. It was described in detail in published books and articles.[15] Many ships, coaches, and newspapers were already called "*The Telegraph*". Some months before the new eastern naval chain started work, the merchants of Yarmouth and Norwich built their own system, using identical six-shutter posts.[16] There were eventually three shutter telegraph stations at Yarmouth: the commercial one on the western tower of the town's South Gate, the Navy's main one on the South Denes, and another naval one on the North Denes for relaying signals up the north Norfolk coast.

Incidentally it was a Frenchman, Chiappe, who had devised the first telegraph back in 1792. The French armed forces had used his system since 1803. It used movable arms on posts instead of balls, flags or shutters, and was copied by the British after the war.

It was probably because of the Martello towers, patrolling gun brigs, and ever-tighter blockade of enemy fleets that the Sea Fencibles were disbanded in 1810 – which incidentally made them liable to naval impressment or the militia ballot. Though some had recently been drilling three times a month, they had hardly ever been alerted for possible action since 1804. As Nelson had accepted, their fishing was more important to them than their defence role, and their discipline also seems to have been in some doubt. Most of the River Colne and River Crouch contingents were oyster-men. The former were in the habit of lifting oysters from the beds tenanted by the latter from Sir Henry Mildmay (the objector to the Moulsham fort). After two previous expeditions, on the evening of 25th January 1808 the Brightlingsea and other Colne men boarded 35 smacks, and, ignoring the entreaties of their Sea Fencible captain, Rutherford, again set off to raid the Crouch. When they arrived next morning they were confronted by Bate Dudley and two other Anglican priest-magistrates in a boat, who tried to warn them off. This they ignored, but when they lowered their dredges these were cut by the Burnham oyster-men with the cutlasses their Sea Fencible captain, Bayley, had issued them. His men seized some of the ringleaders, whom Bate Dudley sent to Chelmsford Gaol. Their followers fled down-river, but were intercepted by the *Turbulent* gun-brig, which had

Major-General John Hope, who commanded the Highland Brigade at Weeley during the 1803-4 invasion alert and later took it to Spain.

The Royal Naval Hospital for the North Sea Fleet was opened in Yarmouth in 1793 and was relocated in 1815. This print is from slightly later in the 19th century, as the Norfolk Pillar, the monument to Nelson, can be seen in the background on the left.

been coming up the Swin and was summoned by the Tillingham signal post. Lt Knopps promptly hauled several of them on board and "pressed" them. The episode was reported in newspapers all over the country, including *The Times* in London – though they made rather a joke of it.[17]

Throughout the war storms and running on rocks and shoals took far more lives at sea than battle. Every winter the coastline was strewn with wrecks and bodies. Disasters like those of the *Lutine* and *Invincible* were only the worst among hundreds. The Admiralty, Trinity House (in charge of buoys and lightships), the newspapers, shipowners, merchants and insurers lamented them, but, like crop failure or falls on the stock market, they were taken as a fact of life. The public sale of ship wreckage – everything from complete hulls down to spars and pieces of mast – was a frequent and popular event at the eastern ports, widely advertised on posters and in the newspapers. Although there was genuine concern about the death toll, no notable steps to diminish it were taken for many years. What made it seem more tragic was that most of the worst disasters did not occur when ships sank out at sea, but when they broke up right onshore, in water deep enough for drowning yet as little as 100 yards from dry land.

In 1801 a pulling (rowing) lifeboat had been installed at Lowestoft of the Greathead or North Country design, and then another at Bawdsey, by Robert Sparrow of Worlingham Hall. The first sailing lifeboat was built at Lowestoft in 1807 to replace the Greathead boat which the local seamen would not use. In December 1806 the troop transport *Peace* was wrecked on Kessingland beach. Beccles surgeon William Crowfoot found a sergeant who had almost died from exposure and exhaustion and resuscitated him. Sparrow then joined him to found a Suffolk Humane Society based in Lowestoft.[18]

On 18th February 1807 the *Snipe* gun-brig ran aground in a storm just outside Yarmouth Haven. Although she was not badly damaged, and was later repaired and put back into service, only 20 survived out of the 93 on board, including a woman and 30 French prisoners. 19 victims were buried at the Yarmouth hospital cemetery. The local lifeboat, which had been moved to Gorleston, had failed to show up.

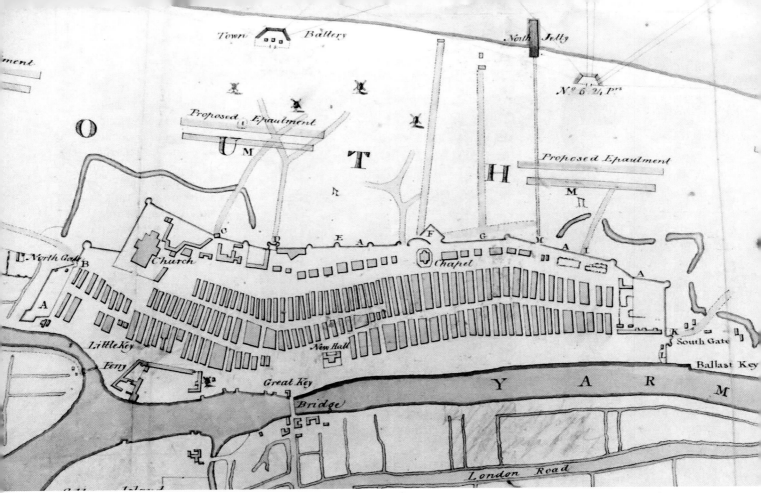

The following labels appear on the map:

Town Battery North Jetty Proposed Epaulment N° 6. 24 P^{rs} O U M T H Proposed Epaulment M North Gate Church B C D E F Chapel G H A I A A K South Gate Little Key Ferry New Hall Great Key Ballast Key Bridge Y A R M London Road

Yarmouth was already a walled town; further defences were proposed during this period.

CAPTH G.W. MANBY, F.R.S.

Captain George Manby, barrack master at Yarmouth, and deviser of Manby's line-throwing mortar, a device which proved effective in its intended role until superseded by the full rocket line.

There were more disasters the following year. In February a ferocious blizzard of gales and snow, apart from cutting the roads from London to Norfolk, sank many ships. The Customs cutter *Hunter* was lost with all hands. A laden collier went onto the West Rocks, off Harwich, where six of her nine crew drowned, and three were rescued by a boat from shore, including one who had clung to the mast for 24 hours. In November a whole series of storms littered the beaches on either side of Yarmouth with wreckage and drowned men.

At that port was Captain George Manby, brother of the captain of the *Africaine* frigate, though in charge of the barracks and not a ship. (They had originated from Downham Market in the same county). He had personally witnessed the *Snipe* disaster. He was inspired to invent a simple rescue apparatus, consisting of a naval mortar firing a line with a hook at the far end.[19] He used it for the first time in rescuing five men from the cargo brig *Elizabeth* off Yarmouth on 12th February 1808. In September 1809 he successfully demonstrated it to a group of naval officers and shipowners. He snagged his hook onto a cable he had suspended between two buoys he had placed just offshore to represent a shipwreck. The line was then held taut from onshore while a boat was secured to it by a looped cable, and rowed out and back.[20] By the next great storm, on 13th January 1810, he had distributed some of his equipment along the nearby coast, and, presumably, trained men how to use it. Two Dutch and one Papenburg merchantmen, defying Napoleon's Continental System, ran ashore and began to break up in the crashing waves. Lt Davies, of the Happisburgh signal post, led the rescue of five of the seven crew of the galliot *Hope*, which had been bound from Emden to London.[21] At the same time the Winterton Sea Fencibles pulled three men off the *Vrow Maria*

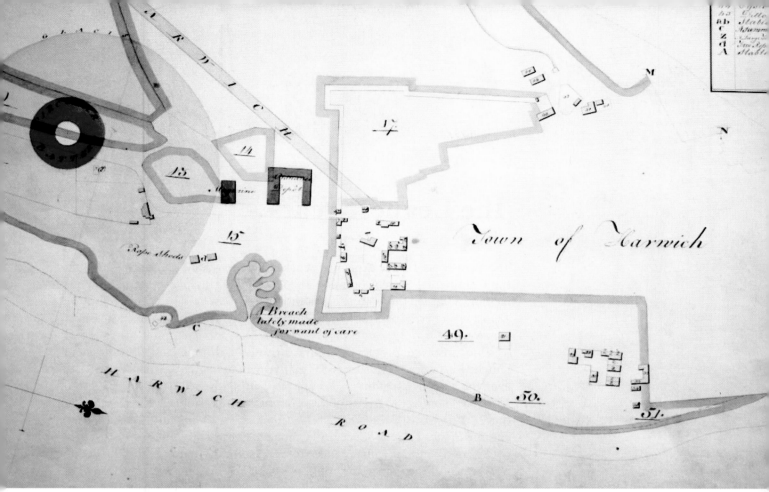

(Delfzyl-London) at Horsey Sand, including the captain and his young son.[22] In both cases "Manby's apparatus" was used. At Kessingland on the *Elizabeth Henrietta* (Lynn-Rotterdam) all but Captain Vanderwall tied themselves to the line thrown to them and were dragged in safely through the surf. There had been a long and anxious wait while the mortar was wheeled from Lowestoft. Captain Manby himself supervised.[23] By the end of the war 169 people had been saved by his invention. The Suffolk Humane Society awarded him one of its silver medals, and he was made a Fellow of the Royal Society.

Unfortunately he could not help everywhere. The storms of early November 1810 were for many the very worst within living memory. At Cromer Manby's apparatus saved four men and the local lifeboat another 15, from the same wreck. But scores died on other merchantmen off Wells, Mundesley and Yarmouth. Most of the smaller craft in Harwich harbour were sunk or driven ashore, and the Angel Gate battery and part of the dockyard were flooded.[24] When the naval cutter *Alban* broke up in a storm off Aldeburgh on 12th December 1812 all but two of her 56 occupants, among them two women, drowned. The surf was so rough that boats from shore could not get through it.[25]

Manby made several other inventions. In 1811 he tested firing the guns of the Yarmouth harbour ship *Utile* with self-igniting chemical injected from tubes, instead of the traditional glowing pieces of cord known as "match". He devised the first modern fire extinguisher and tested an explosive-propelled harpoon on a Greenland whaling ship. He even found time to write a short history of Great Yarmouth.

The Ordnance Board map of the proposed Circular Battery and Ordnance Store at Harwich, 1806.

A contemporary depiction of Captain Manby's line throwing mortar about to be fired.

The Leanest Years 17

The British, as I have explained, cocked a remarkably successful snook at the Continental System between 1806 and 1809. In spite of some dubious farming weather the national wealth and overseas trade expanded. But by 1810 a severe crisis overtook the British economy. The catalogue of woes grew very long.

One unsolved problem was the privateers, who included Danes and Dutch, who were more successful that year than at any time since 1799. As ever, the Navy at Yarmouth was busy combatting them. The *Désirée* captured *Le Norwegian* (21st March) and *Jean Baptiste* (10th October). The *Drake* took the *Tilsit* (9th April), the *Calliope La Comtesse de Hambourg* (5th October), and the *Briseis Le Sans Souci* (15th October). *Quebec* brought in *L'Imperatrice* (21st March) and *La Jeanne Louise* (6th November). That October the 1600th privateer crewman since the resumption of war in 1803 was imprisoned at Yarmouth. The prisoners were even more varied in nationality than those of the previous war. The 47 from *Le Sans Souci* included Frenchmen, Dutchmen, Germans, Swedes, Norwegians and Americans. Her capture had come after an eight-hour pursuit and one-hour gun battle near Heligoland, in which the British had four men killed and 11 badly wounded, the enemy eight dead and 19 wounded. There were further successes in 1811. *Le Vigilant* and her 39 crew were taken off the *Galloper* in March, *L'Olympia* and her 34 off Ostend in October, and Blanckeman's former ship *L'Anachreon* and her 40 near the Dogger Bank in November. Their respective captors were the *Nymphe* frigate, *Quebec* frigate and *Princess of Wales* hired cutter.[1]

However, the privateers were almost the least of the challenges. In 1810 Napoleon ejected his uncooperative brother Louis from the Dutch throne and annexed Holland to the French Empire. He then absolutely banned it from trading with Britain and her colonies. That August he imposed an average 50% import tax on imports into the Continent. He lifted a ban on American vessels which had been in place for some years, so as to divert the trade between the USA and Continental Europe from British carriers and ports. The same month his Danish allies raided a thinly escorted British convoy in the Skagerrak and captured no fewer than 45 of its ships, news conveyed by the cutter *Hero* back to Yarmouth. In September the British trade press declared that "Trade to and from the Baltic still continues brisk", but when another 45 British and British-licensed ships berthed at St Petersburg, flying Spanish flags, they were seized by Tsar Alexander. On 26th October, in compliance with Napoleon's decree, the King of Prussia ordered the confiscation of all British and British-colonial goods in his country. As a result hundreds of British ships were anchored in the Kattegat off Gothenburg, many equipped with bogus neutral (and even French) flags and papers but afraid to enter the

Baltic. Heligoland was so choked with British and British-colonial goods that they were piled up in the open. When part of the Gothenburg convoy finally ventured onwards it met a hostile reception. The Tsar of Russia confiscated 80 of its ships. The Prussians turned it away from their port of Pillau (near Danzig) – though Napoleon had ordered that it be allowed in and then seized. Admiral Saumarez, commanding the British naval squadron off Denmark, finally ordered the merchantmen back home.[2]

In view of the Danish threat unprecedented protection had to be given to the 200 returning ships. Its escort consisted of the frigates *Lynx, Clio, Snake, Rosario, Gluckstad,* and *Centinel*, and sloops *Tartar, Rose* and *Primrose*.

In December Napoleon annexed north-west Germany to France, better enabling him to shut its ports to the British. He also ordered the destruction of all British or British-shipped goods found there and in his other dominions, and of all ships suspected of importing them.

The volume of British overseas trade (import and export, and measured by tonnage) had contracted and then expanded in about the same proportion between 1805 and 1809, but shrank again by 25% in 1810.[3] By then it stood at a lower level than in the 1802–3 peace period (itself mediocre), and though it picked up in 1812, much of this was composed of emergency wheat imports and supplies for the British Army in Spain. This was the poorest performance in decades, and looks even worse when set against the considerable rise in population (around 10%) and productive capacity (factories, machines, enclosures) during the same period.

The South American market, which many exporters and shipowners had switched to in recent years, had become so glutted it had suddenly folded. Bankruptcies were occurring at a record rate. The pound had lost 20% of its international value, and its paper version was said to have depreciated by 30% against gold. This made British exports off-puttingly dear for foreigners, and foreign goods temptingly cheap for Britons – harming profits and employment in the country.

As a result of the very low prices of 1803/4, and consequent landowner protests, the Government had empowered itself to slap a heavy tax on wheat imports when the national average price dropped below 63/- (£3.3s) per quarter, reckoned to be the threshold at which corn growing became commercially viable. But soon it turned out the country had the opposite problem, because poor domestic harvests and the scarcity of imports kept the price above 80/- (£4), and mostly 90/- (£4.10s). During the winter of 1809-10 it hit 130/- (£6.10s) in Essex (the highest since 1801), and after falling in the spring was back up at the winter level in the summer. The 1810 domestic wheat output was the lowest per head of population of any war year, and imports correspondingly highest. Though wages had risen by around one third since the beginning of the war, prices had gone up by over two-thirds. The 1811 harvest was only slightly better, and little wheat imported because of equally bad weather in Britain's usual overseas suppliers and because of Napoleon's annexation of North Sea ports. 1812 saw the peak wheat prices of the entire war – over 155/- (£7.15s)in August.

The English press rued that her economy had fallen into "a horrible crisis".[4] Journalists argued that by becoming so dependent on paper money and neutral as opposed to British shipping the country had brought itself to the edge of ruin. The seaports and shipping of Yarmouth and Lynn had lost most

Harwich from Walton (Felixstowe) shows the signal station on the left, then the low lighthouse, the Circular Battery, the Ordnance Building, the High Light, church and dockyard. This painting, and that below date from about 1811. They are by a Captain Durrant. clearly a talented water colourist.

This painting looks seaward from Harwich dockyard. The Low lighthouse is on the left, then the Circular Battery, the Ordnance Building and on the far right the high lighthouse.

of their Dutch, north-west German, and Baltic business. Lynn's merchant fleet had shrunk, and whereas half of its ships traded with northern Europe before the war, now only one did so. Ten ships had regularly sailed from Yarmouth to Rotterdam pre-war, but none by 1811, though two still ran to Amsterdam and one (the Colchester-owned *Soken*) to Flushing. 33 ships regularly plied between Yarmouth and the Baltic in 1803, but only ten in 1811 – and these were nearly all neutrals.[5]

The shipbuilders also felt the pinch. Encouraged by expanding trade and Admiralty orders between 1803 and 1805, they had laid down more vessels than they could handle and which they could sell within the contracted price. This began to show up as early as the end of 1806. At that juncture Joseph Graham at Harwich was building nothing, Betts of Mistley only one naval ship, and two of the three Lynn yards (Joseph Wales and Mark Watson) were having to operate all their recent ships themselves because the orders for them had been cancelled.[6] There was hardly any Admiralty work for local yards between 1808 and 1811, largely because enough gun brigs and sloops had already been built. The increased cost of Baltic timber must also have been a factor. Custance & Stone at Southtown (Yarmouth) went bankrupt in 1807 and remained so for the next nine years. In 1809 Betts at Mistley and in 1811 Warren at Brightlingsea suffered the same fate. When one of Warren's creditors went to confront him at Ingatestone he hid upstairs and had his wife say she did not know his whereabouts![7] At Yarmouth Nathaniel Palmer and

John Preston stopped building and respectively bought the post office and became Comptroller of Customs.

For several years relations between both Great Britain and France on the one hand and the United States on the other had been poor. French privateers had very often seized American ships and cargoes going to and from Britain and her allies. Back in the late 1790s this had caused a virtual sea war between the two nations. The British had long found Americans on captured French privateers and given them the unpleasant alternative of Norman Cross or service in the Royal Navy. They had also been seizing American merchantmen (trading with the Continental System), and impressing members of their crews. In 1804 six such victims had appealed to Rear-Admiral Russell for release from his Yarmouth squadron.[8] Furthermore, the British claimed that deserters from their warships had been given refuge on U.S. ships – even men-of-war – and were now serving on board. In 1807, after the British had stormed one of his warships in search of one such deserter, and within sight of the American coast, President Jefferson had retaliated, but at the same time sought to preserve his country's neutrality, by banning both British and French ships from his ports. His "embargo" had been lifted in 1809, but an equivalent trade ban had been imposed in 1810 by his successor Madison, with the proviso that if Britain or France agreed to respect U.S. neutrality this would be lifted in her case. Napoleon cleverly agreed, but Britain, whose blockade of France was more important to her than the reverse, refused.

Radically-inclined East Anglians, such as the anti-government Whigs and Norwich manufacturers, deplored this, pointing out that the U.S. embargoes were adding to England's shortages of food and raw materials and loss of export markets.

In June 1812, after fraught negotiations, Perceval's successor Lord Liverpool finally agreed to follow Napoleon and stop the seizures of American ships, cargoes and sailors. But the "War Hawks" within Madison's government and Congress, keen to seize Canada and crush Britain's American–Indian allies, pushed him into declaring war before this news had arrived. And so Britain found herself at war with the U.S.A. just as she was most feeling the strain of the war with France. That summer William Richards of Lynn bewailed

> "the miserable strangulation of trade … it may be very truly said that the trade of Lynn is at this time at a lower ebb than it has ever known to be at any time within the last hundred years…(The war) has saddled upon us at last an unexampled debt of a *thousand* millions! – Such an enormous sum the whole coinage of the universe could not discharge". (*Plus ça change!*)

Yet the eastern economic sky was not entirely dark and stormy. The large military garrisons in the region meant a very considerable extra demand for food and drink, to the benefit of local farmers and brewers. Soldiers are hungry and thirsty people!

Many of the merchant ships absent from local ports were not laid up, but moved off to trade from elsewhere, so that some of their owners' profits and seamen's wages came back to the area. Yarmouth owned slightly more merchant ships (on one estimate over 470)[9] in 1811 than in 1803, and considerably more ships originating from other ports used the harbour. Its English coastwise and Norwegian trade had increased.[10] (Though Norway belonged to hostile Denmark it largely ignored the Continental System). While the quantity of wheat shipped out of Yarmouth (mainly down to London) suddenly halved in 1811, the tonnage of other types of grain product (especially malt) more than offset this. Its largest shipping firm, Palmer's, owned over 40 vessels, more than in 1803 – though their main rival Samuel Padget had sold some of his. Well over 3,000 men from the town (from a population of about 16,000), were employed as merchant seamen, again a slight increase. Lynn switched from shipping wheat to coal. Between 1808 and 1814 the shipbuilder Lovewell dug Yarmouth's first three dry docks across the river at Southtown. They were pumped out with Watt steam engines.[12] There were 12 Harwich Post Office packet ships by the end of the war compared to four at the beginning.[13] All along the coast fishing thrived, with record catches.[14]

The fastest-growing and most modern enterprises in the whole region were the banking and insurance of Norwich. They had only existed for 50 years, but were becoming nationally important. Sir Roger Kerrison's badly managed bank failed when he died in 1808 and left behind a massive debt, but the Gurneys continued to prosper. There had been two insurance "empires" in the city since Thomas Bignold left the Norwich General in 1797 and started his own Norwich Union Fire Society, a "mutual" concern in which numerous "members" shared profits and losses and met to vote on company policy. In 1804 he also launched a bank, and in 1808 a life insurance mutual. His democratic methods had attracted many of the city's radical businessmen and craftsmen. Dr Edward Rigby was one of his directors. But in 1806 Bignold turned Tory and broke with these folk, probably so as to appeal to a wider national clientele – and this paid off as his concerns grew to be some of the largest in the country, operating far beyond Norfolk. Norwich insurance did not cover against business bankruptcy, but it did relieve entrepreneurs and employers of the cost of accidents and unforeseen deaths which otherwise might have ruined them.[15]

The Norwich and Colchester wool business had already partly adjusted itself by shrinking and concentrating on niche markets for special luxury cloth and uniforms for the local troops. Some of the Fenland farmers made good profits from growing hemp – in demand for ships' ropes and sails – to cover the cutting of the normal Baltic supply.[16] Landowners and farmers were beginning to recoup the money invested in enclosures. Several hundred people were even employed around Brandon knapping flints for firearms.[17] The biggest military-industrial employer in Essex was the government's gunpowder mill at Waltham Abbey, which supplied the propelland for army and naval firearms in eastern England and far beyond.

Arthur Young carried out one of his formidable surveys of the situation, questioning bankers, merchants and farmers. His conclusion was that the paper money had not caused the inflation or economic contraction – rather, he argued: "the stoppage of the cash (gold) payments at the Bank not only dissipated the accumulated terrors of 1797, but animated every exertion (in our economy)". The inflation meant that in real terms the peak wheat price of 1812 was actually lower than that of 1795 and 1800. He denied the habitual Whig-radical claim that the war had harmed trade, pointing out that it had considerably expanded, that it had forced businessmen to find new markets and raw materials, and that the increased Government debt was more than offset by the fund it had accumulated to pay it off. The one policy he did regret was the reliance on neutral shipping.[18]

Moreover in 1811, partly due to the tact shown by Admiral Saumarez in handling their merchantmen, the Russians and Swedes gradually detached themselves from the Continental System, and once again traded with us. The Danish gunboats which had been raiding the shipping involved as it passed through the narrows between Copenhagen and Malmö were taught a sharp lesson by Yarmouth-based warships that July, when *Désirée* and boats from *Quebec* and the gun brigs *Acute, Blazer* and *Orion* seized six of them and sent 33 of their crewmen back to the town's prison on the *Redbreast*.[19]

The reopening of the Baltic was attended by one great disaster. When a large convoy was on the way back from there to London and other east coast ports on Christmas Eve 1811 it ran into a mighty storm off the Danish coast. Dozens of its merchantmen were left crippled, or beached, and were taken by Napoleon's friends the Danes. Its escort also suffered. The ships of the line *St George* (once Nelson's flagship) and *Defence*, and sloops *Hero* and *Saldanha*, were lost. Only six out of 700 men survived from *St George*, which had cut off all her masts in the vain hope of escaping destruction, and only 50 out of 550 from *Defence*. *Hero* grounded off the Texel and her crew were rescued by the Dutch Navy. As the English press lamented, the loss of life was equal to that in a great sea battle.[20]

The American War, incidentally, had scant effect on eastern England, which had little transatlantic trade. Edward Morgan's Harwich Excise cutter *Viper* bought a letter de marque to take American ships, but during this additional conflict brought home only one French vessel, the privateer *Louise* from the Dover Strait on 3rd June 1813.[21]

There was one last reason. The illogicalities of blockade and embargo had become even more illogical. Napoleon himself licensed a number of neutral ships to export some of his grain to Great Britain. These vessels had to pay him hefty duties, and could not bring back British exports, but did help this country at its lowest economic ebb. The Emperor apparently thought he was profiting from his enemy's misfortunes! Ten merchant ships were plying between Yarmouth and ports in the French Empire – mainly in Belgium, Holland and north-west Germany, but in two instances Bordeaux.[22]

Another new development was perhaps more of social than economic significance, and is now rather hard to visualise. Before the war Brighton and Weymouth on the South Coast had become gentlefolks' seaside resorts. Recently places on the east coast had joined them. Yarmouth and Harwich built bathhouses, where health-seekers immersed themselves alternately in pools of hot and cold sea water. Lord and Lady Hawkesbury (as Lord and Lady Liverpool were then called) visited the one at Harwich in 1799. At "the south end of Prittlewell" a hotel and terrace of houses had recently been built facing the Thames. Caroline, the estranged Princess of Wales, brought her daughter Charlotte there in the summer of 1804 for the sake of her health. Naval officers came across from the Nore to attend a ball in their honour where Emma Hamilton was the star attraction. It was alleged that one of them, Captain Manby of the *Africaine,* was Caroline's lover. Several aristocrats built summer villas at Aldeburgh, while Lowestoft attracted a larger middle-class clientele. The visitors took the sea and air, not the sun, and there was as yet no sign of the masses. Nevertheless, rather bizarrely for wartime, the local seaside leisure industry had been born.[23]

Victory at Last   18

Wars vary in chronological shape. Some (like 1939-45) are symmetrical, with one side on top in the first half, a great midway turning-point, then the other side dominant through till their final victory. Others (like 1914-18) begin with swift victories by one side, then drag on for many years while the other progressively grinds it down. In both cases the ultimate losers often accelerate their own doom with a desperate eleventh-hour counter-attack. The great conflict of 1792-1815 (to take its full extent), was a mixture of the two. For long the French were victorious – in fact for more like 90% of the war than 50%. The resistance to Napoleon in Spain – by her native guerrillas as well as Wellington – and perhaps the economic pressure of British naval blockade, can be seen as attrition by the other side. But this went on for years before the turning-point, which did not arrive till the French came to grief in Russia late in 1812.

It was a year of very mixed news. The Opposition Whigs of eastern England, like those elsewhere, were reluctant to applaud the British military effort in Spain, partly because of its cost, partly because of their dislike of the Spanish Bourbon dynasty, partly because they rather unjustly hated Wellington's haughty brother the Marquess Wellesley, former Governor-General in India and between 1809 and 1812 Foreign Secretary. In the first few months of 1812 the Spanish border fortresses of Cuidad Rodrigo and Badajoz fell at last. Even the Whigs were impressed. But in April Bishop Bathurst of Norwich privately wrote:

> "Badajos is dearly paid for; so sanguinary a triumph Lord Wellington has never hitherto obtained. I detest war so much I should turn Quaker at last; these conquerors dash on regardless of 'the widow's cries, the orphan's tears' ".[1]

Spencer Perceval was the blackest of *bêtes noires* for the radicals, who loathed him for his infringements of civil liberty, and for bringing back the disgraced Duke of York as army commander-in-chief in May 1811. One year later the prime minister fell victim in the lobby of the House of Commons to a deranged, though non-political, lone assassin. Cobbett gloated that from his cell in Newgate he had heard the crowd applaud the killer as he was led out to execution. The Lynn radical William Richards bluntly commented:

> "much as we may deplore this shocking catastrophe, we would fain hope it will operate as a warning to all future ministers not to trifle with the serious complaints and sufferings of their fellow subjects."[2]

He gloomily added:

"We were not, it seems, sufficiently humbled, or really tired of the horrid game of war, bloodshed and devastation; and so, without taking time to breathe, we rushed headlong into a new war, which has already lasted eight or nine years, and is likely to prove the longest and most disastrous we have been engaged in for many ages. God only knows when and how it will terminate".

He had apparently not yet heard that Napoleon had recently pulled some of his forces out of Spain and invaded Russia. On 27th July the frigates *Aquilon* and *Calipso* called at Harwich to pick up Lords Cathcart and Walpole (one of the Lynn MPs) to take them to Tsar Alexander's military HQ, thereby renewing the Anglo-Russian alliance of 1804-7.[3] Not long afterwards the exciting news came that Wellington had for the first time broken a French army in the open field near Salamanca, advanced to Madrid, and driven Joseph Bonaparte out of the city.

One other promising development had recently come about. Enemy privateering was at last in decline in the North Sea. That summer Yarmouth saw the last of its captured corsairs. The lugger *Eole* was taken west of Heligoland on 17th July by the *Britomart*, *Leveret* and *Osprey* sloops, after she was surrounded and put up a fierce resistance. Two British sailors had been killed in the fight, and nine badly wounded. The captured ship, Capitaine Dubois, and 30 more French prisoners were brought in eight days later.[4] On 4th August the *Leveret* sent in *Le Brave*, Capitaine Girendin, and 22 more prisoners. And on the 13th two Danish privateers and their American prize were brought in by some of the crew of the *Horatio* sloop, which had taken them after a ferocious encounter over a 1,000 miles away off the Arctic north of Norway. On board were Lt Buderhof and 52 other prisoners.[5]

Perceval's death meant a general election in October. His successor Lord Liverpool could not yet be sure the turning-point had come, and that his own party's Tory patriotic fervour would steal a march over Whig negativity. However, as usual, the unreformed voting system, coupled with the propertied classes' fear of French and radicals, gave him a huge head start. In East Anglia the outcome was 29 Tories and 11 Whigs (only five of them radical), a gain of two for the Opposition.

The veteran radical Whig William Smith stood again at Norwich and topped the poll. However, he won less than 40% of its votes, since the Tories split between Charles Harvey, who came second and also took a seat, and the former MP John Patteson, whom he had edged aside as government candidate. At Yarmouth the contest was scarcely ideological at all. All three candidates could be described as Old Whig. The two elected, Edmund Lacon junior and General Loftus, represented the town's merchants and nearby landowners respectively. Both were supported by many "out voters", who had been born in the town, or owned property there, but lived elsewhere. Lacon at least had the distinction of being the first Yarmouth-born man to represent the port for a hundred years. At Lynn the two sitting members, Old Whig Horatio Walpole (then away in Russia) and New Whig Martin Brown-ffolkes were returned, as they had been ever since 1790. Brown-ffolkes had often opposed Government curtailments of personal freedom, but was not a radical. Yet again Coke was returned for Norfolk County.

In Cambridgeshire four Tories and two Whigs were elected. Not one of its seats had even been contested. Since before the war the only changes of MP in this politically somnolent county had been occasioned by a few dying or moving to the House of Lords. Among its representatives the one government minister was the young Lord Palmerston, Secretary at War, at Cambridge University. He had recently taken this seat, which Pitt himself had held till his death, in a by-election. This had been occasioned by George Henry Fitzroy (Earl of Euston, Suffolk) going to the Lords as Duke of Grafton. The other university seat was retained by the moderate Whig Sir J H Smyth. The University seats, for which only its graduates (mostly non-residents) voted, were distinct from the Cambridge *town* seats – since most people could remember these had been held by the loyal and usually absentee Tory Generals Manners and Finch, none other than the Essex-based brigade commanders during the 1803-4 invasion scare. Manners' brother continued in one of the two Cambridge*shire* seats, while the other was taken by Lord Osborne, a Whig so radical that five years earlier he had privately written:

> "The emigration of the House of Braganza is a great event. Why should not the House of Brunswick imitate so noble an example and transport themselves with all the ministers and the German Legion to Botany Bay?"[6]

Between the Waveney and Blackwater, though some MPs were by background Whig, there was little controversy and tame acceptance of the Government and its war methods prevailed. The "rotten boroughs" of Bury, Orford, Aldeburgh and Dunwich were uncontested, and with Eye and Suffolk County, stayed unquestioningly loyal. The same applied to Ipswich and Colchester, with their larger electorates – though their polls were probably swayed in the Tory direction by their many out-voters. Euston's brother Lord Charles Fitzroy, a liberal-minded Whig who was returned yet again for Bury, had until recently been too busy commanding the Ipswich garrison to get much involved in politics. John Hiley Addington continued in his seat at Harwich. Huskisson handed over the other one to Nicholas Vansittart, like Arthur Young a believer in the Government's paper money and high war borrowing and spending. Huskisson was to go on to be a major "Liberal Tory" postwar fiscal reformer, till run over by a train at the opening of the Liverpool-Manchester Railway in 1830. He had not been appreciated at Harwich, which acquired a Vansittart Street but not a Huskisson Street!

In Essex County the election result had been a draw. For the last ten years both its seats had also been held by Tories. One of them was the former Essex Sea Fencibles commander Eliab Harvey. Although described by friends as "church and king to the backbone", he was not quite as uncritical as some assumed, having sided with the radical rear-admiral Cochrane's attack on the sanctimonious Lord Gambier over his mishandling of the attack on the French fleet in the Basque Roads in 1809.

The Essex Whig Club tamely accepted the Tory government's failure to reform. The county's more left-wing Whigs were frustrated by this. On 1st July 1809 one of them, Sir Henry Mildmay, chaired a meeting at Chelmsford Shire Hall which slammed the Government for banning a proposed county meeting to debate its policies.[7] The following April the same Whigs again met at Chelmsford to form the "Essex Freeholders' Club". This was so called because it aimed to mobilise the county's small owner-occupier farmers, who *could* vote, to demand the same right for owner-occupiers in the towns, and to scrap the ridiculous little "borough" constituencies such as Harwich or Orford, thereby both rectifying an injustice and loosening the Government hold on power. Montagu Burgoyne of Harlow took the leadership of this – in spite of being Harvey's son-in-law. The pro-government John Conyers wrote to the *Chelmsford Chronicle* and accused him of being an ex-Tory who had taken up leftist causes only to promote himself. Burgoyne responded that, though a very longstanding defender of his county against the French (he had commanded some of its Fencibles or Volunteers for 15 years), he had also always believed in libertarian reform. He helped his case by resigning a minor tax-collecting post he had been given by Pitt. He had declined to stand in elections, pleading lack of funds, until former Maldon MP C C Western, of Felix Hall, Kelvedon, persuaded him to do so in the Essex December 1810 by-election. He was trounced. In August 1812 he joined his friend Peter Du Cane and the radical Rev. Onley at another Chelmsford meeting, where he again tried to make his county versus rotten boroughs point. He said that power was in the hands of the "moneyed interest", by which he meant, not so much the rich as against the poor, as the Government's tax-collectors, bribers and National Debt interest beneficiaries, as against honest, uncorrupted, gentlemen and middle classes. Attendance was respectable rather than impressive, as the expected farmers were busy harvesting. On this basis Burgoyne stood again, this time alongside Western, in the general election a month later. He was badly beaten, but Western was elected. Eliab Harvey had pulled out through lack of funds.[8]

Socially and ideologically moderate though he actually was, Burgoyne had put off many of his potential freeholder voters by identifying himself with more radical and democratic Whigs such as Burdett, Captain Cochrane RN, William Smith, Samuel Whitbread, Creevey and Wardle. The typical Essex independent farmer hated the Income Tax, the militia randomly taking away his sons and labourers, and the government hirelings in the nearby "boroughs", but mistrusted "unpatriotic" aristocrats who criticised royalty and advocated votes for poor men. Moreover he failed to see why giving the vote to more people in towns – with their desire for lower food prices – would benefit him.

Were these Whigs merely self-interested and opportunistic mudslingers, trying to take advantage of the inevitable problems of a government doing its best to fight a powerful foreign aggressor? This is a tricky question, but I doubt the charge. The Opposition had always maintained three things at the same time. Firstly, that French reform and meritocracy were superior, both morally and in practical effectiveness, to their own government's rigid conservatism; secondly that the war was not inevitable – or at any rate unstoppable – and that a peace with France was possible which would enhance, not damage, the national interest; thirdly that, given that there was still a war, its conduct would improve if taken away from incompetent and corrupt royalty and Tories. The first and second of these points had been soft-pedalled after Napoleon made himself Emperor and threatened invasion of England, but were still there in the Whig repertoire, and had again become audible. The third apparently contradicted them, but the Whigs had a way round this, namely, that liberal reform in this country, and a corresponding encouragement of freedom abroad, were a better way of overcoming Napoleon and thereby obtaining peace than *illiberal* domestic and foreign policies. This was the view of Colonel Money, William Napier and Admiral Cochrane, for instance. Such radicals faulted the Government for backing the cruel old regimes in Spain and Russia. William Taylor claimed that democracy would have freed the former "if our government had not corruptly interfered to royalize the Spanish cause".[9]

Naturally, in this heyday of liberal democracy, we sympathise. Would not Pitt or his successors have hugely embarrassed the French by beating them at their own game of reform? By sticking to the liberalism they themselves had pursued before 1792 would they not have obtained more willing public British (and Irish) support than by riding roughshod over civil liberties? But now we come to the snag. It was precisely in Spain and Russia that Napoleon was to be ruined – and not by liberals. So while on balance I do not find the likes of Vansittart, the two Harveys and Conyers more congenial than those of Coke, Western and Burgoyne, I also believe that the Tories found realistic ways of winning the war which their opponents would have missed, albeit ones only partly of their own making.

The first major question with which the new parliament had to deal was again the Catholic one. The veteran Irish campaigner Grattan had drafted a bill which gave Catholics (i.e. in most cases members of the majority Irish religion) the right to sit at Westminster, and command troops in England. Because the Government included one-time followers of Pitt, as well as Protestant hardliners, it was neutral on the issue and allowed its members a free vote. Grattan dropped his own bill when the independent Pittite Tory Canning took it up and amended it so that Catholic office-holders had to pledge themselves not to aid the country's enemies, and the British government had the power to veto the appointment of disloyal bishops. The bill was debated in the Commons in the early spring of 1813 and rejected by a four-vote majority.

"Catholic relief" had long been discussed in East Anglia, and opinion there was far more divided than over the slave trade.

On the one hand the MPs Popham, Crickitt and Round, the Vanneck family in East Suffolk, Captain Eliab Harvey, and many low-ranking folk had been against change. So opposed were the Norfolk and Norwich parish clergy that they drafted a hostile petition under the nose of one of its leading supporters, their own Bishop Bathurst. The Norwich Tory MP Charles Harvey presented it to Parliament. Another had already been sent from Sudbury. Some backward-looking Old Whigs believed that it was by ousting the Catholic king James II in the "Glorious Revolution" of 1688 their predecessors had given the nation the liberty and security it had enjoyed ever since, and that this legacy should not be tampered with. "Bloody Mary's" burning of Essex and Suffolk Protestants 250 years before was hardly still a folk memory, but was evoked by those who equated it with the massacres of Irish Protestants by their Catholic neighbours in 1798. Orange Lodges had been formed at Norwich, Cambridge and Chelmsford, possibly by some of the Protestant Irish army officers based there.

The only native Catholic congregations in the region were very small ones at Lynn, Norwich, Ipswich (Simon's), Sudbury and a private upper-class residence near Stoke-by-Nayland in Suffolk. However several thousand

"Papists" had recently arrived in the rough shape of the Irish rank and file of the Royal Meath, Wexford and two Mayo Militia Regiments. They soon bloodily clashed with the local militiamen on the streets of Norwich, Yarmouth, Colchester and Chelmsford. This was no doubt due more to drink than religion, but it reminded some local Protestants of the way in which Catholic civilians over in Ireland had been organising themselves into a defiant mass movement. Further links were alleged between Irish Catholics and the war. Some had taken French help to rebel against England in 1798. Since 1801 Napoleon had had a "Concordat" with the Vatican which meant that he and France's Catholic clergy cooperated – by implication in his war against England. And allowing Catholic Irishmen to be British Army officers allegedly risked them helping the enemy.

On the other hand Windham and his friend the Sudbury Old Whig Hippesley, Huskisson, the Cornwallises, Cambridge University and both its MPs, radical Whigs such as Coke, Burgoyne, Maldon MP C C Western, and the two Bishops of Norwich since Horne's death in 1792 – Manners-Sutton and Bathurst – had all long been in favour of "Catholic relief".

Bishop Bathurst, who was, incidentally, a great friend of Coke's, loftily claimed that the survival of Anglican Protestantism should depend on the faith of its adherents, not the law. However, for most of the 1813 bill's supporters the point was political and strategic, not theological. Like Pitt, they realised that Catholicism was a conservative ideological and social force at odds with the radicalism and secularism of the French. Catholic Ireland was no more a natural ally of Napoleon than Catholic Spain. By bringing her within the fold she could be immunised against sympathy with him. Hippesley saw this point most clearly – indeed too clearly for Grattan, the Tories, and the voters of Sudbury. He actually voted against the bill on the day, partly out of jealousy (he was a notorious attention-seeker), but also because he was confident that the Catholic hierarchy was so anti-French that it would sign a wider concordat with the British government without Canning's guarantees.[10]

The would-be reformers claimed that their opponents lived in the past. We have here that common phenomenon, an elite who have indoctrinated the masses into a belief, then change their minds and sniffily dismiss it as vulgar prejudice when later on it comes back to them from critics. It is also striking how very often those Tory MPs who were keenest to help Irish Catholics and African slaves were the most hostile to domestic civil liberties and democracy. Espousing reform overseas conveniently reassured some of them that they could reject it at home, William Richards of Lynn sneered.

Although Catholics were rare in eastern England those other non-Anglicans, the Protestant Dissenters, flourished. Locally their tradition was of course very long, stretching back to Cromwell and beyond, and all their various sects, old and new, had been expanding in the years just before the French Revolution. During the ensuing war they continued to proselytise and grow. In 1800 the Baptists and Congregationalists built their first churches in Bury St Edmunds and Harwich respectively. In 1813 the old radical Mark Wilks laid the first stone of a new Baptist Chapel in Colegate, Norwich. The same year the wealthy Yarmouth shipbuilder Palmer, a Congregationalist, founded and endowed a Mariners' Chapel. In 1808 a local doctor and former Methodist lay preacher founded a little Swedenborgian community at Brightlingsea, which, with help from the sect's London base, put up a 200-seat chapel in 1814. Most of these groups were universalist in sentiment: that is, thought well of humanity and believed all of it could be saved. During the last few years of the war Dissenters of different denominations combined to set up the "Lancaster Schools" (named after the Quaker of that name), England's first cheap primary schools for the poor. By 1814 nearly every East Anglian town had one.

It may well be that critics of the existing social (and moral) order, repelled by the French Revolution, with its paganism and anti-religious violence, yet also politically stifled by their own Government, had re-channelled their energy from radical politics into radical religion. This is more than a psychological theory: some of the Dissenters said as much. Hardline Tories and Anglicans in any case suspected it. In places their fears bubbled up into persecution. In September 1810 the Baptists of Wickham Market in east Suffolk built a chapel and obtained the required magistrate's licence to hold services there. For the next three months they were harassed by mobs who threw fireworks and excrement, shouted down the sermons, mocked the preacher and smashed the windows. The size of the crowd, the persistence of the attacks, and the failure of the authorities to intervene suggest that right-wing "loyalists" organised the campaign.[11]

It was not only some Anglicans who were intolerant of rivals, and political radicals. The fastest growing dissenting sect, the Methodists, had (in the view of William Richards of Lynn) taken to slandering and persecuting the more liberal Independents and Baptists. In 1811, in protest against the dictatorial and self-important attitude of their own preachers, some of Lynn's Baptists broke away and opened the Salem Chapel.[12]

Nonetheless that same year all the dissenters united to shout down a proposal from Home Secretary Lord Sidmouth to refuse licences to itinerant and non-propertied preachers. His repressive intention was all too obvious.

The puritanical and philanthropic Evangelical wing of the Church of England had also been growing, with Clarkson and Young among its membership. It predated the war, but had been fed by it.

In 1811 many of the Anglican Tory and Whig grandees of Suffolk joined the Ipswich Bible Society. Its committee included Bishop Bathurst of Norwich, the Duke of Grafton and other Fitzroys, Lords Cornwallis and Yarmouth, the Bury banker James Oakes, Sir T C Bunbury, Joshua Vanneck and the MP Hippesley. It gave 4,000 New Testaments to the Ipswich poor, Catholic Irish militiamen, the KGL and many parishes. Its first (1812) report said that true biblical knowledge would be the means of uniting and enlightening the world once "the tempest of war is subsiding into calm … and a brighter day begins to dawn". This message was one around which all those educated and propertied people hostile to conquering dictators or revolutionaries could rally.[13]

However, across the River Stour the Colchester and East Essex Bible Society was more overtly political. On 7th December 1812 it met at Colchester Moot Hall to greet the Rev. Steinkoff of the British and Foreign Bible Society, who had landed from Sweden at Harwich the previous day. A Dane, he was back from a six-month tour of northern and central Europe, braving harassment from Napoleon's officials to help publish scriptures. In his welcome speech William Ward, the Rector of Myland, left no doubt of his own bias.

"In France the Age of Reason commenced its reign with the usurpation of the THRONE OF GOD, and still continues to sway its sanguinary sceptre over the fairest portions of Europe ... (Contrast) the PHILOSOPHY of Voltaire and Tom Paine, and the Gospel of Christ. The scenes produced by the one are too horrible and numerous to relate ... The fruit of Infidel PHILOSOPHY ... has been unrelenting Cruelty and insatiable Ambition, and the fruit of the GOSPEL, unbounded Benevolence and universal Love."[14]

Nor did the Rev. Bull, Curate of St Peter's Colchester', who equated England's stands against the Spanish Armada and Napoleon, using the "weathering the storm" metaphor once used in praise of Pitt. He excitedly continued:

"Trace the long line of dire events from the horrors of revolutionary PARIS to the shrieks of flaming MOSCOW – and behold this happy country alone safe, while surrounded by the wreck of nations'! ... Hail noble suffering England. Thy enemies may join in Horrid League against thee, and thy unnatural children may band with them to destroy thy peace".[15]

The Tory MPs Eliab Harvey, Houblon and Thornton were all vice-presidents of the Colchester Society. Lord Chatham, the town's "High Steward", attended the Moot Hall meeting. When Steinkopff reached London he was greeted by Admiral Lord Gambier, who was both a Tory MP and a leading Evangelical. There is little doubt that the Government had been using Steinkopff as an anti-French propaganda weapon.

Bull's Russian reference was a sign that at last the tide of war was turning. The possibility of Napoleon invading England with the help of Irish (or any other kind of) "Papists" was fast receding. The Harwich packets were bringing back a series of cheering dispatches from northern Europe, the contents of which were happily leaked in the town before they reached London. First there was a report that the Russians were counter-attacking and that Napoleon had fled Moscow. On 22nd December news came that he had returned to Paris and left the remnants of his frost-bitten, starved and broken army to stagger back into Poland. In the New Year of 1813 it was learned that the Prussians had switched back onto the Allied side.[16] In mid-March news came that the French had been driven out of Hamburg by the Cossacks. The Frenchmen manning the batteries at Cuxhaven, at the mouth of the Elbe below the city, were forced to surrender by the small British Heligoland flotilla, led by Lt Banks from the gun brig *Blazer*, which sank their gun vessels. By agreement with the local people he raised the Union and Hamburg flags over the town, then sailed up-river and seized a Danish gunboat moored at Brunsbuttel.[17] Via Heligoland the *Lord Auckland*, *Lady Nepean*, *Diana* and other Harwich packets began to take across German expatriates, British merchants, and even preachers and tourists, some heading for as far east as Berlin. One also brought back the exiled Swiss writer Madame de Stael from Gothenburg, after her two years of wandering around the Continent. She was charmed by the frequent mansions, shady trees, little cottages and gardens she saw along the Harwich-London road, and decided that England must be a land of peace and prosperity.[18]

In view of the total removal of the invasion threat the Norfolk Volunteers were disbanded, and the guns removed from the coast and the fortifications at Chelmsford.

The newspapers recorded the various actions that were taken with effigies of Thomas Pain(e), from hanging in a gibbet to burning.

On 14th April 1813 Prince Willem of Orange, the former Hereditary Prince of the Netherlands, landed at Yarmouth jetty from the *Chanticleer* gun brig, which had brought him from Prussia in expectation of an Allied entry into his homeland.[19] It was his second visit to eastern England. Since the first he had been a wanderer, successively supporting his father in England, negotiating with Napoleon (during the Amiens peace), fighting against him in the Prussian and Austrian armies, and taking refuge in England again. Anti-French Dutchmen had recognised him as their leader since his father's death in 1806. Two weeks later the Duke of Cumberland arrived at Yarmouth from London to sail for Cuxhaven and resume his post as regent of Hanover.[20]

The onrush of victories was temporarily halted in the spring. Holland remained quiet and Orange went to London. The French retook Hamburg and its out-ports at the end of May, and there was an armistice between Napoleon and the three east European monarchs while they negotiated in June. But in July the talks collapsed, and on 2nd August 1813 a Harwich packet revealed that the Russians were about to attack Hamburg, and that its French garrison were planning to set fire to it in response. The French abandoned the city and barricaded themselves down-river at Cuxhaven and Gluckstadt, where the Russians and Bernadotte's Swedes besieged them. Meanwhile even more stirring news had arrived from Spain: Wellington had routed Joseph Bonaparte's army at Vitoria and marched right to the French frontier.

As if in harmony with the military turning-point, the harvest of 1813 was the best for many years. As a consequence of this and the renewed availability of cheap Continental imports, food prices tumbled. Suddenly it was not the urban consumers who were angry, but the landowners and farmers. By the end of the year the wheat price was down to 50/- (£2.10s) per quarter. At this level the import tax stipulated in 1804 applied: arguably it stopped the price falling any further, but the home producers claimed that agriculture would be ruined without more protection.

At the end of October Harwich was first to hear that Napoleon had at last been decisively defeated by the combined forces of Russia, Prussia, Austria and Sweden at Leipzig in Germany. He had been driven out of that country for good. However some of his garrisons were left behind on its coasts. Yarmouth-Heligoland men-of-war went into the Rivers Elbe, Weser and Ems to help flush them out. The British gun brigs *Blazer*, *Désirée*, *Hearty* and *Redbreast* helped the Russians take Cuxhaven for the second time.[21] On 11th November 16 of its French 29th Infantry Regiment defenders, together with a surgeon and a customs secretary, were brought back and lodged in the Yarmouth Tolhouse. Eight of them later travelled up-river for parole in Norwich – on that symbol of progress the recently-arrived steamboat.[22]

On the 20th a Dutch envoy landed from a fishing boat at Yarmouth with exciting news for the Prince Regent and Prince of Orange. The Yarmouth naval telegraph signalled across four counties to the Admiralty in London:

"A complete revolution in Holland, the Texel fleet in mutiny, and Dutch baron on his way to the Prince of Orange".[23]

Admiralty Secretary J W Croker relayed the message to Plymouth and from there it went off by ship to Wellington on the Franco-Spanish border. Early on the morning of 23rd November, having travelled from London overnight,

Prince Willem II of the Netherlands.

Charles Grant, a merchant who knew Holland and spoke Dutch, arrived at Harwich and boarded a vessel for Scheveningen. *"Oranje boven!"* ("Long live Orange!") he shouted to the three boats who came out to meet him, and their crews cheered and took him ashore. At the Hague, amid rejoicing crowds, he was greeted by the rebel leader G K van Hogendorp and Admiral Kikkert, who told him that the Russians had reached the north-east of the country, that Amsterdam and the Hague had declared for the exiled House of Orange, and that British military help was urgently needed. Sick of 18 years of French domination, and bitter about the loss of their colonies and overseas trade, and Napoleon's taxes and conscription, the Netherlands had at last thrown off his yoke.[24]

Meanwhile, Major-General Herbert Taylor and the Orangists Colonel Willem Fagel and Piet Gevers had also reached Harwich from London. Just after noon on the 24th, Eepelin, one of Hogendorp's men, came into harbour on a schuyt, to warn that unless immediate assistance reached his countrymen the French would regain control. In the evening Captain May, ex Dutch Navy, also showed up, with the cheering news that arms for the rebels were coming round by sea from London. Next morning Captain King's *Jason* frigate was seen anchoring out in Hollesley Bay, and Taylor and Fagel went out to her. The following day the *Mercurius* sloop, and four transports, arrived. Efforts were made to transfer the arms from the slow transports to the fast *Jason*, but she had too much ballast on board to take many, so on the 27th she proceeded to "beat her way" out of the anchorage while the rest of the guns were loaded onto the *Mercurius*. Against strong south-easterly winds the convoy took a worrying six days to reach Scheveningen, anchoring off the beach there on 3rd December. Meanwhile Prince Willem had left Yarmouth on the *Warrior* ship of the line on the same day as the Hollesey Bay convoy, but taken only three days to reach the same destination. The long-awaited (almost exact) reversal of his miserable departure in 1795 had come. He landed on the same beach he had left 18 years before. Through wild applause (which surprised him) he was driven to the Hague. *En route* over the North Sea he had passed six Scheveningen fishing boats, which that same day reached Yarmouth with another Hague envoy, Cator. The local garrison cheered them from the harbour forts and quays. On 7th December Rear-Admiral Ferrier's three ships of the line reached the Dutch coast from Hollesley Bay to join the smaller British craft. The same day one of Hogendorp's chief associates, Repelaer van Driel, landed at Harwich to liaise with General Taylor and Gevers about the sending of British troops.

That winter numerous British and Dutch army officers, envoys and merchants shuttled back and forth between Harwich and Helvoetsluys. The Dutchmen stayed at the today-extinct *Three Tuns* and *Black Bull* inns. Over 8,000 British troops went across from 14th December onwards, under the command of Lt-Gen Sir Thomas Graham, hitherto Wellington's right-hand man in Spain. They included the 2nd KGL Hussars from Ipswich, under Count Linsingen's son, the West Norfolks, and one battalion of the East and West Essex (44th and 56th Foot) and Cambridgeshires (30th).

With all the victory news from Germany, Holland and Spain there really was plenty to celebrate that Christmas. Every East Anglian town had its church thanksgiving service, fanfare procession, ball and dinner. The end did at last seem in sight.

As it turned out the fourth and last British expedition to Holland was something of a disappointment. After marching down to the Scheldt and bombarding the French fleet there, it pulled back to besiege the enemy garrison in Bergen-op-Zoom while the Prussian corps it was cooperating with moved south and took Brussels. Not only did Bergen hold out till the end of the war, but part of Graham's force got themselves cut off and captured in a premature attack on the town.

Holland's change of side meant that her prisoners at Norman Cross were freed. 1,000 in number, they were formed into an infantry battalion which left Yarmouth for Helvoetsluys on 25th March 1814 – too late to see action against their former French allies.[27] Five Frenchmen went back in the reverse direction – captured by a boat from Southwold on the merchantman *Ann* (of London), which they had been manning as a prize. They brought the number of French prisoners held in Yarmouth Gaol to 2,118 since the resumption of war in 1803, and over 4,000 since 1793.[28]

That winter was long and bitterly cold in East Anglia. For weeks the rivers were frozen and the roads snowed up. The war seemed equally stuck, as Napoleon dodged and delayed the Allied invaders in north-eastern France. But a few days into April the last of the snow melted and the roads were cleared. Along them came the momentous news that the Russians and Prussians were in Paris and that the Emperor had abdicated.

Finale   19

Tories and the officer class could glory in the victory, Whigs in the peace, and the poor in the end of enforced military and naval service.

At Great Yarmouth over £1,000 was spent on a grand celebration. As many as 30,000 people thronged the town on 19th April. In the words of the local publisher, former mayor Robert Cory, who produced a booklet to commemorate the occasion:

> "It is impossible for words to convey an adequate description of this festive scene: it was one of the finest and most delightful spectacles that was ever exhibited. The windows of the houses, the whole way along the Quay, presenting a splendid display of female beauty, and crowded to excess; the number of flags which were flying; the profusion of white ribbons and laurels intermixed, which adorned the houses in endless variety; the multitude of the poorer classes of the inhabitants, with happiness beaming in their faces ... the morning was ushered in by the ringing of bells ... His Majesty's Ships in the roads, and every ship in the harbour, had their colours flying; and a profusion of flags were suspended ... A procession of three barges, decorated with various emblems, and bearing the flags of all nations, left HMS the *Solebay* (Vice-Admiral Murray's flagship) ... and came ashore in a most majestic style, under constant salute".[1]

On board these craft were "Neptune", with his trident, and two of his attendants, who were holding a pistol to the ear, and a sabre over the head, of a chained effigy of "Buonaparte". Onshore a procession, led by a band and including "Cossacks" and 50 girls in white, marched through the town, carrying the Napoleon dummy and banners proclaiming "England the sheet anchor of Europe" and "Louis XVIII restored". The Union flag was flown above the tricolor. At 1pm four thousand ticket-holders sat down to an open-air banquet at tables in the streets. The admiral, the clergy, the Hurrys, Palmers, Palgraves and other notable local families were among them. 6,884 pieces of prime beef, 8,080 loaves, one ton of raisins, and 70 barrels of ale were consumed. Meals were sent to the infirm, and the inmates of the prison, poorhouse and hospital, while some of the ticket-holders were generous enough to pass some of their food to the rest of the crowd. Toasts were drunk to the King (whereupon the naval guns boomed in salute), the Prince Regent, the rest of the royal family, the Navy, the Duke of York and the Army, Tsar Alexander and the other Allied sovereigns, Wellington, the Government, the Bourbons, the peace, the Mayor and Corporation, Yarmouth's fishing, the local men imprisoned in France, and the organisers of the feast. Towards evening the diners formed a great (and probably fairly drunken) procession which marched up to the North Denes, carrying "Buonaparte". As the darkness fell he was incinerated on a 40-foot-high bonfire. The full-bellied and sozzled town ended the day in such "a state of quietness and repose" that the usual night watch were not required!

None of the other celebrations rivalled this. At Lynn there was a rebellious anti-war note: Captain Hedington, the Impress Officer, watched helplessly as the joyous crowd tore down his flagstaff, ripped the Union Jack to shreds, and burned the pole.[2] Predictably Norwich's events seem to have been more about peace than victory, and did not start till news came of the Treaty of Paris in early June. On 7th July a great thanksgiving service was held by Bishop Bathurst at the Cathedral. He had 700 children from the National (Anglican) Schools – just set up in response to the Dissenters' schools – lined up in front to greet the arriving dignatories.[3]

In August the Hon. John Wodehouse proposed a Nelson Column on the Yarmouth South Denes, overlooking the harbour entrance. Surprisingly his old political rival T W Coke became the main sponsor of the scheme, which went ahead.[4] Whether he was defending himself against critics who had accused him of a lack of patriotism, tactically allying with his pro-Corn Law Tory neighbours, or paying genuine tribute to his one-time north-west Norfolk neighbour, is uncertain. Later another monument was proposed for Thetford, which not surprisingly still had nothing to commemorate its famous son, Tom Paine.

The county was quick off the mark with the 'Norfolk Pillar', its memorial to Nelson. Refurbished for the 200th anniversary of Trafalgar in 2005, it continues to be a sea mark, close to the harbour entrance. Britannia, on top of the momument, looks inland to Burnham Thorpe, the place of Nelson's birth.

By the summer the militia and "pressed" sailors had been paid off, and those held prisoner in France came home. By Christmas peace had been made with the USA at Ghent, releasing still more men. Thousands returned to workshops, docks and farms in search of their old jobs. Some had walked hundreds of miles from their place of discharge, begging food and shelter on the road. Fearful of unemployment and disorder, Arthur Young found himself agreeing with the Birmingham working class radical Attwood, who argued that the demobilisation should have been more gradual.[5] The newspapers printed reports of the great peace congress at Vienna, where monarchs and statesmen haggled about who was to rule what. For eastern England the one directly relevant outcome was the unification of Holland, Belgium and Luxembourg under Prince Willem of Orange, now elevated from Stadtholder to King. This seemed to rule out any further threat from the North Sea.

However, the big issue in East Anglia was not the map of Europe, but the low price of corn. The consumers in the towns (and some rural places) wanted it to stay low, the landowners and their tenant farmers wanted it raised. The war, and coincidental bad weather, had inflated the price, but peace, and coincidental fine weather, had lowered it to the point where the livelihoods of the producers (including employees) were in real jeopardy. After 150,000 tons of wheat were imported from France to replace mildewed home stock Arthur Young claimed that "If importation were to be (allowed) at least half the farmers in England would be ruined".[6]

Both rural Tories *and* Whigs believed that if corn imports were banned (and not merely taxed) while the price stood below 80/- (£4) a quarter it could be stopped from dropping much further, and that that would save English farming. In June 1814 a bill to this effect was drafted for Parliament. At Norwich 12,000 (most of the adult population) signed a petition against it, presented by one of the city's MPs, William Smith. The bill was narrowly rejected by the Commons. When this news reached the city the mail coach was dragged round the streets and a bonfire lit in celebration. As a great landowner Coke had voted in favour. For this he was politely taken to task by Cobbett in his *Political Register*:

> "What a lamentable thing would it have been to see Mr Coke regarded as a cause of the people's suffering … They were sure to regard you, who are so liberal a man … as a grasping monopolizer".[7]

The situation was ironic, for recently the leading artist Sir Thomas Lawrence had presented Coke's portrait to the Norwich Corporation, who hung it in Shire Hall – no doubt to the disgust of loyalists who did want to see it near the Nelson sword. Now Coke and the Tory Government shared an economic policy.

As ever, the economics were too intricate – even too apparently arbitrary – for many to appreciate. Corn was cheap because there was a surplus. In which case why the imports? Because they were even cheaper, and by competition drove down the price still further. But in fact there were fewer of them at this period than for most of the war, when prices had been much higher. And who had grown the surplus corn? British farmers.

In March 1815 the bill was again put before the Commons. On the 4th two separate protest crowds (albeit opposed to the same farmers) gathered at Ipswich. In one street they were objecting to the bill, in the next to the charging of eight Gosbeck farm labourers for smashing up the threshing machines which had put them out of work. The magistrate (and former local MP) Middleton hid in the *Great White Horse* inn from the jeering and stones until things quietened down in the evening.[8] On the 6th Arthur Young noted "The most execrable riots begin in London, on account of the Corn Bill".[9] As ever, he blamed the radical press, and approved when "habeas corpus" was again suspended. On the 17th Coke and the Earl of Albemarle were stoned by a mob at the Norwich cattle show for voting for the bill. This was an extraordinary turn-around: in the past they had always been cheered by the radical lower classes of the city for opposing the war and sympathising with their hardships. The Brunswick Hussars rode to their rescue, while the Riot Act was read. The two great landowners hid in the Angel Yard, and then fled the city for Albemarle's Quidenham Hall, twenty miles away. Mayor Yallop thanked von Tempsky, the Brunswicks' colonel, for his intervention.[10] Once again German mercenaries used to oppress the people, said the radicals. Coke, however, complained that the mayor should have called for them earlier. The controversial bill passed.

That month the Whig opposition were in excited mood, demanding the abandonment of all the Government's war measures – the Militia Acts, the enlarged army, the contracts for ships and supplies, the suspension of civil liberties, the Income Tax, Malt Tax, Import Taxes (except on corn) and just about every other tax. They quoted the City of London's recent denunciation of Income Tax as "the most unjust, inquisitorial and degrading impost that ever harassed and oppressed this nation". They got their way in this case, because most backbench Tories hated it too. The east of England MPs to defend it were nearly all in some way employed by the Government: Vansittart and J H Addington (Harwich), Lord Walpole (Lynn), J A Houblon (Essex), J Round (Ipswich), Lacon and Loftus (Yarmouth).[11]

Then the Whigs applauded their leader Tierney when he attacked Vansittart's proposal to offset the abolition of Income Tax by perpetuating the wartime increased Customs duties, thereby maintaining "the vast military system which himself and his colleagues had created".

But meanwhile Napoleon escaped from Elba, returned to France, drove out King Louis XVIII, and reassembled his administration and army. He renounced French territorial expansion, adopted something close to an American-style liberal-democratic constitution, and offered peace to Great Britain. Of course most Englishmen dismissed all this as a trick. The Prince Regent sent back "Buonaparte"'s smarmy letter unopened. The Tory government joined the "legitimate" Continental monarchs in massing armies on the French frontier. Yet even now the usual radical suspects argued that there should be peace with France. Coke, Western and William Smith voted in the Commons against our new declaration of war – along with a surprising one in five other members. Smith rightly claimed that nine out of ten Frenchmen preferred Napoleon to Louis. Creevey, however, was won over to supporting the war by the strange friendship he had struck up with Wellington when they met over in Brussels.

Arthur Young blamed the Government for leaving the way open for Napoleon's return by blaming only him for the previous war and being so lenient on his nation. "It was the vile and sordid devotedness of the French people, the passive instruments of Buonaparte", that shed the blood, he wrote, almost as if he was referring to the German followers of Hitler 130 years later.[12]

Since Napoleon did not control the Low Countries and Germany as he had in the previous war there was no re-assembling of the Navy at Yarmouth and Harwich: the entire North Sea fleet, apart from the Downs squadron opposite France, only numbered 17 or 18 vessels, mostly small gun brigs. Nonetheless, the press gangs showed up and were as usual most unwelcome. When a boat from HMS *Cadmus* entered the River Yare on 11th May it was stoned from both banks, till one sailor was badly injured, the craft was abandoned, and the rioters set fire to it. The Admiralty offered a £20 reward to informers, and a year later seven culprits got short prison sentences at Norwich. There was another ballot for the militia: none of the draftees were assembled in time to fight Napoleon but the West Norfolk battalion were (no doubt to their disgust) shipped from Harwich to police an Ireland still seething over the Union and the defeat of "Catholic Relief".[13]

Wellington was assembling a makeshift army of Britons, Germans and Dutchmen at Brussels. This included the Earl of Uxbridge (formerly Paget) and the Hereditary Prince of Orange, who, as a baby 20 years before, had come ashore at Yarmouth with his mother, now Queen of the Netherlands. Also in its ranks were the Highlanders, riflemen and light dragoons for long based in north-east Essex and south-east Suffolk. In June, en route to Lambert's brigade, an unusual little group stayed at the *Black Bull* at Harwich – Major Harry Smith, his teenage Spanish wife Juana (they had met at Badajoz when he saved her from the rapists), and his brother Charles. The inn landlord, Briton, "a man as civil as full of information", according to the major, introduced him to the skipper of a small trading sloop who agreed to take them along with their five horses, two grooms, and Juana's maid. Briton also supplied them with excellent food at a bargain price. Contrary winds kept them all under his roof for a fortnight: then they got across to Ostend in twenty-four hours. They reached Brussels just one day before the final showdown of the war.[14]

The ferrying demands of the army at Colchester had led to three small ships starting a new packet service between there and Ostend, a route quicker than that via Harwich. Their owner was the Colchester Town Clerk, Tory clubman, Essex Admiralty agent and smuggling boss Daniel Sutton jr. – last mentioned at the Weeley court martial of Mary Ann Clarke's brother. Late on 19th June he came back home on his *Maria* with exaggerated news from the fighting at Quatre Bas three days earlier. Having ridden to London overnight, he got his account – and name – into the *Morning Post*, *Times* and other newspapers. This led to premature rejoicing over a decisive British victory before the genuine news had arrived.[15]

Then it was all over for good. The news of Waterloo spread across East Anglia on 22nd and 23rd June. At Bury St Edmunds the banker and political agent James Oakes wrote in his diary:

> "glorious news from Duke of Wellington … with English and Prussian armys. A most desperate and severe engagement took place on the 17th and 18th, when the French were completely discomfited and fled before them. The slaughter was immense on both sides".[16]

The Norwich crowd held their own unofficial celebration round a bonfire made from stolen wood. From London the painter John Constable wrote to his wife at East Bergholt in Suffolk that he was worried about two of his cousins, who had been in the battle. He thought the War Office were holding back the casualty list. It turned out that one cousin, Peninsula veteran Captain Gubbins of 13th Light Dragoons, had been killed in a cavalry charge, and that the other, Lt Allen of the KGL infantry, was safe.[17] Allen was from Crane Hill near Ipswich. The Norwich press announced that several officers from well-known Norfolk families had also lost their lives, including a Townshend, a Money, a Kerrison and a Hoste. Uxbridge had had his leg shot off. 600 other British wounded were landed at Yarmouth from Ostend and taken to the new hospital on the South Denes. 17 of them died and were buried nearby.[18] By then "Buonaparte" was said to be en route to remote exile in the South Atlantic. Capel Lofft drew a storm of abuse down on his head by calling Napoleon's defeat "most calamitous" and saying that he should have been given political asylum in England![19]

The dominant mood was of course triumphant. The *Suffolk Chronicle* thundered:

> "To Him the Lord of Hosts and Victory, Be Glory, Power and Might and Majesty!"

But there was compassion too. At Ipswich brewer's wife, former employer of the criminal Margaret Catchpole, and minor poet Elizabeth Cobbold, who had never been anywhere near a battlefield, wrote:

> "As victory stretch'd her eagle wing, and wav'd her wreath on high,
> A tear from Pity's holy spring, stood trembling in her eye".[20]

Funds were launched in many places for the wounded, widows and orphans of the battle: Norwich eventually raised £7,000. And again the Whig-radicals celebrated peace rather than victory. The old Norwich radical William Taylor told his friend the poet Southey that "liberty, toleration, art have rather to bewail than rejoice".[21] Bishop Bathurst invited his son Henry, who had recently joined him at Norwich as his archdeacon, to give the sermon at another cathedral thanksgiving. Henry jr told him that:

> "it struck him forcibly that the object of the British government was to root out the principle of resistance to all government, however oppressive … (they were not against Napoleon) as a military despot and tyrant, or even a troublesome neighbour, but merely because he had seated himself on the throne of legitimate kings".[22]

Not only did the Bishop agree, but allowed his son to include an attack on the restoration of the Bourbons in the sermon. He himself supported Coke's putting up a "Napoleon the Great" statue at Holkham, and wrote a laudatory inscription for it. The Tories were enraged. For them Waterloo was the final victory over evil. In an address at the Norwich Shire Hall the Rev. Burges of Halvergate and Moulton was comparatively restrained in observing of the region's most enduring war critic:

> "Whether Mr Coke would have been pleased to have seen the contest decided at Holkham instead of Hougoumont we leave that gentleman to determine".[23]

Bishop Bathurst was nothing if not controversial. His brother-in-law was General Sir Eyre Coote, who had commanded the Bromswell Heath brigade during the 1803 invasion alarm. Soon after Waterloo Coote was disgraced and cashiered for playing sado-masochistic games with schoolboys. Bathurst, in the spirit of Christian forgiveness, got up a petition to have him reinstated and took it in person to the Prince Regent. Considering his recently objecting to the heir to the throne wasting money on the victory celebrations, he had a courteous audience, though the Duke of York, who was present, was visibly embarrassed and the plea was rejected.[24]

Thomas Clarkson, who now lived at Playford Hall, near Woodbridge, joined an anti-militarist "Society for the promotion of permanent and universal peace". He also corresponded with the black ruler of Haiti about preventing France from reconquering and re-enslaving his people now that the war was over. Clarkson was annoyed by the Bourbons' reluctance to abandon the French claim to the island, but applauded the post-war peace congress for condemning the slave trade.[25]

It would be a naïve account of East Anglia's war which summed it up as a unified patriotic struggle against foreign aggression and tyranny, as if we were describing 1939-1945 instead of 1793-1815. If the war leaders Nelson,

Cornwallis and Windham are to be remembered, so also should be the critics Paine, Coke, Bathurst and the Norwich radicals. The conflict never entirely ceased to be a clash between social classes, as opposed to nations. Nonetheless, when Napoleon blatantly reintroduced monarchy, aristocracy and established church even some radicals had to accept that it had become a contest between equally illiberal states, so that it was better to support the homegrown one, which they might one day reform, than the foreign one in which they could have no voice. This necessitated the war for them – but on condition that the Government did not use it to oppress the people and thwart reform. Whenever they suspected these evils they pointed to what the French Revolution and Napoleon *had* done to promote equality and liberty, in France and beyond. This in turn fed the Government's understandable suspicion of them as unpatriotic.

Some have claimed it as the "first total war", because of its politics, economic impact, and state interference with everyday life. However in many other ways it was distinctly "limited". We are often reminded that Jane Austen, in spite of having two brothers in the armed forces, never mentioned it in her novels. Similarly, the painter John Constable and the Bury St Edmunds banker James Oakes hardly ever refer to it their correspondence and diaries. This in spite of week-by-week publication of detailed war news in the local press. In the much shorter 20th century world wars about one in seven Britons served in the armed forces at some stage: between 1793 and 1815 it was around one in 14. (I have left the Volunteers and Home Guard out of both calculations). Although enemy invasion was guarded against almost throughout, it was only a real danger (and then not in everyone's estimation) for three brief periods. The shooting war stopped some miles off the coast, where the nearest enemy privateers and merchantmen were boarded. Though gunfire was very often heard from shore, it mostly came from warships saluting the royal family or "shooting at the mark". The only physical conflict *on land* in East Anglia was the violence between troops and rioters – and between rival riotous troops. The sheer length of the war also meant that other (albeit partially related) concerns – Catholics, corn, electoral reform, the slave trade, social unrest – repeatedly came to the fore and eclipsed it.

All this said, we must remember that the region saw more of the Army and Navy than most, and was a base for many of their operations. It was an anchorage for fleets, a departure point for expeditions, a destination for evacuations and prisoners. The Highland regiments were based in north-east Essex for longer than in the Iberian Peninsula – a period equal to the entire Second World War. The Navy was at Yarmouth for longer than the two world wars combined! Some of the most important war leaders – and war commentators – came from the region, or were based there.

One of them, Arthur Young, addressed a last word to the French from the heart of Suffolk. Having berated them for everything they had done over the past quarter-century, he spoke of their future peace and happiness:

> "Your country, ever since the Revolution, has not found these blessings. I ardently hope that she will at length enjoy them and that her felicity will be uninterrupted. Accept, my friend, of my cordial good wishes".[26]

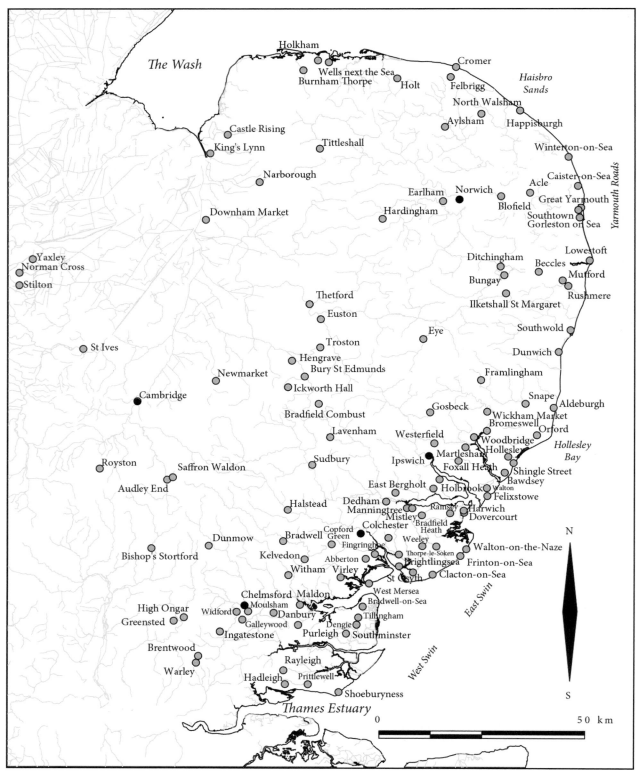

This East Anglian map shows
places mentioned in the book.
The many encampments in Essex
and south Suffolk crowd between
the rivers and estuaries.

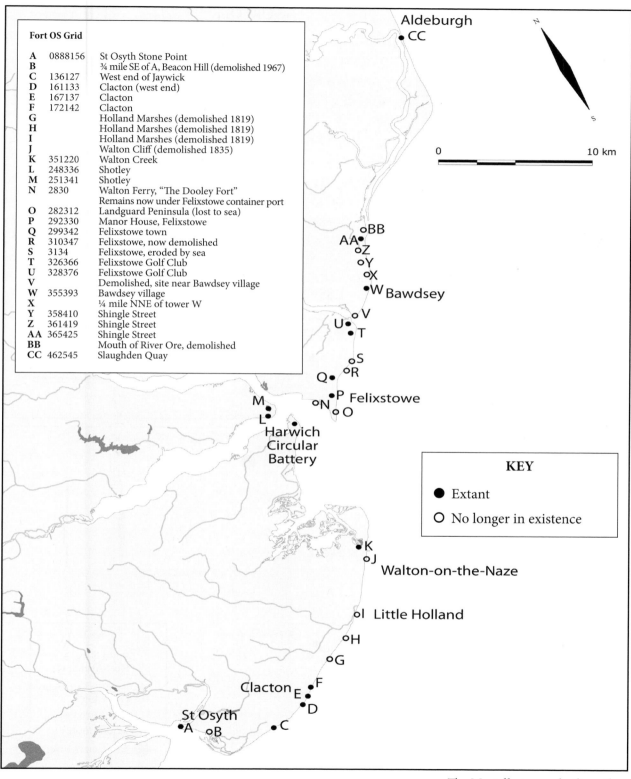

Fort OS Grid

A	0888156	St Osyth Stone Point
B		¾ mile SE of A, Beacon Hill (demolished 1967)
C	136127	West end of Jaywick
D	161133	Clacton (west end)
E	167137	Clacton
F	172142	Clacton
G		Holland Marshes (demolished 1819)
H		Holland Marshes (demolished 1819)
I		Holland Marshes (demolished 1819)
J		Walton Cliff (demolished 1835)
K	351220	Walton Creek
L	248336	Shotley
M	251341	Shotley
N	2830	Walton Ferry, "The Dooley Fort"
		Remains now under Felixstowe container port
O	282312	Landguard Peninsula (lost to sea)
P	292330	Manor House, Felixstowe
Q	299342	Felixstowe town
R	310347	Felixstowe, now demolished
S	3134	Felixstowe, eroded by sea
T	326366	Felixstowe Golf Club
U	328376	Felixstowe Golf Club
V		Demolished, site near Bawdsey village
W	355393	Bawdsey village
X		¼ mile NNE of tower W
Y	358410	Shingle Street
Z	361419	Shingle Street
AA	365425	Shingle Street
BB		Mouth of River Ore, demolished
CC	462545	Slaughden Quay

KEY

● Extant

○ No longer in existence

The Martello towers built on the
east coast 1809-1812. A number
have been lost to coastal erosion.

The Army Order of
Battle, 1803

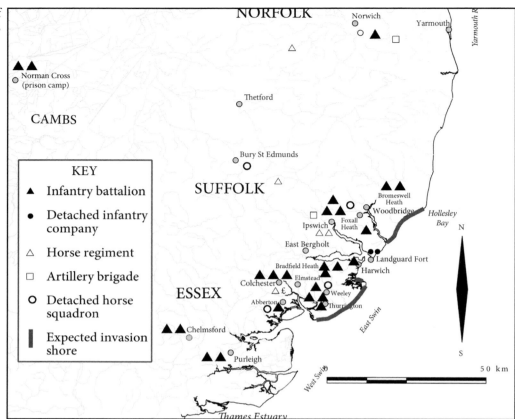

Royal Navy Bases
and Guardships

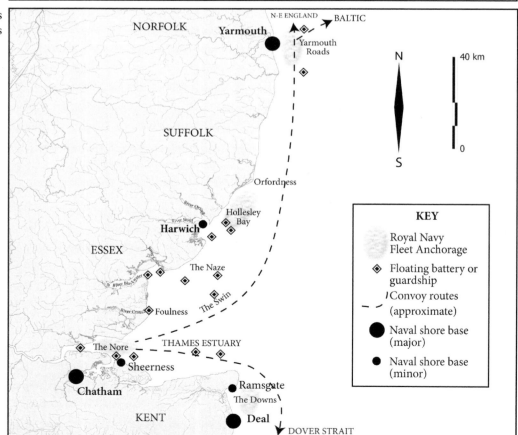

References

1 News from the Revolution

1. Ian Scott: *Reactions to Radicalism in Norwich 1789-1802* (online dissertation)
2. C. Knight: *The Popular History of England* (1870); *Autobiography of Arthur Young* (1898)
3. G. P. Gooch in *Cambridge Modern History*, Vol VIII (1907), C B Jewson (*Jacobin City: A Portrait of Norwich & Its Reaction to the French Revolution* (1975). The label "Jacobin City" was Pitt's.
4. R. G. Thorne: *The History of Parliament* (1986). Thorne's research, in the spirit of Sir Lewis Namier, delves into the fine details of candidates, constituencies and elections, and brings out personal and local factors which seldom show up in histories written more from national or ideological perspectives. It is now all found on the official website "Parliament Online".
5. Jewson.
6. Scott.
7. *The Theological & Philosophical Works of Joseph Priestley* (1972)
8. *The Trial of John Joseph Tooke for High Treason* (Joseph Gurney's trial transcript (1795)
9. Thorne.
10. *Trial of Tooke*. Jewson.
11. *The Political Works of Thomas Paine* (1817).
12. Charlotte Barrett: *Diary & Letters of Madame d'Arblay* (1854). Madame d'Arblay was Fanny Burney's married name, and Mrs Barrett was her niece.
13. *Monthly Review* (Jan 1793)
14. *Ipswich Journal*.
15. The fact that Paine was holding public office in an enemy country, as he already had in the previous war, obviously told against him. He had a defence barrister at the trial, the senior Scottish Whig lawyer Sir Thomas Erskine, but he himself was soon to become an enemy of the Revolution.
16, *Ipswich Journal*
17. *Ibid*
18. *Ibid*
19 *Ibid*
20. Scott.

2 The Beginning of the Sea War

1. Letter from "a Leicester clergyman" in *Gentleman's Magazine*, Nov.1793.
   "Journey from London through Holland" in *Christian Observer* Vol. 15 (1816)
2. *Ipswich Journal*; various naval logs.
3. *Agamemnon* Logs & Muster Rolls (National Archive)
4. *Navy Lists*
5. *Racehorse* Log & Muster Rolls. HO 42/231 (N.A.)
6. I .E.Land: *Domesticating the Maritime* (1999). This misspells Collis's name as "Coller".

7. Henceforth all reports of merchant ship attacks and captures by enemy privateers are from *Lloyd's List* – usually they were also published in the *Gentleman's Magazine* and in various east coast newspapers.
8. N. Gallois: *Les Corsaires francais sous la République et l'Empire* (1847)
9. *Savage* log. Captured papers from *Custine* (N.A.)
10. *Ipswich Journal*; *Iris* logs; captured papers from *Sans Culotte* & *Le Vaillaint Custine*; Norwich naval prison book, ADM 103/103 (N.A.) Henceforth the movements and actions of British men of war, the details of ship captures, and of enemy privateer or naval prisoners, are from such logs, captured documents and prison books respectively.
11. *Lizard* logs. Prison Book, ADM 103/103(N.A.) Isaac Schomberg: *Naval Chronology* (1802)
12. *Ibid.*
13. *History & Proceedings of the Debates in the House of Commons* (1804).
14. *Navy Lists.*
15. *Scots Magazine* (April 1794)

3 Jacobins & Loyalists

1. Isaac, Jane & Ann Taylor: *The Family Pen* (1867)
2. *Cambridge Modern History,* Vol VIII. C.H. Cooper: *Annals of Cambridge,* Vol IV (1852)
3. *Monthly Review,* Vol XI (1793)
4. *The Trial of Thomas Hardy for High Treason,* Vol 2 (1795)
5. *Jordan's Parliamentary Journal* (1793); *The Parliamentary Register,* Vol 4 (1794)
6. Edmund Burke: *Letter to His Grace the Duke of Portland* (1793)
7. C. Rawcliffe: *Norwich Since 1550, (2004)*
8. G. Matchett: *Norfolk & Norwich Remembrancer & Vade-mecum* (1802)
9. Jewson.
10. J. Mingay: *An Address to the Electors of Norwich (1794)*
11. *Ibid.*
12. Arthur Young: *An Idea of the Present State of France* (1795)
13. *The Cabinet,* Vol.3 (1795)

4 The Émigrés

1. *Memoires Inédits de Madame la Comtesse de Genlis,* Vol 2 (1825); d'Arblay.
2. *Ipswich Journal*
3. A. le Braz: *Aux Pays d'Exil de Chateaubriand* (1907). It has also been suggested that Chateaubriand's visits were prompted by a desire to evade fellow exiles recruiting for an Anglo-French expedition to help the Breton Vendée rebels, though this does only seem to be   supposition.
4. F-R de Chateaubriand: *Memoires d'Outre-Tombe* (1849-50)
5. C.Hayward: *A Sermon Preached at the Parish Church of Copford* (1793)
6. W.Betham: *The Baronetage of England* (1801)
7. *Handbook for Essex, Suffolk, Norfolk & Cambridgeshire* (1870)
8. C.McKie: *Norfolk Annals* (1901). McKie's material came mainly from the *Norwich Chronicle. The Month,* Vol 168 (1936)
9. *Gentleman's Magazine,* 1795.
10. *History of St Mary's Church, Ipswich. From the Church Archives, St Pancras Catholic Church* (websites).
11. Advertised in *Gentleman's Magazine.*

5 Defeats & Discontent

1. G W Manby: *History of Great Yarmouth* (1806).
2. Home Office letter HO 42/54 (N.A.).
3. *Gentleman's Magazine,* Vol. 7 (Feb, 1795).
4. W Woodfall: *Parliamentary Reports* (1795).

5. *Gentleman's Magazine.* This printed tables of county-by-county wheat prices throughout the period.

5. B.A.Holderness & Michael Turner: *Land, Labour & Agriculture 1700-1820* (1991). Liam Brunt: *Estimating English Wheat Production in the Industrial Revolution* (Oxford University discussion paper, 1999).

6. Scott

7. Adam Smith: *The Wealth of Nations*, Vol II (1776).

8. Arthur Young: *Annals of Agriculture* Vol XXV (1796). *Gentleman's Magazine* (Dec.1795)

9. as in 4. Arthur Young later blamed some of the food price inflation on the higher wages paid to local labourers because many were employed by the Army building defence works – but in fact most of these were erected in 1796-7 and 1803-4, when wheat prices were fairly low. Moreover most of the labour was imported from London.

10. Parliamentary Inquiry Into Grain Prices (1798).

11. D.G. Burns: *A History of the Corn Laws* (1930).

12. *The Autobiography & Services of Sir James McGrigor* (1861). McGrigor went on to be Wellington's Surgeon-General in Spain.

13. *Ipswich Journal.*

14. Letters in *Gentleman's Magazine.*

15. Thorne, *Ipswich Journal.*

16. John Thelwall: *An Appeal to Public Opinion Against Kidnapping & Murder* (1796).

17. E.P.Thompson: *The Making of the English Working Class* (1963).

18. David Addy: *St.Edmundsbury* history website.

19. *Monthly Magazine* Vol 3 (1797).

20. Woodfall: *Parliamentary Debates.*

21. Thurlow featured as a befuddled, easily-led, personality in the film *The Madness of King George.*

6 From the Quota Act to Camperdown

1. *Statutes at Large*, Vol XL (1795).

2. *Ipswich Journal*, 11 April 1795.

3. D. MacPherson: *Annals of Commerce* (1805).

4. Palmer, though he accidentally says 1796.

5. R.Knight & M.Wilcox: *Sustaining the Fleet 1793-1815* (2010).

6. *Ipswich Journal.*

7. J.Debrett: *A Collection of State Papers Relative to the War* (1796). William James: *Naval History of Great Britain* Vol I (1839).

8. *Ibid.*

9. W.J.Neale: *The Mutiny at Spithead and the Nore* (1805).

10. The term seems to have been popularised by the leftwing London newspaper *The Courier.*

11. *Leopard* and *Monmouth* muster rolls (N.A.) Only ten men from the former were listed as East Anglians, and a dozen from the latter, though many (homes unrecorded) had transferred from other ships.

12. Neale.

13. C.Lloyd: *The Nation & the Navy* (1954)

14. Neale.

15. Duncan's despatches in *London Gazette*; H W Wilson in *Cambridge Modern History*, Vol VIII (1907). The muddle about signalling must partly be blamed on Duncan's over-optimistic belief that his captains could understand at least three sudden changes of plan. Indeed there was so much confusion that some recent accounts of the onset of the battle have been mutually, and even self, contradictory!

16. *London Gazette*; William James, Vol II (1847).

17. McKie.

7 Corsairs of the Republic

1. *Lloyd's List.*
2. Yarmouth naval prison book, ADM 103/103 (N.A.) See Chapter 2, reference 9.
3. *Lloyd's List* (24th July 1795)
4. Gallois. C.B.Norman: *The Corsairs of France* (1887)
5. *London Gazette.* As 2.
6. Yarmouth Prison Book, ADM 103/103.
7. *Ibid.*
8. W C Oulton: section on Yaxley in *Traveller's Guide* (1805). Oulton refers to gross exaggerations by "a prostituted French journalist" writing long before Pillet; T J Walker: *Norman Cross* (1913).
9. *Ipswich Journal.*
10. *London Gazette*, July 1797; Prisoner interrogation report for *l'Espoir* (N.A.); Harwich Prison Book (ADM 103/103); *New Annual Register*, Dec.1797; *London Chronicle* Vol 82 (1798)
11. Journal de Francfort
12. Harwich & Yarmouth prison books, ADM 103/103 (N.A.).
13. "T.Gaspard Malo" on Geneanet Website.
14. William James, Vol II
15. *Gentleman's Magazine*, Vol.LXVIII (1798)
16. *London Gazette* (7 Dec.1799). *Naval Chronicle* (July-Dec.1799).
17. *European Magazine & London Review* (Vol.77, April 1800)
18. *Naval Chronicle*
19. *London Chronicle* (Vol 87, 1800)
20. *Facts Opposed to Falsehood in the Prize Case Clarissa* (c.1800)
21. William Cobbett: *Political Register*, Vol 21 (1812)
22. *Weekly Despatch* (27 Sept.1801)

8 The First Invasion Scare

1. Thomas Paine: *Observations on the Construction and Operation of Navies with a Plan for an Invasion of England* (1798).
2. Michael Glover: *Wellington as Military Commander* (1968).
3. *List of the Officers of the Fencibles, Cavalry, Infantry, Volunteers etc.* (War Office, 1797).
4. Troop Returns, Eastern District, WO 17/384 (1795).
5. *Ipswich Journal*, 16th Feb.1793.
6. *Ipswich Journal*, 20th April 1793 .
7. *List of the Officers of the Fencibles, Cavalry, Infantry, Volunteers etc.* (War Office, 1797).
8. *Gentleman's Magazine.*
9. *Scots Magazine*, Feb.1796.
10 *List of the Officers of the Fencibles, Cavalry, Infantry, Volunteers etc.* (War Office, 1797).
11. *Lady's Magazine* (Dec.1796). J.W. Burrow: *The Essex Yeomanry* (1925).
12. J. Chambers: *A General History of the County of Norfolk* (1820).
13. J. Phillippart: *The Royal Military Calendar* (1815).
14. *The Georgian Era: Memoirs of the Most Eminent Persons*, Vol II (1833).
15. *Gentleman's Magazine.*
16. Eastern District defences, WO 30/67 (N.A.) James Carrick Moore: *The Diary of Sir John Moore.*
17. WO 30/67.
18. *Ibid.*
19. *Ibid.*
20. *Ibid.*
21. R.Philips: *Essays on the Theory & Practice of War*, Vol II (1809); Journal of the House of Commons, Vol 53 (1797).
22. McKie.
23. *Sporting Magazine* Vols 10 & 13 (1797). Note that duelling is classed as a sport, not a crime!
24. *Monthly Magazine*, Vol 3 (1797).

25. R.Hellman: *Bloody British History: Chelmsford* (2012).
26. *Gentleman's Magazine*.
27. WO 30/100.
28. *Ibid.*
29. W.Mudge, I.Dalby, T.Colby: *Trigonometrical Survey of England & Wales* (1799). Navy Lists.
30. *Gentleman's Magazine*, Feb.1799.
31. *Braakel* logs & muster rolls.
32. *Naval Chronicle*, Vol. 6.
33. *Navy Lists*. Sea Fencible muster and pay rolls, ADM 26/25, 26/26, 27/25 (N.A.).
34. Arthur Young: *An Inquiry into the Rise of Prices during the Last 25 Years* (1815).
35. McKie.
36. *Lady's Magazine*.
37. M. H. Wilkin: *Joseph Kinghorn of Norwich, a Memoir* (1855); *Baptist Quarterly* (1972)
38. Thomas Paine: *The Age of Reason* (1795)

9 Turn of the Century Travail

1. Statutes, Vol III (1799).
2. Arthur Young: *Autobiography*.
3. *A Complete History of the Rise, Progress and Termination of the Late War* (1802).
4. *Anti-Jacobin*, Vol IV (1799).
5. J. Baron: *The Life of Edward Jenner* (1827).
6. Young: *Annals of Agriculture*.
7. *Ipswich Journal*.
8. Young: *Annals of Agriculture*.
9. *Chelmsford Chronicle*. A J Peacock: *Bread or Blood* (1965). A J F Brown: *Prosperity and Poverty in Rural Essex 1700-1815*. Holderness & Turner. Brown tells us the ringleaders were from Steeple, three miles north-west of Southminster.
10. *Chelmsford Chronicle*.
11. *Ipswich Journal*.
12. Holderness & Turner.
13. Parliamentary Report on the Herring Fisheries, 1798.
14. M.E. Turner: *English Parliamentary Enclosure* (1990). *St Edmundsbury* website. Arthur Young: *General Report on Enclosures* (1808).
15. F.J.Jackson: *Laws of the Sea* (1818).
16. *Reports of Cases Determined in the High Court of Admiralty* (1853).
17. Palmer (1816). McKie.(1816).
18. Schomberg. James. *Gentleman's Magazine*, March 1801.
19. *Edinburgh Magazine*, Vol 18 (1801).
20. *The Trial of J.Taylor for Forgery* (1800). *The Criminal Recorder*, Vol 1(1815); John Glyde: *The New Suffolk Garland* (1816); V.A.C. Gatrell: *The Hanging Tree: Execution & the English People 1770-1868* (1994); *St Edmundsbury* website.
21. *Chelmsford Chronicle* (1802).
22. Arthur Young: Autobiography. T.K.Cromwell: *Excursions in the County of Suffolk* (1818)
23. *Weekly Despatch*, 27th Sept.1801. The Rev. Bate Dudley was thick-skinned enough to write to the press in very similar terms, calling for legislation to safeguard some independence and "a small share" of agricultural land and income for the poor. Note the word "small"!
24. *Navy Lists*.
25. Sir Nicholas Nicholas: *Nelson's Letters & Despatches* (1895).

10 Amiens Interlude

1. *The Substance of the Speeches of the Rt.Hon.William Windham on Measures Connected with the Defence of this Country* (1804).
2. McKie.
3. Amelia A. Opie & Cecilia L. Brightwell: *Memorials of the Life of Amelia Opie* (1854).
4. Thorne.
5. *Speeches of Mr William Pitt in the House of Commons*, Vol.IV (1804).

11 Waiting for Napoleon

1.   Arthur Young: *Autobiography*.
2.   *Ipswich Journal*.
3.   W.G.Perrin: *Keith Papers* (1927).
4.   *Naval Chronicle*, May 1803.
5.   Yarmouth Naval Letters, ADM 1/1424 (N.A.).
6.   C.S.Forrester: *Adventures of John Wetherall* (1954).
7.   North Sea correspondence, ADM 1/536 (N.A.).
8.   W.MacFarland & C.Weobly: *A Collection of Remarkable & Interesting Criminal Trials*, Vol II (1804).
9.   *Aimwell* Muster Book (N.A.).
10. North Sea correspondence, ADM 1/540. Yarmouth Naval Letters, ADM 1/1424. Sea Fencible Pay Lists, ADM 27/25 (N.A.).
11. *Eastern District Defences*, WO 30/100 (N.A.)
12. *Ibid*.
13. *Ibid*.
14. *Ibid*.
15. *Ibid*.
16. *Ibid*.
17. W.Sheardown: *Origins & Services of the Third West Yorkshire (Light) Militia* (1870).
18. *Keith Papers*.
19. *Sketches of Life & Manners with Descriptions of Scenery in England, Scotland & Ireland*, Vol II (1811).
20. Cecilia L. Brightwell: *Memorials of the Life of Mr.Brightwell of Norwich* (1869).
21. *Speeches of William Pitt in the House of Commons* (1804).
22. J.W. Robberds: *A Memoir of the Life of the Late William Taylor* (1843).
23. WO 30/100 .
24. William Cobbett: *Political Register*, Vol 12 (1807) .
25. *Keith Papers*. *Naval Chronicle* Vol.12 (1804).
26. *Naval Chronicle*, Vol 12 (1804).
27. H.F.B.Wheeler & A.M. Broadley: *Napoleon & the Invasion of England* (1908).
28. J.Holland Rose & A.M: *Dumouriez & the Defence of England against Napoleon* (1908).
29. *Ipswich Journal*.
30. *The Writings of Jane Taylor*, Vol.I (1832).
31. Sheardown.
32. J.H. Evans: *The Poems of George Crabbe* (1933).
33. ADM 1/540..
34. Warship Logs (N.A.).
35. Jane Taylor.
36. Cecilia Brightwell.
37. Jane Taylor.

12 The Crisis Passes: Pitt, Trafalgar & All the Talents

1.   *Defences of the Eastern District* (N.A.).
2-5 *North Sea Correspondence*, ADM 1/542 (N.A.).
     J.Barrow: *Life & Correspondence of Admiral Sir William Sidney Smith* (Vol 2) (1848).
     Naval Chronicle, Vol 12.
6.   *Tom Paine National Historical Association website* (Eric Foner's introduction).
7.   *Ipswich Journal*.
8.   *Speeches in Parliament of William Windham* (1804).
9.   *Speeches of William Pitt in the House of Commons* (1804).
10. McKie..
11. *Naval Chronicle*, Vol.12. The Warrens stayed the night at Colchester.
12. *Ipswich Journal*.
13. D.Harris & A.Cross: *Nelson Almanac* (1998).
14. Roger Knight: *Pursuit of Victory: The Life & Achievements of Horatio Nelson* (2005).

15. Boyd Hilton, in his *A Mad, Bad & Dangerous People: England 1783-1846*, stresses this boycotting of Nelson's funeral. But was it jealousy, an English distaste for glorifying a self-publicist, or the Emma Hamilton scandal?
16. Paul Richards: *History of Lynn*.
17. Thorne.
18. *The Late Negotiation* (speech in Parliament by Canning, 1807).
19. J.McAlister & C.Petley: *The Royal Navy & the British Atlantic World* (2016). McKie. G.Matchett: *Norfolk & Norwich Remembrancer*.
20. Thorne.

13 Dockyards & Shipyards

1. R.Winfield: *British Warships in the Age of Sail. Naval Chronicle. Navy Lists*.
2. E.P. Dicken: *A History of Brightlingsea* (1913).
3. *Harwich Guide* (1808). *Navy Lists*.
4. G.A.Clarke: *The History and Description of the Town & Borough of Ipswich* (1830). *Navy Lists*.
5. Palmer. McKie.
6. *Lloyd's Register*.
7. *Ipswich Journal*.
8. ADM 106/1974 (N.A.).
9. *Navy Lists*.

14 Privateering & Blockading

1. *Lloyd's Lists. London Gazette.Newcastle Courant*.
2. *Newcastle Courant*.
3. Yarmouth Naval Letters ADM 1/1424. Yarmouth Naval Prison Book ADM 103/461 (N.A.).
4. Yarmouth Naval Letters ADM 1/1424. *Lloyd's List*.
5. Yarmouth Naval Prison Book ADM 103/461.
6. Yarmouth Naval Letters ADM 1/1425.
7. *London Gazette*.
8. Gallois. *Cruizer's Log. London Gazette. Naval Chronicle Vol 12* (1804). *The Battle and the Breeze* (1804).
9. *Lloyd's List*.
10. *Gentleman's Magazine*, Vol 76 (1806).
11. Gallois.
12. *London Gazette*.
13. Gallois. *Ipswich Journal*.
14. Yarmouth Naval Letters ADM 1/1427.
15. *Ipswich Journal*.
16. John Brown: *The Mysteries of Neutralisation* (1806).
17. *Cambridge Modern History*, Vol IX (1906).
18. *Ipswich Journal*.
19. *Lloyd's Register*.
20. *Navy Lists*. Graham Smith: *Smuggling in Essex* (2003).
21. H. Benham: *Once Upon A Tide* (1986).
22. Yarmouth Naval Letters, ADM 1/1424.

15 Continental Expeditions

1. L-A. Fauvelet de Bourrienne: *The Life of Napoleon Bonaparte*, Vol 3 (1831).
2. *Ipswich Journal, Harwich Guide* (1808) .
3. W.Surtees: *Twenty-Five Years in the Rifle Brigade* (1833).
4. *Edinburgh Medical & Surgical Journal* (1808). The medical press agreed that the illness was self-inflicted, claiming that the malingerers were playing on the fact that British

troops had been genuinely affected in Egypt.

5. H.A. Bruce: *Life of Sir William Napier KCB*, Vol.I (1864).
6. Palmer: *The History of Gt.Yarmouth* (1856).
7. *Gentleman's Magazine*.
8. G.A.Clarke: *The History and Description of the Town & Borough of Ipswich* (1830).
9.& 10. Cobbett/Hansard: *Parliamentary Debates*, Feb.1809 (Vol.XII).
11. McKie.
12. Lt-Col C Greenhill Gardyne: *The History of the Gordon Highlanders* (1901).
13. Troop Returns for Eastern District WO 17/384 (N.A.).
15. *Official Documents Relative to the Disputes between the Doctors of the Late Medical Board* (1810).
   Minutes of the Evidence taken before the House relating to the Expedition to the Scheldt (1810) .
16. Arthur Young: *Autobiography*.
17. *An Account of the Celebration of the Jubilee on the 20ᵗʰ of October 1809* (1809).
18. Paul Richards: *History of Lynn*.
19. Palmer: *History of Gt Yarmouth*.
20. *Monthly Magazine*, March1803.
21. *Gentleman's Magazine*, Dec.1808.
22. *Ibid*, Jan.1809.
23. *Universal Magazine*, June 1814.
24. Walker: *Norman Cross*.

16 Forts, Signal Posts & Lifesavers

1. *North Sea naval correspondence* 1810-1812; ADM 571-573 (N.A.).
2. Cobbett: *Parliamentary Debates*, 20 June 1808.
3. Harwich Guide (1808). *Reports from the Commissioner*, Vol IV (1811).
4. WO 30/67.
5. Map drawn by Col. Bryce, MR1/1388 (N.A.).
6. K.Walker: *Martello Towers and the Defence of North East Essex in the Napoleonic War* (Essex Review, Oct.1938).
7. *United Service Magazine*, Part 1 (1842).
8. It may be that the towers were manned from time to time for exercises, perhaps by the new Local Militias.
9. Palmer: *History of Gt Yarmouth*.
10. *United Services Magazine* (1842).
11. *Navy Lists*
12. *Ibid*.
13. *Gentleman's Magazine*. Ibbotson is buried in the Church.
14. Signal chain, *Navy Lists*.
15. Warships' logs.
16. History has some very strange twists. The idea of an electric telegraph was proposed around 1800 by Godoy, the Spanish minister who became a by-word for corruption and treachery when he influenced his king and queen to invite Napoleon into the Iberian Peninsula in 1807.
17. J.Storer: *Antiquarian & Topographical Cabinet*. McKie.
18. *Chelmsford Chronicle*.
19. R.W. Malster: *The Minutes of the Suffolk Humane Society* (2013).
20. G.W. Manby: *An Essay on the Preservation of Shipwrecked Persons* (1812). *Transactions of the Royal Society* (1808).
21. *The Tradesman* (1810).
21. *Naval Chronicle*, Vol 23 (1810).
22. *Athenaeum*, Vol 3 (1808).
23. *Universal Magazine* Vol XIII (1810).
24. *Lloyd's Lists*.
25. *Ibid*, McKie.

17 The Leanest Years

1. Yarmouth Prison Book, ADM 103/461. Warship logs. (N.A.).
2. Sir James Ross: *Memoirs & Correspondence of Admiral Lord de Samaurez*, Vol II (1838). Saumarez, a Jerseyman by origin, lived at Shrublands, a mansion at Coddenham, north of Ipswich, during his visits ashore.
3. P. Colquhoun: *Treatise on the Wealth, Power & Resources of the British Empire* (1815). H.W. Wilson in *Cambridge Modern History*, Vol IX (1906).
4. *The Tradesman* (1810).
5. *Lloyd's Register.*
6. *Reports on the Navigation & Trade of Great Britain* (1807). *Lloyd's Registers. The Tradesman*, Vol 5 (1810).
7. *Literary Panorama* (1807). *National Register* (1808). B3/5643 (N.A.).
8. ADM 1/1424.
9. A.D. Bayne: *A History of the Industry & Trade of Norwich & Norfolk* (1858) – quoting C.J.Palmer.
10. *Lloyd's Register.*
11 & 12. Bayne.
13. *Navy Lists.*
14. *General View of the Agriculture of the County of Essex*, Vol II (1813).
15. C. Rawcliffe: *Norwich Since 1550.*
16. W. Marshal: *Review of the Reports to the Board of Agriculture* (1811).
17. *St Edmundsbury* website.
18. Arthur Young: *An Inquiry into the Rise of Prices in Egland during the last Twenty-five Years* (1815).
19. James Vol V. Yarmouth Prison Book.
21. J. Ross: *Memoirs & Correspondence of Admiral Lord de Saumarez* (1838); J.D. Grainger: *The British Navy in the Baltic* (2014); James Vols V & VI.
22. *Letters of Marque*, HCA 2/279 (N.A.).
23. James Vol V. Yarmouth Prison Book.
23. John Feltham: *A guide to all the watering and sea-bathing places; with a description of the lakes* (1813).

18 Victory at Last

1. *Memoirs & Correspondence of Dr. H.E.Bathurst, Bishop of Norwich* (1833).
2. Paul Richards: *History of Lynn.*
3. Matchett.
4. *Naval Chronicle* Vol 40.
5. *Naval Chronicle* Vol 28.
6. Thorne.
7. *National Register; The London Chronicle*, Vol 107.
8. Thorne, Bathurst, *Summary of the Speeches of Sir J.C. Hippisley* (1811).
9. J.W. Robberds: *A Memoir of the Life of the Late William Taylor* (1843).
10. Thorne.
11. A.K. Cowell: *A Short Biography of the Late Mr John Thompson* (1827). *Baptist Quarterly*, Vol 40, Issue 5 (2004).
12. Richards.
13. *Report of Suffolk Auxiliary Bible Society* (1812).
14 & 15. *Proceedings of Colchester & East Essex Bible Society* (1812).
16. *Gentleman's Magazine.*
17. James, Vol VI. Yarmouth Prison Book, ADM 103/460 (N.A.).
18. *Ouvres Completes de Madame la Baronne de Staël* (1820).
19. McKie. *Chanticleer* log.
20. McKie. *Gentleman's Magazine.*
21. James, Vol VI.
22. Yarmouth Prison Book, ADM 103/460 (N.A.).
23. *Correspondence & Memoranda of Field Marshal Authur Wellesley, 1ˢᵗ Duke of Wellington* (1858).
24. *The Rise of the Dutch Kingdom* (1815). E Taylor: *The Taylor Papers.*

19 Finale

1. Robert Cory: *A Narrative of the Grand Festival at Yarmouth* (1814).
2. McKie.
3. *Ibid.*
4. W. Finch-Crisp: *Great Yarmouth Chronological Retrospect* (1877).
5. Thomas Attwood: *Observations on Currency, Population & Pauperism* (1818).
6. Young: *Autobiography.*
7. *Cobbet's Political Register* Vol 25 (1814).
8. *Monthly Magazine*, Vol 39 (1815).
9. Young: *Autobiography.*
10. McKie.
11. Thorne.
12. Arthur Young: *An Inquiry into the Rise of Prices during the Last 25 Years* (1815).
13. McKie.
14. William H Seymour: *On Active Service* (1939).
15. Patrick O'Keefe: *Waterloo; the Aftermath* (2014).
16. Jane Fiske (edit): *James Oakes' Diaries* (1990).
17. *John Constable's Correspondence*, Vol 12.
18. McKie.
19. *New Monthly Magazine*, Vol 4 (1815).
20. *Augustan Review* (1815). Mrs Cobbold's other claim to fame was as the one time employer and subsequent patron of the prison escaper and autobiographer Margaret Catchpole.
21. J.W. Robberds: *A Memoir of the Life of the Late William Taylor* (1843).
22. *Memoirs & Correspondence of Dr. H.E.Bathurst, Bishop of Norwich* (1833).
23. George Burges: *A Letter to T.W.Coke* (1817)
24. *Memoirs & Correspondence of Dr. H.E.Bathurst, Bishop of Norwich* (1833).
25. E.L. Griggs & C.H. Prator: *Henry Christophe & Thomas Clarkson – Correspondence* (1952).
26. Arthur Young: *An Inquiry into the Rise of Prices during the Last 25 Years* (1815).

BIBLIOGRAPHY

These are the main works consulted in writing this book, as opposed to a wider reading list on the period. I have not listed publishers, as the great majority of the original firms are no longer in existence. Many of the texts have now appeared in full or in part online.

Books

d'Arblay, Madame (Fanny Burney), *Memoires Inédits de Madame la Comtesse de Genlis, Vol II* (1805)

Barrow, J., *The Life and Correspondence of Admiral Sir William Sidney Smith, Vol 2* (1848)

Barney, John *The Defence of Norfolk 1793-1815* (2000)

Bathurst, Dr. H E, : Bishop *Memoirs and Correspondence* (1833)

Barrett, Charlotte, *Diaries and Letters of Madame d'Arblay* (1854)

Bayne, A.D., *A History of the Industry and Trade of Norwich and Norfolk* (1858)

de Bourrienne, L-A Fauvelet, *The Life of Napoleon Bonaparte, Vol 3* (1831)

de Braz, A., *Aux Pays d'Exil de Chateaubriand* (1907)

Brightwell, Cecilia L., *Memorials of the Life of Mr Brightwell of Norwich* (1869)

Brown, John, *The Mysteries of Neutralisation* (1806)

Bruce, H.A., *The Life of Sir William Napier KCB, Vol I* (1864)

Burns, D.G., *A History of the Corn Laws, 1660-1846* (1930)

Chateaubriand, F.R., *Memoires d'Outre Tombe* (1849-50)

Clarke, G.A., *The History and Description of the Town and Borough of Ipswich* (1830)

Colquhoun, P., *Treatise on the Wealth, Power and Resources of the British Empire* (1815)

Cooper, C.H., *Annals of Cambridge, Vol IV* (1852)

Debrett, J., *Collection of State Papers Relative to the War Against France* (various vols. 1793-1797)

Dicken, Dr. E.P., *A History of Brightlingsea* (1913)

Facts Opposed to Falsehood in the Prize Case Clarissa (c.1800)

Finch-Crisp, W., *Yarmouth Chronological Perspective* (1877)

The Anti-Gallican (1804)

Fiske, Jane, (Edit), *James Oakes' Diaries* (1990)

Gallois, N., *Les Corsaires francais sous la République et L'Empire*

General View of the County of Essex (1813)

Greenhill Gardyne, Lt-Col C., *The History of the Gordon Highlanders* (1901)

Gurney, J., (edit), *The Trial of John Joseph Tooke for High Treason* (1795)

Hayes, Derek R. *His Majesty's Late Ship the Invincible* (1985)

Hellman, R., *Bloody British History*, Chelmsford (2012)

Holderness, B.A. and Turner, Michael, *Land, Labour and Agriculture 1700-1821* (1991)

Holland Rose. J., and Broadley, A.M., *Dumouriez and the Defence of England against Napoleon* (1908)

James, William, *The Naval History of Great Britain* (1822)

Jewson, C. B., *Jacobin City: A Portrait of Norwich and its Reaction to the French Revolution* (1975)

Kent, Peter *Fortifications of East Anglia* (1988)

Knight, R. and Wilson, M., *Sustaining the Fleet 1793-1815* (2010)

Knight, Roger, *Pursuit of Victory: The Life and Achievements of Horatio Nelson* (2005)

Matchett, G., *Norfolk and Norwich Remembrancer and Vade-mecum* (1802)

McKie, C., *Norfolk Annals* (1901)

Malster, R.W., *The Minutes of the Suffolk Humane Society* (2013)

Manby, G.W., *A Historical Guide to Great Yarmouth* (1806)

Moore, James Carrick, (edit), *The Diary of Sir John Moore* (1833)

Nicholas, Sir N., *Nelson's Letters and Despatches* (1895)

Neale, W.J., *The Mutiny at Spithead and the Nore* (1805)

Norman, C.B., *The Corsairs of France* (1887)

O'Keefe, Patrick, *Waterloo; the Aftermath* (2014)

Opie, Amelia Alderson, *The Works of Mrs Amelia Opie* (1848)

Paine, Thomas, *The Rights of Man* (1795 edition)

Palmer, Charles, *The History of Great Yarmouth* (1856)

Perrin, W. G., (edit), *The Keith Papers* (1927)

Preston, John, *The Picture of Yarmouth* (1819)

Rawcliffe, Carol, *Norwich Since 1550* (2004)

Richards, William, *History of Lynn* (1812)

Ross, Sir James, *Memoirs and Correspondence of Admiral Lord Samaurez, Vol.II* (1838)

Schomberg, I., *Naval Chronology* (1802)

Scott, Ian, *Reactions to Radicalism in Norwich, 1789-1802*

Seymour, William H., *On Active Service* (1939)

Sheardown, William, *Origin and Services of the Third West Yorkshire (Light) Infantry Regiment of Militia* (1870)

Smith, Graham, *Smuggling in Essex* (2005)

Surtees, W., *Twenty Five Years in the Rifle Brigade* (1833)

Taylor, E., (edit), *The Taylor Papers* (1913)

Taylor, Jane, *The Writings of Jane Taylor, Vol I* (1832)

Taylor, Isaac, Jane and Ann, *The Family Pen* (1870)

Thompson, E. P., *The Making of the English Working Class* (1963)

Thorne, R. G., *The History of Parliament* (1986)

The Trial of Thomas Hardy for High Treason (1795)

Walker T. J., *Norman Cross* (1913)

Wheeler, H.F.B., and Broadley, A.M., *Napoleon and the Invasion of England* (1908)

Winfield, R., *British Warships in the Age of Sail* (2005)

Woodfall. William, *Parliamentary Reports, various vols* (1793-1797)

Young, Arthur *Autobiography* (edit. by Knight, C., 1898)

        France, a Warning to England (1793)

        An Idea of the Present State of France (1795)

        An Inquiry into the Rise of Prices during the last Twenty-Five Years (1915)

Newspapers & Periodicals

The Anti-Jacobin
Annals of Agriculture (edit.by Arthur Young)
Annual and New Annual Register
The Cabinet (1795)
Chelmsford Chronicle
Essex Review
Gentleman's Magazine
Ipswich Journal
London Chronicle
London Gazette
Lloyd's Lists
Lloyd's Registers
Monthly Magazine
Monthly Review
National Register
Naval Chronicle
Navy Lists
Norfolk Chronicle
William Cobbett's Political Register
Scots Magazine
Sporting Magazine
Suffolk Chronicle
The Tradesman
Transactions of the Royal Society
United Service Magazine
Universal Magazine
Weekly Dispatch

Documents

These are referenced as they crop up in the footnotes for each chapter. Most are National Archive documents from the following categories:

ADM 1/ 536-542, 571-573 – Yarmouth Naval Correspondence
ADM 1/1424-1426 – North Sea Naval Correspondence
ADM 36 series – Warship Muster Rolls (crew lists)
ADM 51, 52 series – Warship Masters' Logs.
These records have been used whenever details of a ship's movements or actions are given.
ADM 103/103, 460-462 – Naval Prison Record Books (mainly Yarmouth and Harwich)
HCA 32 series – Prize Court and other papers of captured enemy privateers
HO 42 series – Various Home Office letters and papers.
MP1 series – Various maps of coastline, forts, etc.
WO 17/384 – Troop Returns, Eastern District
WO 30/67, 100 – Army's Eastern District

Index

Vessels

Army Units

Regulars

Other Regiments

Militia & Fencibles